W9-CFL-489

Tools of the Mind

The Vygotskian Approach to Early Childhood Education

Second Edition

Elena Bodrova
Mid-continent Research for Education and Learning

Deborah J. Leong
Metropolitan State College of Denver

PEARSON

Merrill
Prentice Hall

Upper Saddle River, New Jersey
Columbus, Ohio

Library of Congress Cataloging-in-Publication Data

Bodrova, Elena.
 Tools of the mind: the Vygotskian approach to early childhood education
/Elena Bodrova and Deborah J. Leong.—2nd ed.
  p. cm.
Includes bibliographical references and index.
ISBN 0-13-027804-1 (alk. paper)
1. Early childhood education—Philosophy. 2. Child development. 3.
Constructivism (Education) 4. Learning, Psychology of. 5. Play. 6. Early
childhood education—Activity programs. 7. Vygotskii, L. S. (Lev
Semenovich), 1896–1934. I. Leong, Deborah. II. Title.
LB1139.23.B63 2007
372.21—dc22   2006021779

Vice President and Executive Publisher: Jeffery W. Johnston
Publisher: Kevin M. Davis
Acquisitions Editor: Julie Peters
Editorial Assistant: Tiffany Bitzel
Senior Production Editor: Linda Hillis Bayma
Production Coordination: Norine Strang, Carlisle Editorial Services
Design Coordinator: Diane C. Lorenzo
Cover Designer: Kristina Holmes
Cover images: Morey Kitzman *(top, left)*; Danielle Erickson *(right)*
Production Manager: Laura Messerly
Director of Marketing: David Gesell
Marketing Manager: Amy Judd
Marketing Coordinator: Brian Mounts

This book was set in New Baskerville by Carlisle Publishing Services. It was printed and bound by R.R. Donnelley &
Sons Company. The cover was printed by R.R. Donnelley & Sons Company.

Photo Credits: Morey Kitzman, pp. 3, 15, 28, 78, 95, 104, 111, 120, 126, 130, 194; Felicia Martinez/PhotoEdit.
Courtesy of Robert Solso, p. 7; Danielle Erickson, pp. 39, 50, 64, 137, 141, 179; Ginni Kinder, pp. 59, 60, 158; Nicole
Hensen, p. 103; Amy Hornbeck, p. 121; Elena Bodrova, p. 123; Mark Drews, p. 164.

Copyright © 2007, 1996 by Pearson Education, Inc., Upper Saddle River, New Jersey 07458. Pearson Prentice Hall.
All rights reserved. Printed in the United States of America. This publication is protected by Copyright and
permission should be obtained from the publisher prior to any prohibited reproduction, storage in a retrieval
system, or transmission in any form or by any means, electronic, mechanical, photocopying, recording, or likewise.
For information regarding permission(s), write to: Rights and Permissions Department.

Pearson Prentice Hall™ is a trademark of Pearson Education, Inc.
Pearson® is a registered trademark of Pearson plc
Prentice Hall® is a registered trademark of Pearson Education, Inc.
Merrill® is a registered trademark of Pearson Education, Inc.

Pearson Education Ltd.   Pearson Education Australia Pty, Limited
Pearson Education Singapore Pte. Ltd.   Pearson Education North Asia Ltd.
Pearson Education Canada, Ltd.   Pearson Educación de Mexico, S.A. de C.V.
Pearson Education—Japan   Pearson Education Malaysia, Pte. Ltd.

10 9 8 7 6 5 4 3 2 1
ISBN: 0-13-027804-1

This book is lovingly dedicated to our families:

Dmitri and Andrei Semenov

Robert and Jeremy Leitz

Discover the Companion Website Accompanying This Book

The Prentice Hall Companion Website: A Virtual Learning Environment

Technology is a constantly growing and changing aspect of our field that is creating a need for content and resources. To address this emerging need, Prentice Hall has developed an online learning environment for students and professors alike—Companion Websites—to support our textbooks.

In creating a Companion Website, our goal is to build on and enhance what the textbook already offers. For this reason, the content for each user-friendly website is organized by topic and provides the professor and student with a variety of meaningful resources. Common features of a Companion Website include:

- **Introduction**—General information about the topic and how it is covered in the website.
- **Web Links**—A variety of websites related to topic areas.
- **Timely Articles**—Links to online articles that enable you to become more aware of important issues in early childhood.
- **Learn by Doing**—Put concepts into action, participate in activities, examine strategies, and more.
- **Visit a School**—Visit a school's website to see concepts, theories, and strategies in action.
- **For Teachers/Practitioners**—Access information you will need to know as an educator, including information on materials, activities, and lessons.
- **Observation Tools**—A collection of checklists and forms to print and use when observing and assessing children's development.
- **Current Policies and Standards**—Find out the latest early childhood policies from the government and various organizations, and view state, federal, and curriculum standards.
- **Resources and Organizations**—Discover tools to help you plan your classroom or center and organizations to provide current information and standards for each topic.
- **Electronic Bluebook**—Paperless method of completing homework or essays assigned by a professor. Finished work can be sent to the professor via email.

To take advantage of these and other resources, please visit Merrill Education's **Early Childhood Education Resources Website**. Go to **www.prenhall.com/bodrova**, click on the book cover, and then click on "Enter" at the bottom of the next screen.

Foreword

Very few would disagree with the famous adage, variously attributed to William James and Kurt Lewin, that there is nothing as practical as a good theory. At the same time, it is very rare for practicing teachers to find anything useful to their everyday work in the theories of developmental and educational psychologists. A major exception to this dismal state of affairs is Elena Bodrova and Deborah Leong's outstanding introduction to Lev Vygotsky's theory, *Tools of the Mind*. In the first chapter of this fine book, written specifically for practitioners of early childhood education, Bodrova and Leong provide a lucid introduction to Vygotsky's ideas based on four key principles:

1. Children construct knowledge using cultural tools that become "tools of the mind."
2. Development must always be studied in its sociocultural context.
3. Learning can be organized in such a way that it promotes development.
4. The development of language is central to the intellectual development of the child.

These ideas are explained lucidly in a clear, accessible way, and relevant comparisons are made to the ideas of such major developmentalists as Montessori, Piaget, and those who favor the use of behavior modification techniques in the classroom. A variety of experimental examples are provided to make the basic concepts clear and then these examples are broadened to link them to a variety of classroom practices that teachers can implement themselves.

In this carefully revised edition of *Tools of the Mind*, Bodrova and Leong have retained all the outstanding features of the first edition and made several additions that will make the book even more useful for practicing teachers and teachers in training. In addition to a readable, understandable exposition of Vygotsky's theories, this new edition is chock full of practical examples that bring the theoretical ideas to life in ways that teachers can put to immediate use. There is also a timely discussion of children with special needs that will not only prove practical to teachers, but also will make clearer the deep connection that Vygotsky sees between the organization of the social environment of children in the classroom and the way that it is possible to create special zones of proximal development for such children by applying Vygotsky's ideas.

The first edition of *Tools of the Mind* was a major milestone in providing teachers with a really useful set of tools for their own work. This new edition will prove even more useful.

Michael Cole
Sanford I. Berman Chair in Language, Thought and Communication
University Professor of Communication, Psychology and Human Development
Director, Laboratory of Comparative Human Cognition
University of California, San Diego

About the Authors

Elena Bodrova and Deborah J. Leong have co-authored numerous books and articles on the Vygotskian approach since they began writing together in 1995. They have written on play, self-regulation development, and early literacy development as well as articles on state standards and on early childhood assessment. With Oralie McAfee, they co-authored *Basics of Assessment: A Primer for Early Childhood Educators* published by the National Association for the Education of Young Children. They have a series of videos with Davidson Films: *Vygotsky's Developmental Theory: An Introduction; Play: A Vygotskian Approach; Scaffolding Self-Regulated Learning in the Primary Grades;* and *Building Literacy Competencies in Early Childhood.* Their work was featured in the video *Growing and Learning in Preschool* (National Institute for Early Education Research). Their early childhood program was named an exemplary program by the International Bureau of Education (UNESCO) in 2001.

Elena Bodrova is a senior researcher at Mid-continent Research for Education and Learning (McREL) in Denver, Colorado. Prior to her coming to the United States, she was a senior researcher at the Russian Center for Educational Innovations and the Russian Institute for Preschool Education. She received her Ph.D. from the Academy of Pedagogical Sciences, Moscow, Russia, and her M.A. from Moscow State University. In addition to her work with Dr. Leong, she co-authored the book *For the Love of Words: Vocabulary Instruction That Works, Grades K–6* (Jossey-Bass) with Diane E. Paynter and Jane K. Doty.

Deborah J. Leong is a professor of psychology and the director of the Center for Improving Early Learning (CIEL) at Metropolitan State College of Denver. She received her Ph.D. from Stanford University and her M.Ed. from Harvard University. In addition to her work with Dr. Bodrova, she is co-author with Oralie McAfee of *Assessing and Guiding Young Children's Development and Learning* (Allyn & Bacon) that is now in its fourth edition.

Preface

In the second edition of this book, we have attempted to stay true to our original purpose and to add new information that is currently available from the work of post-Vygotskians in Russia who have made great strides in the application of the theory in the classroom. Since the first edition there has been growing interest in Vygotsky and in the work that followed his death in which his colleagues and students went about applying the ideas in the classroom, developing classroom interventions, and verifying and extending his ideas as the work evolved. This has led to additions to the chapters on development and a new section on special education.

The title for this book, *Tools of the Mind*, reflects its purposes, which are to enable teachers to arm young children with the mental tools necessary for learning and to act as tools for teachers. Mental tools are ideas that we learn from others, modify, and then pass on. Vygotsky, his students, and his colleagues have given us wonderful mental tools that we in turn hope to pass on to our readers. This book and four related videos[*]— *Vygotsky's Developmental Theory: An Introduction; Play: A Vygotskian Approach; Scaffolding Self-Regulated Learning in the Primary Grades;* and *Building Literacy Competencies in Early Childhood*—will give teachers a strong foundation in Vygotsky's ideas.

The book is still organized as a set of concentric circles, or a spiral, in that the content becomes more and more tightly focused as the book progresses. Section I (Chapters 1 through 3) introduces the major ideas in the Vygotskian approach and compares and contrasts them with perspectives that will be familiar to early childhood teachers and psychology students. Chapter 2 contains a new section describing the Vygotskian approach to special education. Section II of the book (Chapters 4, 5, 6, and 7) revisits the points made in the first section and applies them to the learning/teaching process. Section II has been substantially reorganized and now describes general strategies for approaching learning/teaching and specific tactics that can be used for scaffolding this process. Section III (Chapters 8 through 14) is even more detailed, with specific applications provided. The second edition expands the first edition's coverage on the specific developmental features of children at specific ages: infants and toddlers, preschoolers and kindergarteners, and primary grade students. Separate chapters were added to specify the nature of learning and teaching that fosters development at different ages. Examples of Vygotsky-based classroom practices that were previously discussed in a single chapter are expanded in this edition and presented in three separate chapters according to the ages of children. The second edition ends with a special chapter on dynamic assessment.

---

[*]For further information, contact Davidson Films, Inc., 735 Tank Farm Road, Suite 110, San Luis Obispo, CA 93401. Phone: (805) 594-0422. FAX (805) 584-0532. Toll-free number: (888) 437-4200.

Examples and activities in this book are a product of 15 years of collaboration with preschool, kindergarten, and first- and second-grade teachers all over the United States. The programs ranged from Head Start to public school preschools, state- supported universal pre-K programs, private schools, child care, and federal Early Reading First and Reading First programs. The vast majority of the programs have been for at-risk children. The classrooms ranged from traditional to multiage groups (combining three- and four-year- olds, but also kindergarten, first grade, and second grade) and were philosophically diverse. For example, some employed traditional ways of teaching reading and others used the Whole Language approach. Some of the classrooms provided bilingual instruction.

One of the most exciting things we have found in our work with teachers is that the Vygotskian approach works in all of the classrooms we have described. Many of the concerns addressed in this book go beyond socioeconomic class or classroom philosophy. Vygotsky helps us examine our roles as the adults in the classroom in a different way, providing many more alternatives for action. He helps us see ourselves as partners with children in the great journey to learn, rather than as taskmasters or followers. Our work with teachers and children in these various classrooms has been a liberating, exhilarating, and exciting endeavor, reminding many of us why we became teachers in the first place!

Throughout the book, we have balanced the examples by using children of different ages, so that all of the early childhood period is presented. Because English lacks a gender-neutral pronoun for *child* and *teacher*, we alternate between using *he* and *she*.

Acknowledgments

We have many people to thank for their contributions to this book. In addition to the people who contributed to the first edition, we would like to thank the teachers, coaches, and administrators in the Vygotskian-based programs in New Jersey, Colorado, Oregon, Wyoming, Wisconsin, Iowa, Illinois, Missouri, California, and Arizona who have contributed to our work. The following people require special thanks: Sharon Saunders, Loretta Merritt, Laura Morana, Rita Mendez, Gisela Ferrer Bullard, Sally Millaway, Steffen Salfer, Lena Ko, Sandy Martin, Rebecca Fuerstein, Shawna Fagnant, Ann Lundt, Lynn Soat, JoAnn Christofferson, Laura Abruzzezze, Pat Chamberlain, Peggy Ondera, Louise Nelson, Tammy Upton, and Robin Bulterd.

We would like to thank a group of people who have become our partners in training people in the Vygotskian approach: Ruth Hensen, Amy Hornbeck, Danielle Erickson, Judy Edwards, and Gwen Coe.

The following people contributed by helping us to work through the new chapters and the ideas in the second book: Fran Davidson, Kathleen Roskos, Ellen Frede, Peg Griffin, Gary Price, Aaron Leitz, and Marianne (Mimi) Bloch.

We would like to thank our colleagues in the psychology department of Metropolitan State College of Denver. In particular, we appreciated the support of President Stephen Jordan, Lyn Wickelgren, Ellen Susman, Carol Svendson, Susan Call, and Betsy Zeller. We are also thankful for the support of present and past staff of Mid Continent Research for Education and Learning (McREL)—Tim Waters, David Frost, Diane

Paynter, Jennifer Norford, and Salle Quackenboss—who allowed us to expand the reach of Vygotsky's ideas to many schools and centers all over the country.

We would also like to thank reviewers Holly Lamb, Tarleton State University; Judith Niemeyer, University of Northern Carolina at Greensboro; and Deborah Zurmehly, Ohio University–Chillicothe.

"Bol'shoe spasibo" to our Russian colleagues—Elena Yudina, Lubov Klarina, Boris Gindis, Galina Zuckerman, and Vitall Rubtsov—who gave us valuable feedback on the first edition and helped us shape the post-Vygotskian sections of the second edition.

Finally, we would like to thank the following people for their support of our work: Adele Diamond, Barbara Goodson, Steve Barnett, M. Susan Burns, David Dickinson, Fred Morrison, Jean Layzer, Carolyn Layzer, Marylou Hyson, Jacqueline Jones, Ed Greene, Carol Copple, Douglas H. Clements, Julie Sarama, Laura Berk, Michael Cole, Irv Sigel, Courtney Cazden, and Chris Lonigan.

Teacher Preparation Classroom

TEACHER PREP

MERRILL
PRENTICE HALL

See a demo at
www.prenhall.com/teacherprep/demo

Your Class. Their Careers. Our Future. Will your students be prepared?

We invite you to explore our new, innovative and engaging website and all that it has to offer you, your course, and tomorrow's educators! Organized around the major courses pre-service teachers take, the Teacher Preparation site provides media, student/teacher artifacts, strategies, research articles, and other resources to equip your students with the quality tools needed to excel in their courses and prepare them for their first classroom.

This ultimate on-line education resource is available at no cost, when packaged with a Merrill text, and will provide you and your students access to:

Online Video Library. More than 150 video clips—each tied to a course topic and framed by learning goals and Praxis-type questions—capture real teachers and students working in real classrooms, as well as in-depth interviews with both students and educators.

Student and Teacher Artifacts. More than 200 student and teacher classroom artifacts—each tied to a course topic and framed by learning goals and application questions—provide a wealth of materials and experiences to help make your study to become a professional teacher more concrete and hands-on.

Research Articles. Over 500 articles from ASCD's renowned journal *Educational Leadership*. The site also includes Research Navigator, a searchable database of additional educational journals.

Teaching Strategies. Over 500 strategies and lesson plans for you to use when you become a practicing professional.

Licensure and Career Tools. Resources devoted to helping you pass your licensure exam; learn standards, law, and public policies; plan a teaching portfolio; and succeed in your first year of teaching.

How to ORDER *Teacher Prep* for you and your students:

For students to receive a *Teacher Prep* Access Code with this text, instructors **must** provide a special value pack ISBN number on their textbook order form. To receive this special ISBN, please email **Merrill.marketing@pearsoned.com** and provide the following information:
- Name and Affiliation
- Author/Title/Edition of Merrill text

Upon ordering *Teacher Prep* for their students, instructors will be given a lifetime *Teacher Prep* Access Code.

Brief Contents

Contents

CHAPTER 3

The Vygotskian Framework and Other Theories of Development and Learning   *28*

SECTION II

Strategies for Development and Learning   *37*

CHAPTER 4

The Zone of Proximal Development   *39*

CHAPTER 5
Tactics: Using Mediators   *50*

CHAPTER 6
Tactics: Using Language   *64*

NOTE: Every effort has been made to provide accurate and current Internet information in this book. However, the Internet and information posted on it are constantly changing, so it is inevitable that some of the Internet addresses listed in this text book will change.

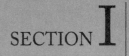

The Vygotskian Framework: The Cultural–Historical Theory of Development

This section introduces the major principles in the Cultural-Historical Theory of development proposed by L. S. Vygotsky and implemented by scholars in Russia and the United States. In addition, it compares Vygotsky's perspective with other theories of child development. There are three chapters in this section:

Chapter 1   Introduction to the Vygotskian Approach

Chapter 2   Acquiring Mental Tools and Higher Mental Functions

Chapter 3   The Vygotskian Framework and Other Theories of Development and Learning

CHAPTER **1**

Introduction to the Vygotskian Approach

Sun-mei, who is 4 years old, draws a picture of what she wants to do when she and Johan go to the dramatic play area to play spaceship. She draws a picture of herself and Johan with helmets. Next to them she draws some rocks. "We are going to make a space walk and look at moon rocks. We're scientists on the ship," she says when the teacher asks her what she is doing. When she goes to the play center, she and Johan play spaceship, starting out with moon rocks and then doing repairs on the ship. They stay involved for more than an hour and continue their play when they go outside.

Seven-year-old Juan has written his own version of a story he has read. The teacher asks him to "edit" his work by looking for spelling and capitalization errors. He puts on a pair of special glasses called "Editor's Eyes" to help him step out of his role of writer and into the role of editor. With the glasses on, he notices many more mistakes in his own writing.

Maura, a sixth grader, is a thoughtful, deliberate problem solver. When she has to answer a question, her answers seem intentional, and she thinks before she speaks. She ponders complex problems, planning her approach before she begins and looking over her work.

What do these three children have in common? Each is using "tools of the mind" to help them solve problems and remember. The idea of tools of the mind was developed by Lev Vygotsky, a Russian psychologist (1896–1934), to explain how children acquire increasingly advanced mental abilities.

Tools of the Mind

A tool is something that helps us solve problems, an instrument that facilitates performing an action. A lever helps us lift a rock that is too heavy to move with only our arms. A saw helps us cut wood that we cannot break with our hands. These physical tools extend our abilities, enabling us to do things beyond our natural capacities.

Just as we humans have invented physical tools, like hammers and forklifts, to increase our physical capacities, we have also created mental tools, or *tools of the mind,* to extend our mental abilities. These mental tools help us to attend, remember, and think better. For example, mental tools such as memory strategies enable us to double and triple the amount of information we recall. Mental tools, however, do more than extend our natural abilities. Vygotsky believed that they actually change the very way we attend, remember, and think.

Because Vygotskians believe that mental tools play a critical role in the development of the mind, they have explored ways in which children acquire these tools. They propose that these tools are learned from adults and suggest that the role of the teacher is to "arm children" with these tools. This sounds simple, but the process involves more than merely direct teaching of facts or skills. It involves enabling the child to use the tool independently and creatively. As children grow and develop, they become active tool users and tool makers; they become crafters. Eventually, they will be able to use mental tools appropriately and invent new tools when necessary (Paris & Winograd, 1990). The teacher's role is to provide the path to independence—a goal of all educators.

Why Mental Tools Are Important

When children lack mental tools, they don't know how to learn in a deliberate fashion. They are unable to focus their minds on purpose, and consequently their learning is less effective and efficient. As we will see, children develop the ability to use different mental tools at different ages. Their "tool chests" aren't filled all at once but gradually. Here are some examples of children who do not have mental tools.

Four-year-old Amanda is sitting in group time when the teacher asks the children to hold up their hand if they are wearing yellow. Amanda looks down at her dress and sees a gigantic brown kitty. She forgets all about "yellow," but she still holds up her hand.

Jane, who is 5, knows that she is supposed to hold up her hand when another child is talking and wait until the teacher calls on her. However, she can't seem to stop herself from talking out of turn. When you ask her, she can tell you the rule. In fact, she is always telling other children the rule, even as she is blurting out answers herself.

Second-grader Ben is working on his journal in a small group. He gets up to sharpen his pencil, but as he walks past the book section, he stops and looks at a book. Soon another book catches his eye. When it is time to change activities, he notices he is still holding a dull pencil, and he no longer has any time left to complete his work.

Eight-year-old Tony is solving a word problem: There are some birds sitting on a tree. Three flew away and seven are left. How many birds were there in the tree in the beginning? Tony keeps subtracting 3 from 7. Instead of adding, he subtracts because of the word "away." He doesn't self-regulate or check his thinking. Even though his teacher has just explained that estimating will help, he doesn't apply the strategy to this problem.

Young children *are* able to think, attend, and remember. The problem is that their thinking, attention, and memory are very reactive; what ends up holding their attention may or may not have anything to do with the task they are expected to perform. Think about how many things children learn by watching television, especially commercials. Very simply, television exploits reactive thinking, memory, and attention. Television is loud, has lots of movement, changes scenes every few seconds, and is colorful. This format is used to teach basic skills in many educational television programs and computer "teaching games," but many teachers complain that the fast-paced sensory bombardment makes it difficult to teach some children in other ways. In fact, many early childhood teachers complain that they have to "sing, dance, or act like Big Bird" in order to teach. Without the acquisition of mental tools, this attention-grabbing approach would be the only way for children to acquire information, because children could not direct and focus their attention, memory, and problem-solving skills on their own. It would take many more exposures to information to learn very simple information.

When children have mental tools, they are no longer reactive learners. They can take more responsibility for learning on their own because learning becomes a self-directed activity. The teacher no longer has to take total responsibility for every aspect of the learning process. Tools relieve teachers of this unnecessary burden, and more important, they can be applied across the curriculum, from reading to math or manipulatives to dramatic play.

One of the great strengths of the Vygotskian approach is that the mechanisms for teaching mental tools have been tried and tested. Instead of just expecting the tools to be learned and leaving children to struggle on their own, Vygotsky shows us ways to facilitate acquisition. Teachers in the United States and Russia who use these techniques report that they can see changes in the way that children think and learn (Cole, 1989; Davydov, 1991; Palincsar, Brown, & Campione, 1993).

The absence of mental tools has long-term consequences for learning because mental tools influence the level of abstract thinking a child can attain. To understand abstract concepts in science and math, children must have mental tools. Without them, children can recite many scientific facts, but they cannot apply the facts to abstract problems or problems that are slightly different from the ones presented in the original learning situation. Vygotskians trace this lack of transfer from one setting to the next to an absence of mental tools. Abstract problems are the concern of teachers in the upper elementary grades, therefore, tools learned during the early childhood period have a direct bearing on later abilities.

Logical, abstract thought is needed not just in school but in making informed decisions in many areas of adult life. How to buy a car, manage one's finances, decide how to vote, participate in a jury, and raise children all require mature thinking skills.

History of the Vygotskian Approach

The Life of Vygotsky

The Russian psychologist Lev Vygotsky lived from 1896 to 1934 and produced more than 180 articles, books, and research studies (see Figure 1.1). Vygotsky suffered from tuberculosis from a young age, and the disease eventually killed him at the age of 37. Throughout his life, he triumphed over difficulties. He faced difficulty getting an education. Born in the small town of Orshe near the city of Gomel (currently Republic of Belarus), Vygotsky was a Jew. In prerevolutionary Russia, strict limits were set on the number of Jews that could be educated at the university level, but Vygotsky won a place and became an exceptional student. As a psychologist, Vygotsky faced intense pressure to modify his theory to fit the prevailing political dogma. He did not succumb to the pressure. Several years after his death, however, his ideas were repudiated and expunged. The problem of political correctness also affected the work of his students, who courageously continued to expand and elaborate on his theory in spite of the risks. We have these scholars to thank for keeping Vygotsky's ideas alive. When the intellectual thaw of the late 1950s and early 1960s occurred, these scholars revived Vygotsky's ideas, applying them in many areas of education.

Vygotsky's interests ranged from cognitive and language development to literary analysis and special education. He taught literature in a secondary school and then went on to lecture at a teacher-training institute. He became very interested in psychology and gave a presentation in St. Petersburg on consciousness that brought him much acclaim. After moving his family to Moscow, he began a collaboration with Alexander Luria and Alexei Leont'ev that resulted in the rich theory and body of research that we have come to know as the Vygotskian approach.

Figure 1.1   Lev Vygotsky

If you are interested in learning more about Vygotsky and his colleagues and students, Van der Veer, Valsiner, and Kozulin give detailed accounts of Vygotsky's life and ideas both in and outside of Russia (Kozulin, 1990; Van der Veer & Valsiner, 1991). In addition, Alexander Luria's autobiography (1979) makes fascinating reading. Finally, memoirs written by Vygotsky's daughter, Gita Vygodskaya, provide unique personal "brush strokes to the portrait" (Vygodskaya, 1995, 1999).

Vygotsky's theory of development, which was unique and distinct from those of his contemporaries, is often called the *Cultural-Historical Theory*. Because his life was so short, his theory leaves many unanswered questions and is not always sufficiently supported by empirical data. Over the years, however, many of his concepts have been elaborated and studied by scholars in Russia and the West. Presently, his theory is changing the way psychologists think about development and the way educators work with young children.

In a strict sense, Vygotskian theory is really a framework for understanding learning and teaching. It gives the early childhood educator a new perspective and helpful insights about children's growth and development. Although it does not define a set of premises and present empirical studies that provide recipes for any classroom situation, teachers can expect his ideas to inspire them to see children in a different way and consequently to modify the ways they interact with and teach them.

Vygotsky's Contemporaries

Among the major Western theorists that Vygotsky studied and reacted to were psychologists such as Piaget (constructivism), Watson (behaviorism), Freud (psychoanalysis), Kohler and Koffka (Gestalt psychology) as well as educators, anthropologists, and linguists. In his theoretical papers and empirical studies, Vygotsky proposed alternative explanations for several of Piaget's early works concerning the development of language in young children. Vygotsky frequently referred to Kohler's work on the use of tools by apes to discuss various similarities and differences in animal and human behavior. Vygotsky also commented on the work of Montessori. For a discussion of the similarities and differences between the Vygotskian framework and other developmental psychologists, see Chapter 3.

Post Vygotskians: Russian Colleagues and Students

Vygotsky collaborated with Alexander Luria (1902–1977) and Alexei Leont'ev (1903–1979) on many of his early experiments, and they contributed to the development of the framework. After Vygotsky's death, Luria, Leont'ev, and other Vygotskians faced increased pressure to cease their research. Many of them continued but did not openly acknowledge the tie to Vygotsky until the political winds changed. They elaborated on the major principles and applied them to various areas of psychology.

Luria, one of Vygotsky's most prolific colleagues, pioneered studies in such varied areas as cross-cultural psychology, neuropsychology, and psycholinguistics. He applied Vygotskian principles to the study of neuropsychology by looking at brain damage and possible ways of compensating for it (Luria, 1973). In cross-cultural psychology, Luria (1976) also studied how cultural influences shape cognition. Luria's psycholinguistic research probed the role of private speech in the regulation of motor actions and examined the ties between language and cognition from a developmental as well as clinical perspective. Vocate (1987) gives an excellent summary of Luria's work.

Leont'ev studied deliberate memory and attention, and developed his own theory of activity, which linked the social context or environment to developmental accomplishments through the child's own actions (Leont'ev, 1978). Leont'ev's theory is the basis of much current research in Russia, especially in the areas of play and learning. Some of these studies and their application to early childhood development will be discussed in detail in Chapters 10 and 12.

Piotr Gal'perin (1902–1988), Daniel Elkonin (1904–1985), and Alexander Zaporozhets (1905–1981), three of Vygotsky's students, focused on the structure and development of learning/teaching processes. Zaporozhets founded the Institute of Preschool Education where he and his students applied the Vygotskian approach to early childhood education.

Today, the Vygotskian tradition in educational and developmental psychology is being carried on in Russia by what can be called third- and fourth-generation Vygotskians (Karpov, 2005). The ranks of these neo-Vygotskians include, among others, such scholars as Vasili Davydov, Maya Lisina, Leonid Venger, Vitali Rubtsov, Galina Zuckerman, and Elena Kravtsova. Their elaborations of Vygotsky's original ideas have led to many of the innovations in teaching practices discussed in this book.

Research and Applications of Vygotsky's Theory in the West

Western psychologists first became interested in Vygotsky in the late 1960s following the translation of his *Thought and Language* (Vygotsky, 1962). Psychologists in Scandinavia, Germany, and Holland have addressed broad philosophical issues in this framework. American psychologists Michael Cole and Sylvia Scribner (1973), Jerome Bruner (1985), and Uri Bronfenbrenner (1977) first brought Vygotsky to the attention of psychologists and educators in the United States. From the 1970s to the 1990s, interest in the social-cognitive aspects of the Vygotskian framework was promoted by other researchers such as Wertsch (1991), Rogoff (1991), Tharp and Gallimore (1988), Cazden (1993), Campione and Brown (1990), and John-Steiner, Panofsky, and Blackwell (1990).

At first, American researchers were interested in the global aspects of Vygotsky's theory, but more recent research has been more specialized, studying how the framework applies in different areas of psychology and education. For example, several researchers have focused on a comparison of Vygotskian and non-Vygotskian approaches to play (Berk, 1994; Berk & Winster, 1995) or to joint problem solving (Newman, Griffin, & Cole, 1989). The Vygotskian framework has been used in a number of programs in the United States and in other countries outside of Russia. Most of the efforts have involved elementary, middle school, and high school students (Campione & Brown, 1990; Cole, 1989; Feuerstein & Feuerstein, 1991; Moll, 2001; Newman, Griffin, & Cole, 1989).

However, a few programs have used the Vygotskian approach with preschool and kindergarten children such as in the Reggio Emilia programs and our own work in the classroom in the *Tools of the Mind* (Bodrova & Leong, 2001) and *Scaffolding Early Literacy Programs* (Bodrova, Leong, Paynter, & Hensen, 2001; Bodrova, Leong, Paynter, & Hughes, 2001). Articles about the application of many of Vygotsky's ideas have been published widely, and the popularity of the approach has only grown in the last 15 years.

This book synthesizes Vygotskian works; the work of Vygotsky's colleagues; and contemporary research in Russia, the United States, and Europe to explain how the Vygotskian framework applies to the early childhood classroom. Vygotsky's ideas form a general approach that is helpful for examining developmental processes and for finding creative ways to enhance and further a child's development.

The Vygotskian Framework: Principles of Psychology and Education

The basic principles underlying the Vygotskian framework can be summarized as follows:

1. Children construct knowledge.
2. Development cannot be separated from its social context.
3. Learning can lead development.
4. Language plays a central role in mental development.

The Construction of Knowledge

Like Piaget, Vygotsky believed that children construct their own understandings and do not passively reproduce what is presented to them. However, for Piaget, cognitive construction occurs primarily in interaction with physical objects (Ginsberg & Opper, 1998). People play an indirect role, for example, in planning the environment or creating cognitive dissonance. For Vygotsky, cognitive construction is always *socially mediated;* it is influenced by present and past social interactions (Karpov, 2005). The things that a teacher points out to her student will influence what that student "constructs." If one teacher points out that the blocks are of distinct sizes, the student will construct a concept that is different from the one constructed by the student whose teacher points out the blocks' color. The teacher's ideas mediate what and how the child will learn; they act as a filter in a sense, determining which ideas the student will learn.

Vygotsky believed that both physical manipulation and social interaction are necessary for development. Trudy must touch, physically compare, arrange, and rearrange the blocks before she acquires the concept of "big and little" and incorporates it into her own cognitive repertoire. Without manipulation and hands-on experience, Trudy will not construct her own understanding. If she has only her teacher's ideas or words, chances are that Trudy will not be able to apply the concept to slightly different materials or to use it when the teacher is not present. On the other hand, without her teacher the child's learning would not be the same. Through social interaction Trudy learns which characteristics are most important and what to notice and act upon. The teacher has a direct influence on Trudy's learning through shared activity.

Because of the emphasis on the construction of knowledge, the Vygotskian approach stresses the importance of identifying what the child actually understands. Through sensitive and thoughtful exchanges with the child, the teacher discovers exactly what the child's concept is. In the Vygotskian tradition, it is common to think of learning as *appropriation* of knowledge, which underscores the active role that the learner plays in this process.

The Importance of Social Context

For Vygotsky, the *social context* influences more than attitudes and beliefs; it has a profound influence on how and what we think. The social context molds cognitive processes and is part of the developmental process. Social context means the entire social milieu; that is, everything in the child's environment that has been either directly or indirectly influenced by the culture (Bronfenbrenner, 1977). The social context should be considered at several levels:

1. The immediate interactive level, that is, the individual(s) the child is interacting with at the moment

2. The structural level, which includes the social structures that influence the child such as the family and school

3. The general cultural or social level, which includes features of society at large such as language, numerical systems, and the use of technology

All of these contexts influence the way a person thinks. For example, the child whose mother emphasizes learning the names of objects will think in a different way from the child whose mother issues terse commands and does not talk with her child. The first child will not only have a larger vocabulary but will also think in different categories and use language differently (Luria, 1979; Rogoff, Malkin, & Gilbride, 1984).

Social structures also influence a child's cognitive processes. Russian researchers found that children raised in orphanages did not have the same level of planning and self-regulatory skills as children raised in families (Sloutsky, 1991). American researchers found that schools, one of the many social structures outside of the family, directly impact the cognitive processes presumed to underpin IQ (Ceci, 1991).

The general features of the society also influence the way we think. Asian children who used an abacus had different concepts of number than children who did not (D'Ailly, Hsiao, 1992). These examples illustrate the pervasive influence of the social context on cognition.

The Characteristics of Cognition: Content and Processes.   A number of theorists have discussed the idea that development requires the acquisition of culturally generated knowledge. Vygotsky extended this idea to include both the content and form of knowledge, the very nature of the mental processes. For example, children in Papua, New Guinea, will not only know different types of animals from children in the United States, but the strategies they use to remember these animals will also differ. Children who attend school and are taught scientific categories for classifying animals will actually group animals in a different way from children who do not attend school. Luria found that illiterate adults from a herding community in central Asia used situationally based categories, and therefore placed hammer, saw, log, and hatchet in the same category because they are all needed for work (Luria, 1976, 1979). Adults with varying amounts of school experience grouped the objects into two categories, tools (hammer, saw, and hatchet) and objects to be worked on (log).

The idea that culture influences cognition is crucial because the child's entire social world shapes not just what he knows but how he thinks. The kind of logic we use and the methods we use to solve problems are influenced by our cultural experience. Unlike many Western theorists, Vygotsky did not believe that there are many logical processes that are universal or culture-free. A child does not just become a thinker and a problem solver; she becomes a special kind of thinker, rememberer, listener, and communicator, which is a reflection of the social context.

Social context is a historical concept. For Vygotsky, the human mind is the product of both human history, or *phylogeny*, and a person's individual history, or *ontogeny*. The modern human mind has evolved with the history of the human species. Each individual's mind is also a product of unique personal experiences. Therefore, Vygotsky's approach to development is often called the Cultural–Historical Theory.

Before they began producing tools and developing a social system for cooperation, human beings evolved in a way similar to other animals. When humans began to use language and to develop tools, *cultural evolution* became the mechanism that shaped further development. Through culture, one generation passes knowledge and skills on to the next. Each generation adds new things, and thus the cumulative experience and information of the culture are passed on to succeeding generations. Vygotsky assumed that children do not invent all of their knowledge and understanding but appropriate the rich body of knowledge accumulated in their culture. The developing child acquires this information and uses it in thinking. Thus the cultural history of our ancestors influences not just our knowledge, but our very thought processes.

Vygotsky believed that an individual's mind is also formed by individual history. Even though there are common aspects to mental processes, a child's mind is the result of his interactions with others within a specific social context. The child's attempts to learn and society's attempts to teach through parents, teachers, and peers all contribute to the the way a child's mind works.

The Development of Mental Processes.   Social context plays a central role in development, because it is critical for the acquisition of mental processes. Vygotsky's unique contribution was to see the possibility of the sharing of higher mental processes. Mental processes not only exist internally to the individual but can occur in an exchange among several people. Children learn or acquire a mental process by *sharing*, or using it when interacting with others. Only after this period of shared experience can the child internalize and use the mental process independently.

The idea of socially shared cognition is very different from the idea of cognition commonly accepted in Western psychology. Western tradition has viewed cognition as a set of internal mental processes accessible only to the individual. However, as researchers have studied the Vygotskian framework, a growing number have begun to examine the idea of cognition as a shared process and to recognize the importance of social context in the acquisition of these mental processes (Karasavvidis, 2002; Rogoff, Topping, Baker-Sennett, & Lacasa, 2002; Salomon, 1993).

To understand the idea of a shared mental process, let's look at Western and Vygotskian descriptions of how memory develops. In the Western tradition, we would attribute Ariel's ability to remember something to the fact that she possesses a set of memory strategies and that she encodes the information in memory. Memory is something that is internal. Because Ariel is 4 years old, she will probably not remember certain things because her strategies are immature. How will she acquire mature strategies? With age, her mind will mature and she will have them.

In contrast to seeing memory only as an internal process, Vygotsky believed that memory can be shared between two people. For example, Ariel and her teacher share memory; their interaction contains the mental process of memory. Ariel has forgotten the directions to playing a game. The information is stored somewhere in her memory, but she cannot retrieve it by herself. Her teacher, on the other hand, knows some strategies for recalling the information, but he doesn't know this particular game. Therefore, recalling the directions of the game requires both participants. The child cannot do it alone, but the teacher cannot either. It is through their social exchange, dialogue, or interaction that they can remember. The teacher says, "What do you do with the dice?" The child says, "You throw them and they tell you how many you can move." It is in the interchange that the memory exists for now. As Ariel grows she will appropriate the strategy that she currently shares. Soon she will ask herself questions about what the rules of the game might be. At this point in her development, however, she cannot generate the questions independently.

Andre, a first grader, is trying to read a particularly difficult passage in a book. He comes across a word that he can "read" but does not understand. His mother proposes two different reading strategies to help him figure out what the word means. He can guess at the meaning based on the meaning of the sentence or he can look the word up in the dictionary. Andre chooses one of these strategies and confirms his understanding of the sentence with his mother. Several days later, when Andre comes across an analogous situation, he thinks of the strategies that his mother told him. He uses both strategies independently.

Stephen, a second grader, is trying to solve a chess problem. His father identifies the problem and suggests several alternative moves. The child chooses a move and successfully captures the pawn. The problem is solved in a shared way with both participating. Playing chess several days later, Stephen uses his father's moves independently.

Natasha and Joseph are working on a project together. Neither of them remembers exactly what the teacher wants them to do. "I think he said we are supposed to look in the library first," Natasha says. "Right, but first we have to pick from one of these topics," contributes Joseph. Together they reconstruct the steps that they are supposed to follow to create the project.

Therefore, for Vygotsky, all mental processes exist first in a shared space, and then move to an individual plane. The social context is actually part of the developmental and learning process. Shared activity is the means that facilitates a child's internalization of mental processes. Vygotsky did not deny the role of maturation, but he emphasized the importance of shared experience for cognitive development.

The Relationship of Learning and Development

Learning and development are two different processes that are complexly related to each other. Unlike behaviorists who believe that learning and development are the same thing (see e.g., Horowitz (1994)), Vygotsky argued that there are qualitative changes in thought that are not accounted for only by the accumulation of facts or skills. He believed that the child's thinking gradually becomes more structured and deliberate.

Although Vygotsky believed that there were maturational prerequisites for specific cognitive accomplishments, he did not believe that maturation totally determines development. Maturation influences whether the child can do certain things. For example, children could not learn logical thinking without having mastered language. However, theorists who stress maturation as the major developmental process believe that a specific level of development must exist *before* the child can learn new information (Thomas, 2000). For example, Piaget (1977) suggests that a child must attain the stage of concrete operations before she can think logically. In this view, the internal reorganization of thinking precedes the ability to learn new things. Thus, when information is presented at a higher level, the child cannot learn it until that developmental level has been attained.

In the Vygotskian framework, not only can development impact learning, but *learning can impact development*. There is a complex, nonlinear relationship between learning and development. Although Vygotsky did not question the existence of developmental prerequisites that limit a child's ability to learn new information at any time, he also believed that learning hastens and even causes development. For example, 3-year-old Cecily is classifying objects, but she cannot keep the categories straight. Her teacher gives her two boxes, each marked with a word and a picture. One box has the word *big* in large letters with a picture of a large teddy bear. The other has the word *little* in small print with a picture of a small teddy bear. The teacher helps Cecily learn by giving her the boxes to help her keep the categories straight. Soon Cecily is categorizing other objects without the benefit of the boxes. The learning of the words *big* and *little* in association with the images will hasten the development of categorical thinking.

Vygotsky insisted that we must consider the child's developmental level and also present information at a level that will lead the child into development. In some areas, a child must accumulate a great deal of learning before development or qualitative change occurs. In other areas, one step in learning can cause two steps in development. If we insist that development must come first, we reduce teaching to presenting material that the child already knows. As experienced teachers know, children quickly become bored when teachers review a skill that the children have already mastered. But if we completely ignore the child's developmental level, we would miss the moment when children are ready to learn and consequently present material that is frustratingly difficult. An example of this type of error would be introducing addition before a child can count accurately.

Vygotsky's ideas about the relationship between learning and development are also helpful in explaining why teaching is so difficult. We cannot make exact prescriptions that produce developmental changes for every child since individual differences are to be expected. We cannot say to a teacher, "If you do this six times, every child will develop a particular skill." The exact relationship between learning and development may be different for each child and for different areas of development. Teachers must constantly adjust their methods to accommodate the learning and teaching process for each child. This is a great challenge for all educators.

The Role of Language in Development

We tend to think that language's primary impact is on the content of a person's knowledge. What we think about and what we know are influenced by the symbols and concepts that we know. Vygotsky believed that language plays a greater role in cognition. Language is an actual mechanism for thinking, a mental tool. It is one of the processes through which external experience is converted into internal understandings. Language makes thinking more abstract, flexible, and independent from the immediate stimuli. Through language, memories and anticipations of the future are brought to bear on the new situation, thus influencing its outcome. When children use symbols and concepts to think, they no longer need to have an object present in order to think about it. Language allows the child to imagine, manipulate, create new ideas, and share those ideas with others. It is one of the ways we exchange social information with each other. Therefore language has two roles: it is instrumental in the development of cognition and it is also part of cognitive processing.

Because learning occurs in shared situations, language is an important tool for appropriating other mental tools. To share an activity, we must talk about that activity. Unless we talk, we will never be able to know each other's meanings. For example, Joshua and his teacher are working with Cuisenaire rods. Unless they talk about the relationships between the blocks, the teacher will not know if Joshua has built the quantity five out of the units because he understands the relationship between the small rods and the larger rods. Perhaps Joshua is focusing on the color of the smaller rods and doesn't even notice that five little ones make a rod the same size as the fives rod. Only by talking can the teacher distinguish relevant from irrelevant attributes. Only by talking can Joshua make known how he understands the activity. Only by talking can Joshua and the teacher share this activity.

Language facilitates the shared experiences necessary for building cognitive processes. Six-year-old Lucy and her teacher are watching butterflies breaking out of their cocoons and drying their wings. Lucy says, "Look, they don't look bright to begin with." The teacher says, "When do they become bright? Look at that one that is just pulling itself out. Why would its wings be a different color compared with the wings of a butterfly that has been flying around for a while?" Lucy and the teacher discuss the butterflies they both see. Through many dialogues like these, Lucy will not only learn about butterflies and caterpillars, but will also acquire the cognitive processes involved in scientific discovery.

For Further Reading

Karpov, Y. V. (2005). *The neo-Vygotskian approach to child development.* New York: Cambridge University Press.

Kozulin, A. (1990). *Vygotsky's psychology: A biography of ideas.* Cambridge: Cambridge University Press.

Luria, A. R. (1979). *The making of mind: A personal account of Soviet psychology.* Cambridge, MA: Harvard University Press.

Van der Veer, R., & Valsiner, J. (1991). *Understanding Vygotsky: A quest for synthesis.* Cambridge: Blackwell.

CHAPTER 2

Acquiring Mental Tools and Higher Mental Functions

For Vygotsky, the purpose of learning, development, and teaching is more than acquiring and transmitting a body of knowledge; it involves the acquisition of tools. We teach to arm children with tools, and children appropriate these tools to master their own behavior, gain independence, and reach a higher developmental level. Vygotsky associated the higher developmental level with the use of mental tools and the emergence of higher mental functions.

The Purpose of Tools

Vygotsky believed that the difference between humans and lower animals is that humans possess tools. Humans use tools, make new tools, and teach others how to use them. These tools extend human abilities by enabling people to do things that they could not do without them. For example, although you can cut cloth to a certain extent with your teeth or hands, you can do it more easily and more precisely using scissors or a knife. Physical tools enable humans to survive in and to master a changing environment.

Humans, unlike all other animals including apes, invent both physical and mental tools. The whole history of human culture can be viewed as the development of increasingly complex mental tools:

> [T]he use of notched sticks and knots, the beginnings of writing and simple memory aids all demonstrate that even at early stages of historical development humans went beyond the limits of the psychological functions given to them by nature and proceeded to a new culturally-elaborated organization of their behavior. (Vygotsky, 1978, p. 39)

Mental tools have evolved from the first scratches on cave walls representing numbers to the complex categories and concepts used in modern science and mathematics. The use of the mental tools in processes such as memory and problem solving has been transmitted from generation to generation.

Extending the Mind's Capacities

Vygotsky's extension of the idea of tools to the human mind is a novel and unique way of viewing mental development. Vygotsky proposed that mental tools are to the mind as mechanical tools are to the body. Mental tools extend the mind's capacity to allow humans to adapt to their environment, and thus have a function similar to that of mechanical tools:

> [E]ven such comparatively simple operations as tying a knot or marking a stick as a reminder change the psychological structure of the memory process. They extend the operation of memory beyond the biological dimensions of the human nervous system and permit it to incorporate artificial, or self-generated, stimuli. (Vygotsky, 1978, p. 39)

Just like mechanical tools, mental tools can be used, invented, and taught to others. Unlike mechanical tools, however, mental tools have two forms. In the early stages of development (both phylogeny *and* ontogeny), mental tools have an external, concrete, physical manifestation. At more advanced stages, these become internalized; that is, they exist in the mind without external support. An external manifestation of a mental tool is the use of a string around your finger to help you remember to buy apples at the grocery store. You would be using an internalized mental tool if you categorized groceries by the food groups or by the meals you plan to cook.

Mastering Behavior

Another difference between mental and mechanical tools is their purpose. Mental tools help humans to master their own behavior, not just the environment. According to Vygotsky, "humans master themselves from the outside—through psychological tools" (Vygotsky, 1981, p. 141). Without mental tools, humans would be limited to reacting to the environment as animals do. Mental tools enable humans to plan ahead, to create complex solutions to problems, and to work with others towards a common goal.

For example, the ability of humans to remember how to navigate long distances is limited compared with that of songbirds or other animals that use biologically programmed responses to outside stimuli, such as light patterns. Humans use mental tools to compensate for the lack of innate navigational abilities; they might leave a pile of stones to mark the way, make a scratch on a tree, or compose a song about the landmarks along the way. Maps and compasses are physical tools that reflect advanced mental processing about the problem of navigating long distances.

Mental tools help children master their own physical, cognitive, and emotional behaviors. With mental tools, children make their bodies react in a specific pattern, for example, to music or a verbal command. Planning, problem solving, and memory are not possible without tools. Tools also help children master emotions. Instead of hitting another person when angry, they learn ways of thinking, or strategies, to control their feelings. Counting to 10 and thinking of something else are tools to subdue anger.

Let's look at how mental tools, such as language, help children to control their behavior. Toddlers are not able to resist touching objects with dials and knobs because they do not have control over their impulses. In Vygotsky's words, children who lack this self-control have not yet "mastered their own behavior." When children begin to acquire this mastery, they will issue commands to themselves to help them stop doing something. Two-and-a-half-year-old Thomas says "No, no" when coming near the stereo he knows he shouldn't touch. Six months earlier, Thomas did not have this tool and would run to touch the stereo. Only his mother's words and presence in front of the stereo would stop him. His actions were a reaction to the buttons and levers on the machine. When Thomas can stop himself by saying "No, no," Vygotsky would say he has learned a mental tool and has become the master of his own behavior. Thomas' speech is the mental tool that enables him to regulate his actions on his own.

Gaining Independence

Vygotsky believed that when children have acquired mental tools, they will use the tools in an independent manner. Children begin by sharing the process of using the tool with others; the process is *interpersonal* at this stage. In the Vygotskian framework, the words *shared, distributed,* and *interpersonal* all stand for the idea that mental processes exist between two or more people. As children incorporate the tool into their own thought processes, a shift occurs and the tool becomes *intrapersonal,* or *individual.* Children no longer need to share the tool, because they can use the tool independently. Thus, gaining independence is associated with a child's moving from shared possession of tools to individual possession, where the tool is, in a sense, inside the child.

Nadia has a hard time concentrating during the morning group meeting. She lies down on other children, pokes them, and constantly talks, interrupting the teacher. The teacher has said "I like the way Mindy is paying attention" or "Pay attention" hundreds of times without the slightest impact on Nadia's behavior. The teacher realizes that Nadia does not possess the tools that will help her to concentrate on purpose. So she sits Nadia in the front of the meeting where she can put her hand on her shoulder. Then she gestures to the book and says "Nadia, listen." She gives her a picture of an ear to hold to help her remember to listen. At this point, attention still exists in a shared state, between Nadia and the teacher. After a number of group meetings, Nadia begins to concentrate on her own. Now attention is individual; Nadia is able to do it by herself.

Reaching the Highest Level of Development

The highest level of development is associated with the ability to perform and self-regulate complex cognitive operations. Children cannot reach this level through maturation or the accumulation of experiences with objects alone. The emergence of this higher level of cognitive development depends on the appropriation of tools through formal and informal instruction.

Language: The Universal Tool

Language is a universal tool that has been developed in all human cultures. It is a cultural tool because it is created and shared by all members of a specific culture. It is also a mental tool because each member of the culture uses language to think.

Language is a primary mental tool because it facilitates the acquisition of other tools and is used for many mental functions. Tools are appropriated or learned through shared experience, which exists, in part, because we talk to each other. Two-year-old Frank and his teacher are putting together a puzzle. They share the experience through their physical interaction over the puzzle. However, the learning that Frank will take away from the experience depends on the language that he and his teacher share. The teacher says, "Look for a piece that has blue, because the piece next to this one is blue." Frank says, "Dis?" The teacher says, "Yes, that is blue. It matches this spot here. Keep turning it until it fits." The dialogue elevates Frank's learning to a higher level, arming him with strategies for other puzzles. Without language, Frank would not even know that there are strategies!

Language can be used to create strategies for the mastery of many mental functions, such as attention, memory, feelings, and problem solving. Saying to yourself "Only color matters" will focus your attention to the color of an object and help you ignore the other attributes. Language plays a large role in what we remember and how we remember. Because of its application to so many mental functions, we devote all of Chapter 6 to the discussion of the various aspects of language in the Vygotskian framework.

The Concept of Higher Mental Functions

Like many of his contemporaries, Vygotsky divided mental processes into lower mental functions and higher mental functions. However, unlike his contemporaries, Vygotsky did not consider lower and higher mental functions to be completely independent of each other but instead proposed a theory of how these two sets of functions interact.

Characteristics of Lower Mental Functions

Lower mental functions are common to both higher animals and human beings. Lower mental functions are innate and depend primarily on maturation to develop. Examples of lower mental functions are cognitive processes such as sensation, reactive attention, spontaneous memory, and sensorimotor intelligence. Sensation refers to using any of the five senses in mental processing and is determined by the anatomy and physiology of a particular sensory system. For example, different animals are capable of discrimination between different number of colors—from almost color-blind marine mammals to birds and fish who can discriminate between more shades of color than humans do. Reactive attention refers to attention that is dominated by strong environmental stimuli, as when a dog suddenly reacts to the sound of a car coming up the driveway. The dog's attention is drawn by the noise. Spontaneous memory, or associative memory, is the ability to remember something after two stimuli are presented together many, many times, such as associating a tune from a commercial with a company logo or a dog that salivates when it associates a bell with being fed. Sensorimotor intelligence in the Vygotskian framework describes problem solving in situations that involve physical or motor manipulations and trial and error. Table 2.1 provides some examples of lower and higher mental functions.

Characteristics of Higher Mental Functions

Unique to humans, *higher mental functions* are cognitive processes acquired through learning and teaching. The main difference between lower and higher mental functions is that the latter involve the use of mental tools.

> The central characteristic of elementary functions is that they are totally and directly determined by stimulation from the environment. For higher functions, the central

Table 2.1   Lower and higher mental functions

Lower Mental Functions	Higher Mental Functions
humans and higher animals	*humans only*
Sensation	Mediated perception
Reactive attention	Focused attention
Spontaneous or associative memory	Deliberate memory
Sensorimotor intelligence	Logical thinking

feature is self generated stimulation, that is, the creation and use of artificial stimuli which become the immediate causes of behavior. (Vygotsky, 1978, p. 39)

Higher mental functions are *deliberate, mediated, internalized* behaviors. When humans acquired higher mental functions, thinking became qualitatively different from that of the higher animals and evolved with the development of civilization. Higher mental functions include mediated perception, focused attention, deliberate memory, and logical thinking. When we distinguish between different colors, placing sky blue in a different category from turquoise blue, we are using mediated perception. Focused attention describes the ability to concentrate on *any* stimulus, whether or not it is exceptionally salient or striking. Deliberate memory refers to the use of memory strategies to remember something. Logical thinking involves the ability to solve problems mentally using logic and other strategies. All these higher mental functions are built upon lower mental functions in a culturally specific way. In current cognitive theories, many of the mental processes described by Vygotsky as higher mental functions are commonly referred to as *metacognitive*.

Higher mental functions are *deliberate* in that they are controlled by the person, and their use is based on thought and choice; they are used on purpose. The behaviors can be directed or focused on specific aspects of the environment, such as ideas, perceptions, and images, while ignoring other inputs. Young children lacking deliberateness react to the loudest noise or the most colorful picture. When children acquire higher mental functions, they direct their behavior to the aspects of the environment most pertinent to solving a problem. These aspects may not necessarily be the most perceptually obvious or noticeable (see Table 2.2).

Mediation is the use of certain signs or symbols to represent behavior or objects in the environment. These signs and symbols may be external as well as internal (see Table 2.3). Vygotsky considered mediation an essential characteristic of higher mental functions. "All higher mental functions are mediated processes. A central and basic aspect of their structure is the use of the sign as a means of directing and mastering mental processes" (Vygotsky, 1987, p. 126). The signs or symbols can be universal, specific to a small group such as a family or classroom, or specific to a particular person. For

Table 2.2   Examples of nondeliberate and deliberate mental behaviors

Nondeliberate Behavior	Deliberate Behavior
Cannot find a hidden figure in a picture because she searches in an unsystematic way or is distracted by other figures	Searches for hidden figure in a systematic and deliberate way, ignoring other distracting figures
Cannot listen to the teacher when other children are talking	Listens to the teacher and blocks out distracting noises
Begins building with blocks that are nearest at hand and keeps stacking them on top of each other with no idea what the structure is going to be	Begins building with blocks using a mental plan, so blocks that will be best for the future structure are chosen

Table 2.3 Examples of nonmediated and mediated behaviors

Nonmediated Behavior	Mediated Behavior
Trying to remember a complicated dance pattern you have just watched	Saying the names of the steps to yourself, such as "two right, three left, kick, kick"
Trying to visually estimate the number of items	Counting the items
Blurting out your comment after the teacher's question	Holding up your hand as a sign that you are ready to answer the question

example, a stop sign or red light is a universal sign for stopping forward motion and is understood the world around. On the other hand, when a teacher places a red dot next to a student's name, it can mean different things depending on the particular classroom. In one classroom it might mean that all children with red dots will go to the blocks area while all children with green dots will do an art project. However, in a different classroom it might mean that a child who received a red dot just got his last warning and if he continues to misbehave he will be sent to a time-out. Sometimes a sign has meaning only for the individual who uses it and is meaningless for everybody else. For example, a circled date on a calendar may be a very important reminder for the person who circled it, but it can mean anything to a stranger—from an anniversary to a dental appointment.

Internalized behaviors exist in a person's mind and may not be observable. Internalization happens when external behaviors "grow into the mind," maintaining the same structure, focus, and function as their external manifestations (Vygotsky & Luria, 1993). Adding a group of numbers using your fingers is an external behavior. Adding the numbers in your head is basically the same behavior, but it is internal.

In young children, most behaviors are external and visible. When young children are beginning the process of internalization, we can see the roots of higher mental functions in their overt actions, such as attempts to control memory by chanting or singing something repeatedly to themselves. Older children possessing deliberate memory may not show any overt strategies.

The Development of Higher Mental Functions

Vygotsky believed that higher mental functions develop in a specific way:

1. They are dependent on lower mental functions.
2. They are determined by the cultural context.
3. They develop from a shared function to an individual function.
4. They involve internalization of a tool.

Building on Lower Mental Functions

Higher mental functions are built upon lower mental functions that have developed to a specific level. Two-year-old Elena cannot remember all the words to "Itsy Bitsy Spider" because her spontaneous memory has not sufficiently developed. Presently, her ability to remember deliberately is limited primarily by the immaturity of the underlying lower mental functions, not by the absence of specific strategies.

When higher mental functions develop, a fundamental reorganization of lower mental functions occurs (Vygotsky, 1994). It means that as children start utilizing higher mental functions more frequently, their lower mental functions do not disappear completely but are used less and less often. For example, as children acquire language, they continue to use their associative memory, but now they depend less and less on their ability to recollect things spontaneously and more and more on the use of various memory strategies.

The Influence of Cultural Context

Culture affects both the essence of the higher mental functions and the way mental functions are acquired. A classic example of this is found in Luria's studies of classification in the 1930s. Luria found that the classification system used by people who do not have formal schooling is quite different from those who do. People without formal schooling use an experience-based system of classification that depends on where they have encountered the objects. When asked which object does not belong—apples, watermelon, pears, or plate—they are likely to say all of the objects go together. Since people with formal schooling develop more abstract ways of categorizing, such as fruit and nonfruit, they are likely to exclude plates from the group. Luria's findings have been confirmed in several cross-cultural studies (Ceci, 1991).

The acquisition of higher mental functions also depends on the cultural context. Abstract thinking, such as using numbers, is learned differently depending on cultural background. In some African cultures children use their hands in a specific rhythm to help them add, in parts of Asia they use an abacus, and in some North American classrooms, children count using Cuisinaire rods. The children in all three cultures learn the same mental skills but in different ways. Individuals may have the same higher mental functions, but the paths to their development may be different.

Moving from Shared to Individual Functions

Higher mental functions first exist in shared activity between two or more people and only later become *internalized* by an individual. Vygotsky called this transition from shared to individual *the general law of cultural development*, emphasizing that in the course of development of higher mental functions, "social relations, real relations of people, stand behind all the higher mental functions and their relations" (Vygotsky, 1997, p. 106).

Comprehension of complex texts is a process calling for the use of higher mental functions. As primary students are learning strategies such as asking questions or making predictions, there is a time when the entire process is distributed between the teacher and the group of students. At this stage, it is mostly the teacher who models both how to apply a specific strategy and how to know which strategy works for which kind of text. Later, students take over some parts of this process with one child asking a question about the text, the second one answering the question, and the third one checking if the answer is correct. Finally, each student is able to carry out all of these processes independently, as everyone has mastered the use of comprehension strategies. At this point, what was previously shared becomes individual. To apply the earlier Vygotskian quote, relationships between the teacher and students, in the context of text comprehension, were transformed into the relationships between specific comprehension strategies that each student is now able to apply independently. We will discuss this process in more detail in Chapter 7.

To acquire higher mental functions, the child must have already learned the basic mental tools of her culture. Children use mental tools to modify and restructure lower mental functions into higher mental functions. Mental tools such as language will reorganize the child's lower mental functions. We will discuss several tools and their relationship to higher mental functions in the chapters that follow.

Individual Differences in the Development of Mental Functions

Lower Mental Functions

Vygotsky proposed that lower mental functions were culture-free, or independent of any cultural context. They seem to be part of our biological heritage. All people can solve sensorimotor problems regardless of whether they live in Papua, New Guinea, or the United States. Lower mental functions depend primarily on maturation and growth, and not on any particular type of instruction. However, all people do not develop the same level of lower mental functions. The problem may be organic and due to the underdevelopment of, or damage to, a particular area of the brain. Children with certain learning disabilities lack some aspects of lower mental functions, such as being able to discriminate between some visual or auditory stimuli or to hold a specific amount of information in their memory. Sensorimotor stimulation, the opportunity to manipulate objects and explore the environment, also affects lower mental functions. Extreme deprivation can lead to individual differences, especially in the first years of life when lower mental functions are developing.

Higher Mental Functions

Individual differences in higher mental functions may be influenced by factors described previously, but there are other contributing factors. One is the quality of language environment. Opportunities to hear and practice language will directly influence the future development of higher mental functions.

Another factor is social context. Some social contexts are more conducive to the development of higher mental functions. Vygotsky insisted that formal schooling was one of the most beneficial social contexts. Some aspects of higher mental functions can be learned only by going to school. The development of taxonomic categories (mammal, carnivore) is an example of "schooled" behavior. However, a child's informal experiences may be very different from those taught at school, especially when the child's culture is different from the mainstream culture. Most likely, white, middle-class children will have an informal context that is quite similar to that found in most schools in the United States. For them, the process of developing higher mental functions builds upon their previous accomplishments. Children from other cultural backgrounds have varying degrees of similarity between school and their other social contexts. The degree of dissimilarity will influence how much mental restructuring must occur before the child can acquire the higher mental function presented in school. This is an important point for parents and educators to understand. This mental restructuring will require special support. It cannot happen by just dropping the child into that setting.

Compensating for the Deficits in the Development of Higher and Lower Mental Functions: Vygotskian Approach to Special Education

Abnormal psychology and special education for Vygotsky were more than simply the applications of his general ideas on learning and development. In fact, Vygotsky was able to formulate or refine some of his major theoretical principles while studying the development of children and adults with disabilities. Vygotsky's view of disabilities is consistent with his major principle of social determination of the human mind: for him a disability is a sociocultural and developmental phenomenon and not a biological one.

Social and Cultural Nature of Disabilities

Vygotsky strongly opposed views that were dominant in special education during his time where the focus of diagnosis and intervention was on the handicap itself. He argued that these views reflect a simplistic—he called it "arithmetic"—view of a human as a "sum of its parts." From this perspective, a child with an auditory or visual impairment is considered to be no different than a normally developing child—"minus the disability." In contrast, for Vygotsky, the development of children with sensory, cognitive, or speech impairments takes a completely different course from the development of their healthy peers. To emphasize the complex and systemic nature of this development, Vygotsky used the term "disontogenesis" or "distorted development."

The major components that determine the course of this developmental path include the primary disability (e.g., visual impairment or restricted movements) and the social context in which the child develops. This social context would determine the extent to which this child would be considered (and will consider himself) "disabled." According to Vygotsky, "For the daughter of an American farmer, for the son of a Ukrainian landowner, for a German duchess, for a Russian peasant or a Swedish proletarian, blindness represents absolutely different psychological factors" (Vygotsky, 1993, p. 82). Another way to illustrate this principle is to compare children experiencing similar problems in coordinating movements of their eyes while focusing on near objects. For a child living in a Western industrialized country, this problem will interfere with his ability to track print when reading. On the other hand, a child living in a herding community might not even have a need for tracking small objects since most of his daily tasks involve looking at larger objects at a distance. Evidently, the same visual "deficit" may go virtually unnoticed in a society that does not rely on written texts for carrying out essential tasks. But it might put another child at risk for developing a reading disability and even for academic failure associated with the possibility of subsequent social and emotional complications.

As a result of the interaction between the primary disability and the social context, a secondary disability can develop. While the child's primary disabilities affect primarily lower mental functions, secondary disabilities are the distortions of higher mental functions. Secondary disabilities develop because primary disabilities often prevent a child from mastering cultural tools that are critical for engaging in social interactions. In turn, limited social interactions prevent the child from acquiring even more cultural tools, which eventually leads to systemic distortions in the child's mental functioning. On the other hand, if the social context provides this child with an opportunity to learn an alternative set of cultural tools, the child may be able to participate in a wide range of social interactions and, as a result, develop higher mental functions.

In his own writings, Vygotsky frequently used examples of children who were deaf or blind (primary disability) and who did or did not develop secondary disabilities depending on whether or not they were able to master alternative tools, such as sign language instead of oral language and Braille instead of written language. Today, with an ever-increasing number of assisting devices, the mastery of cultural tools is becoming possible for children with various primary disabilities.

Remediation as a Means of Remediation

Vygotsky's approach to remediation differs greatly from the approaches of his contemporaries, as well as many of today's educators. The proponents of the "arithmetic" approach to disabilities believed that remediation is possible at the level of an isolated function—the one affected by the primary disability. The way to "fix" this isolated function was to provide training to overcome the deficit (e.g., doing numerous exercises in blending isolated sounds into syllables and then into words to compensate for an auditory processing deficit) or to train an alternative function to take over for the one that is not working (e.g., training a blind person to develop more acute hearing or more differentiated tactile perception).

For Vygotsky, however, the primary disability should not be the main focus of the remediation efforts. He argued that, contrary to common wisdom, the primary disability is the hardest one to remediate because it affects lower mental functions. As we discussed earlier in this chapter, lower mental functions are biologically determined (in today's language, we would call them "hardwired"). It is exactly because of their biological nature that they cannot be changed by any means other than radical medical intervention such as inserting a hearing implant to improve hearing. On the other hand, higher mental functions are culturally and socially determined and as such can be successfully remediated in the course of specifically designed educational interventions. Vygotsky advocates focusing on higher rather than lower mental functions in remediation contending that "the developmental limitations in higher knowledge go beyond sensorimotor training which is possible in the elementary processes. Thought is the highest form of compensation for the insufficiencies of visual perception" (Vygotsky, 1993, p. 204).

For Vygotsky and his students, the way to engage higher mental functions to compensate for the deficiencies in lower mental functions is to use mental tools such as language. In a series of studies focusing on the self-regulatory role of speech in motor behaviors, Vygotsky's colleague Alexander Luria observed changes in behaviors of extremely impulsive children after they were taught to verbalize their actions while carrying them out (Luria, 1979). At the beginning of the study, these children had a hard time following an experimenter's directions to press a rubber bulb when a green light came on and not to press it when a red light came on. Instead, they pressed the bulb every time they saw the light—any light—or did not press it at all. After being taught to say "press" in response to the green light and "no" or "do not press" in response to the red light, these children were able to gain control over their reactions and began to respond according to the directions. In essence, Luria had re-built the behavior that was lacking internal regulatory mechanisms by replacing the mechanisms with the children's own self-directed speech. This speech mediated the children's responses to external stimuli; therefore their new, more self-regulated behavior was not simply the result of remediation but also the result of re-mediation (Cole, 1989).

Application of Vygotsky's Theory to Special Education

Vygotsky's ideas had a profound impact on the field of special education in Russia and are gaining popularity in the West (Gindis, 2003). We will not be able to describe the specific intervention strategies or particular programs that have been developed, but we will summarize two major ways Vygotsky's approach is being currently applied to special education.

Differential Diagnosis of Impairment of Higher and Lower Mental Functions.   In extreme cases of severe visual or hearing impairment, it is clear which of the lower mental functions is affected. However in most early childhood classrooms, we are dealing with a system of interactions between a primary disability and subsequent deficiencies in social interactions and the acquisition of mental tools. Often children with neurological or sensory conditions exhibit symptoms similar to those of children with no such conditions who have been subject to cultural deprivation or educational neglect. Differentiated diagnoses of these cases is critical for planning successful instructional interventions. In his work with special needs children, Vygotsky pioneered a new type of assessment that allows for such a differentiated diagnosis. Based on the idea of Zone of Proximal Development (see Chapter 4), this assessment provides information not only about children's current mastery of certain content and skills but also about their responsiveness to adult assistance and their amenability to instruction in general (Gindis, 2003). In contemporary literature, this type of assessment is called Dynamic Assessment (see Chapter 14). A special type of dynamic assessment has been developed for cases in which a child's low performance is thought to be fully or partially due to the gaps in the child's acquisition of certain mental tools. Some examples of such cases—studied at the time by Vygotsky himself and now studied by R. Feuerstein and his associates (Feuerstein, Rand, & Hoffman, 1979; Kozulin, 1999)—include children brought up in poverty or displaced as a result of war. Other cases include children who have been institutionalized and/or adopted internationally (Gindis, 2005).

Preventing "Secondary Disabilities" by Promoting the Development of Higher Mental Functions.   According to Vygotsky, the major efforts of special education should focus on creating alternative pathways of development for children with special needs. These pathways involve introducing special mental tools geared toward the unique needs of children with different kinds of disabilities and designing strategies to facilitate their acquisition. An example of this approach can be found in the work of the Russian Institute of Corrective Pedagogy—the Institute that emerged from the laboratory of abnormal developmental psychology founded by Vygotsky. Methods of corrective pedagogy developed by the researchers working in this institute included an innovative approach to teaching 2- and 3-year-old children who are deaf to read in order to equip them with a tool alternative to oral language early enough to participate in a wider variety of social interactions (Kukushkina, 2002).

Probably the most impressive example of the implementation of Vygotsky's ideas in special education is the unique system of educating children who are born blind and deaf. Developed by Luria's student, Alexander Meshcheryakov, this approach builds on the intact lower mental functions of these children, such as their sense of touch or muscle memory, to develop complex higher mental functions (Meshcheryakov, 1979). Teachers in the school for children who are blind and deaf founded by Meshcheryakov help their students engage in a series of joint activities focused first mainly on their self-help routines. Gradually, movements used by children in performing these routines (e.g., pulling on pants or holding a dish) develop into symbolic gestures used to communicate to adults and other children. For example, holding a dish acquires a generalized meaning of "eating" and the gesture imitating pulling on pants would mean "going ouside." After children develop simple gestures that serve as "symbolic equivalents" for the words, they proceed to learning special (dactylic) language based on different combinations of hand and finger movements. This allows children to develop progressively more abstract concepts. A graduate of Meshcheryakov's program who himself became a psychologist and who researches the development of children who are deaf and blind says, "Gesture equivalents become a kind of prism through which the child sees the real world" (Sirotkin, 1979, p. 58). At this point, children have developed higher mental functions using alternative but essentially equivalent pathways to cultural development that Vygotsky placed in the center of remediation efforts.

For Further Reading

Gindis, B. (2003). Remediation through education: Socio/cultural theory and children with special needs. In A. Kozulin, B. Gindis, V. S. Ageyev, & S. M. Miller (Eds.), *Vygotsky's educational theory in cultural context* (pp. 200–222). New York: Cambridge University Press.

Luria, A. R. (1979). *The making of mind: A personal account of Soviet psychology.* Cambridge, MA: Harvard University Press.

Vygotsky, L. S. (1981). The instrumental method in psychology. In J. V. Wertsch (Ed.), *The concept of activity in Soviet psychology* (pp. 134–143). Armonk, NY: M. E. Sharpe.

CHAPTER 3

The Vygotskian Framework and Other Theories of Development and Learning

In this chapter, we will first compare Vygotsky's theory with other theories of child development and then give a general critique of the Vygotskian approach. These comparisons focus on the major principles of his Cultural-Historical Theory described in Chapter 1. More detailed comparisons of specific concepts appear in later chapters as each Vygotskian concept is introduced.

Vygotsky studied and commented on the work of constructivists (Piaget), behaviorists (Watson), Gestalt psychologists (Koffka), and psychoanalysts (Freud), as well as the work of educators (Montessori). Vygotskian theory also complements many of the ideas in information processing theory, which was developed after his death.

Piaget's Constructivist Approach

Vygotsky was familiar with the early works of Jean Piaget such as *The Language and Thought of the Child* (Piaget, 1926). In his book *Thought and Language* (Vygotsky, 1962), Vygotsky criticized the Piagetian perspective on the relationship between thought and language, and proposed his own approach. Piaget accepted some of Vygotsky's criticisms and modified some of his later ideas, but this did not happen during Vygotsky's lifetime (Tryphon & Vonèche, 1996). The works of some of Vygotsky's students (e.g., Leont'ev) have more in common with Piaget than the works of Vygotsky himself. These similarities have caused many psychologists to erroneously consider the Vygotskian framework as part of Piaget's constructivist tradition.

Similarities

Both Piaget's and Vygotsky's theories are best known for their insights into the development of thought processes. Piaget placed thinking at the center of child development (Beilin, 1994; DeVries, 1997). Although the bulk of Vygotsky's work was concerned with the development of thinking, Vygotsky had planned to study other areas of development that he considered equally important (such as emotions), but his early death did not allow him to complete this work.

Piaget and Vygotsky agree that a child's development is a series of qualitative changes that cannot be viewed as merely an expanding repertoire of skills and ideas. For Piaget, these changes occur in distinct stages (Ginsberg & Opper, 1988). Vygotsky, however, proposed a set of less well-defined periods. He wrote primarily about the restructuring of the child's mind that takes place during the periods of transition from one stage to another and placed less emphasis on each stage's characteristics (Karpov, 2005).

Both Piaget and Vygotsky believed that children are active in their acquisition of knowledge. This belief differentiates them from the proponents of behaviorism, who view learning as determined primarily by external (environmental) variables. Instead of seeing the child as a passive participant, a vessel waiting to be filled with knowledge, both Vygotsky and Piaget stress the active intellectual efforts that children make in order to learn (Cole & Wertsch, 2002).

Both theories describe the construction of knowledge in the mind. Piaget believed that young children's thinking is different from that of adults and that the knowledge children possess is not *just* an incomplete copy of what adults have. Vygotsky and Piaget agree that children construct their own understandings and that with age and experience these understandings are restructured.

In his later writings, Piaget acknowledges the role of social transmission in development (Beilin, 1994). Social transmission is the passing of the accumulated wisdom of the culture from one generation to the next. Vygotsky also believed in the importance of culture in transmitting knowledge. Piaget, however, believed that social transmission influences primarily the content of knowledge. For Vygotsky social transmission plays a much greater role; it influences not only content but the very nature and essence of the thinking process.

Finally, for both theorists the elements of mature thought are quite similar. Piaget describes formal operational thinking as abstract, logical, reflective, and hypothetical-deductive. Vygotsky's higher mental functions involve logic, abstract thinking, and self-reflection.

The emphasis on abstract, logical thinking has led some psychologists to criticize Piaget and Vygotsky for being Eurocentric because they place a higher value on the mental processes that are more prevalent in Western, technologically advanced societies (Ginsberg & Opper, 1988; Matusov & Hayes, 2000; Wertsch & Tulviste, 1994). Although Vygotsky did place more emphasis on logical thought, he believed that, given exposure, all humans are capable of developing it, and that the lack of development of logic in a particular culture was due to the fact that it was not "useful" in that culture.

Differences

Initially for Piaget, intellectual development has a universal nature independent of the child's cultural context. Thus, all children reach the stage of formal operations at about the age of 14. For Vygotsky, the cultural context determines the very type of cognitive processes that emerge. Cultures that do not employ formal reasoning extensively would not foster the development of formal operations in their young. Vygotsky's ideas have been supported by the data obtained in cross-cultural studies of societies where children do not develop formal operations (Bruner, 1973; Jahoda, 1980; Laboratory of Comparative Human Cognition, 1983; Scribner, 1977). The research of some of Piaget's students (Perret-Clermont, Perret, & Bell, 1991) has led to a greater stress on the contribution of the cultural context.

While Piaget emphasizes the role of the child's interactions with physical objects in developing mature forms of thinking (Beilin, 1994), Vygotsky focuses on the child's interactions with people. For Piaget, people are of secondary importance, and the objects and the child's actions on objects are of primary importance. Peers may create cognitive dissonance, but they are not an integral part of the learning process. For Vygotsky, a child's actions on objects are beneficial for development only as long as they are included in a social context and mediated by communication with others.

For Piaget, language is more a by-product of intellectual development than one of its roots (Beilin, 1994). Language can increase the "power of thought in range and rapidity" by representing actions, liberating thought from space and time, or organizing actions (Piaget & Inhelder, 1969). However, the way a child talks merely reflects the present stage of the child's cognition; it has no impact on the progression from one stage to another. For Vygotsky, language plays a major role in cognitive development and forms the very core of the child's mental functions.

Piaget views the child as an "independent discoverer" who learns about the world by creating his own construction of it on his own. (DeVries, 2000 Wadsworth 2004). Vygotsky argues that there is no such thing as completely independent discovery for children who grow up in human society. Instead, a child's learning takes place in a cultural context, and both the things to be discovered and the means of discovery are products of human history and culture.

Piaget believed that only the discoveries children make independently reflect their current intellectual status. Knowledge of how children acquire or apply knowledge that is transmitted by adults is not relevant in determining a child's developmental level. Vygotsky, in contrast, believed that appropriation of cultural knowledge is key to a child's cognitive development. Therefore, a child's shared performance is as valuable as her independent performance for determining her intellectual status (Obukhova, 1996).

The effect of learning on development is viewed differently by Piaget and Vygotsky. For Piaget, a child's current developmental status determines his ability to learn. Accordingly, all teaching should be adjusted to the existing cognitive abilities of a child. For Vygotsky, the relationship between learning and development is more complex. For certain knowledge or content and for certain ages, one step in learning may mean two steps in development. In other cases, learning and development proceed at a more even pace. However, teaching should always be aimed at the child's emerging skills, not at the existing ones.

Behaviorist Theories

In Russia during the 1920s and 1930s, when Vygotsky did most of his writing, behaviorism in its various forms was one of the most influential psychological theories. Vygotsky lived in the epoch of early behaviorism represented by John B. Watson (Watson, 1970) and was not familiar with later developments within this framework. Although Vygotsky disagreed strongly with behaviorists, the influence of this theory is evident in his language.

Similarities

Like the behaviorists, Vygotsky favored the use of objective methods in psychology. His approach was not purely speculative but was based on observations, measurements, and experiments. Vygotsky criticized the use of introspection as an experimental method, as did the behaviorists.

Although Vygotsky stressed unique features of the human mind, he also recognized that humans and animals have certain common behaviors. Like the behaviorists, Vygotsky believed that animals and humans are part of the same evolutionary continuum, not completely different forms.

Another similarity of the behaviorists and Vygotsky is their mutual interest in learning. Behaviorism and the Vygotskian framework both focus on the learning process, although they approach it from different directions.

Differences

Unlike early behaviorists, Vygotsky was not satisfied with measuring only overt behaviors. Vygotsky did not believe that thinking could be understood by considering only

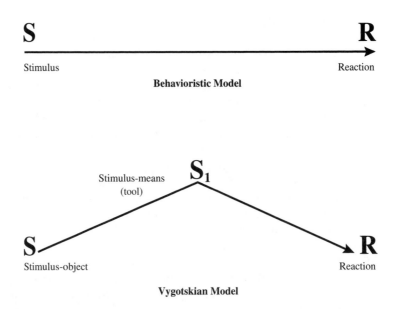

Figure 3.1   Comparison of behaviorist and Vygotskian views of behavior

those behaviors that can be measured and observed by another person. He always tried to explain covert behaviors using inferences based on broader theoretical categories. Later theories of behaviorism also use concepts that are inferred from overt behaviors but cannot be directly observed (Horowitz, 1994).

The major disagreement Vygotsky had with the behaviorists concerned the nature of the "stimuli" that trigger certain behaviors in animals and humans. Behaviorists assert that the relationship between stimuli and behavior is the same for all organisms. For Vygotsky, the fundamental difference between humans and animals lies in the fact that humans are able to respond to stimuli that they generate for themselves. By responding to these specifically created stimuli, or "tools," humans actually gain control over their own behavior (see Figure 3.1).

In addition, Vygotsky opposed Watson's view of speech as no different from other overt behaviors. Watson believed that thinking was just "silent speech." For Vygotsky, speech plays a unique role in the process of mental development, and thinking is substantially different from speech in its form and function (see Chapter 6).

The views of Vygotsky and the behaviorists on the relationship between learning and development also differ. Behaviorists do not distinguish between these two processes and do not address development as a separate concept. From this, Vygotsky concluded that behaviorists believe that learning *is* development. Behaviorists, indeed, maintain that a developing child is always the same child but becomes more knowledgeable and skillful as a result of learning. For behaviorists, there are no qualitative changes in mental structures; learning is simply cumulative (Thomas, 2000). Vygotsky argues that there are qualitative changes not explained by growth in the number of things a child knows. He states that certain learnings can reorganize and qualitatively change the structure of thought. For example, when children acquire language, they begin to think in words, thereby changing both their sensorimotor thinking and their problem-solving abilities.

Finally, Vygotsky and the behaviorists differ on the idea of construction of knowledge. Behaviorists see the child as relatively passive, with knowledge being a product of associations strengthened through reinforcement (Thomas, 2002). Vygotsky claims that children construct knowledge and are active in acquiring knowledge. Children act based on these mental structures and understandings. For behaviorists, the environment (including physical objects and other people) is in control of the child's thoughts and actions, selecting the appropriate ones and increasing them through reinforcement. In contrast, Vygotsky argues that the acquisition of knowledge and tools gives the child a means to control her own thoughts and actions.

Information Processing Theory

Information processing theory (Atkinson & Shiffrin, 1968) was developed long after Vygotsky's death. Even so, many of the concepts that Vygotsky developed and predicted are consistent with the research findings of information processing theory.

Similarities

Both the Vygotskian framework and information processing theory stress the importance of metacognition in mature thinking and problem solving. In both theories, metacognition includes the concepts of self-regulation, self-reflection, evaluation, and monitoring. Both theories are concerned with self-regulation of mental processes as a key to effective problem solving. Information processing theorists use the terms *executive function* and *inhibitory control* to describe the ability to stop one's first reaction to something and to enact a different strategy. Both theories agree that this is fundamental to effective problem solving. Recent brain research (Blair, 2002) supports the importance of self-regulation as a central process.

In addition, information processing theorists and Vygotsky agree that the child must make a mental effort to learn. There is nothing passive about this process. Furthermore, new learning is not merely added to existing structures but modifies present knowledge. Vygotsky speaks of comprehension as a dialogue in which the child communicates with the teacher or the author of a text to build new meanings rather than simply copying existing ones.

Finally, information processing theorists and Vygotsky stress cognitive processes and semantics, or the meaning of words. Both theories place attention, memory, and metacognition at the center of the learning process (Cole & Wertsch, 2002; Frawley, 1997).

Differences

Information processing theory is not really a developmental theory. It describes processing at different ages but does not explain why children are better at it as they grow older. On the other hand, Vygotsky is primarily concerned with how these processes develop and how they are taught to children.

Since information processing theory uses the computer as the primary analogue for the human mind, the social context and the way it forms thinking processes are not considered. Culture influences input—knowledge and facts—but not the method of processing information. For Vygotsky, culture influences both the content of thinking and the way humans process information; it affects the nature of attention, memory, and metacognition. For example, Vygotskian researchers found that primacy and recency effects, which are described by information processing theorists as universal phenomena in memory, are influenced by the type of schooling children have. Whether children remember only the last thing they heard (recency effect) or the first and the last things they heard (primacy and recency effects) depends on the culture they belong to (Valsiner, 1988). Recent research done within the information processing paradigm confirms that formal education does affect such cognitive processes as visual-perceptual processing, attention, and visual and verbal memory (Ostrosky-Solis, Ramirez, & Ardila, 2004).

Finally, emotional and motivational aspects of learning are ignored by information processing theorists. Vygotskians believe that emotions and motivation are important in the learning process. Children learn best when they feel emotionally engaged in learning activities. Leont'ev (1978) did extensive research to identify what makes an activity motivating and beneficial to young children (his research is summarized in Chapter 5). Furthermore, Vygotskians believe that cognitive and social-emotional self-regulation are linked and that the development of one influences the development of the other.

Montessori's Approach

Maria Montessori and Lev Vygotsky were of the same era and although Montessori never wrote about Vygotsky, Vygotsky was aware of her methods (Bodrova, 2003). Montessori came from a different research paradigm than Vygotsky, developing her theory through observational methods and borrowing from anthropology and medicine (Montessori, 1912, 1962). Vygotsky came from the psychological tradition with its use of testing and experimentation.

Similarities

Both Montessori and Vygotsky argued for the importance of instruction and learning in development, however, their definitions of development differed. Montessori believed that development was the natural unfolding of innate abilities, but Vygotsky argued that the nature of development was actually determined by the cultural tools that children acquired in the course of instruction. Both are constructivists, believing that children learn by developing their own understandings of phenomena. Montessori called this autoeducation (self-education), in which the teacher supports the child's quest for discovery and learning. For Vygotsky, learning occurs through co-construction. The child requires the mind of another person to learn.

Differences

There are two main points on which Montessori and Vygotsky disagree. The first is the role of language in development, and the second is the role of play. Montessori, similar to Piaget, believed that language was a by-product of knowledge and that it expressed what the child had already perceived or concluded on his own (Montessori, 1912). For example, learning words to describe different colors was the outgrowth of the child's eye already being trained to see the differences. Vygotsky argued that language was the engine of development, that it helped children to acquire concepts. Knowing the words for the colors orange and red helped children to see that there was a difference between the two colors. The role and importance of written language was another point on which they differed. For Montessori, children learned to write to help them meet the demands of primary grades and to practice motor control. For Vygotsky, writing was a cultural tool whose acquisition influenced the child's mental processes. It was given a much more elevated position in development.

Montessori and Vygotsky also differed on the importance placed on play in development. Montessori believed that play was not necessary and that children should forgo play for more productive activities. Vygotsky argued that play was a central activity to preschool and that without it children did not develop the creativity, self-regulation, and other underlying skills necessary for later development.

Critique of the Vygotskian Approach

Vygotsky died before many of the ideas he proposed were researched so many of the questions he posed were left unanswered. Therefore, his writings do not form a coherent, well-organized theory. Consequently, his ideas about some areas of development, such as the relationship between emotions and learning, are not fully explained, elaborated, or demonstrated empirically.

One common criticism is that Vygotsky placed too much emphasis on the role of speech in cognitive development and did not adequately explore how other types of symbolic representations contribute to higher mental functions. Later research completed by Zaporozhets and Venger showed how nonverbal cultural tools promote the development of perception and thinking in young children (Venger, 1977; Zaporozhets, 1977).

Another criticism is that Vygotsky himself, as well as his followers, focused on the role of social factors in child development at the expense of biological factors such as heredity or maturation. Summarizing recent findings of behavioral geneticists and other developmental scientists, Karpov (2005) suggests that an incorporation of these findings interpreted from the cultural-historical perspective will enrich the Vygotskian theory of child development "without losing its emphasis on the role of mediation in the context of children's joint activity with adults and peers as the major determinant of their development" (Karpov, 2005, p. 239).

Vygotsky has also been criticized for placing too much emphasis on the role that others play in shared activity and not enough on what the child must do to be an active participant. It was partly in response to this criticism that his colleague Leont'ev developed his "activity theory," which stresses the child's active participation in shared activity (Leont'ev, 1978).

As we will see in the following chapters, the Vygotskian framework provides a view of the developing child that is distinct from the ideas in Western psychology. The framework has the potential to help us understand the learning and teaching process in a more precise way.

For Further Reading

Bodrova, E. (2003). Vygotsky and Montessori: One dream, two visions. *Montessori Life, 15*(1), 30–33.

Tryphon, A., & Vonèche, J. J. (Eds.). (1996). *Piaget-Vygotsky: The social genesis of thought.* Hove, UK: Psychology Press.

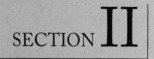

SECTION **II**

Strategies for Development and Learning

The concepts presented in the first section of the book are discussed as they apply to the learning/teaching process. In this section, we will discuss the Vygotskian idea of zone of proximal development (ZPD) and describe general tactics for promoting development and learning based on the idea of ZPD. These tactics have been used in Russian classrooms and pilot-tested in the United States. Teachers can use these tactics to improve the contextual support they give to the child's learning, but to use them properly they must keep in mind the child's ZPD and the leading activity and developmental accomplishments of the child's age level. In addition, these tactics provide teachers with another way of looking at the learning/teaching process. In practice, the various tactics are intertwined, but for the purpose of fully understanding each tactic, we will discuss them as separate entities here. The tactics are organized under three general headings—mediators, language, and shared activities. There are four chapters in this section:

Chapter 4   The Zone of Proximal Development

Chapter 5   Tactics: Using Mediators

Chapter 6   Tactics: Using Language

Chapter 7   Tactics: Using Shared Activities

CHAPTER **4**

The Zone of Proximal Development

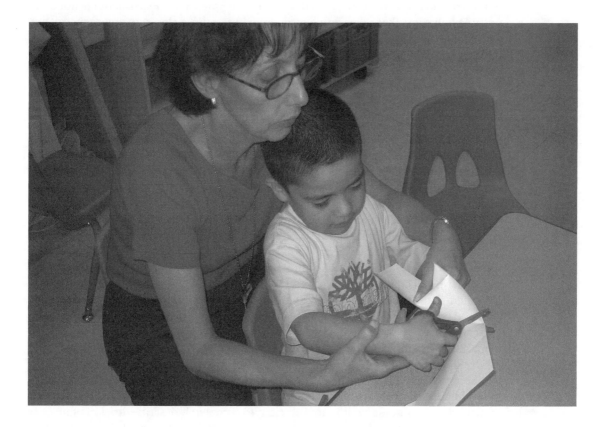

 Both the acquisition of a specific cultural tool and further mental development depend on whether or not that tool lies within the child's ZPD. Vygotsky considered the ZPD a strategy for development and learning.

Defining the Zone of Proximal Development

The *Zone of Proximal Development,* or *ZPD,* one of the most well known of all of Vygotsky's concepts, is a way of conceptualizing the relationship between learning and development. Vygotsky chose the word *zone* because he conceived development not as a point on a scale, but as a continuum of behaviors or degrees of maturation. Vygotsky writes about this zone as a "distance between the actual developmental level as determined by independent problem solving and the level of potential development as determined through problem solving under adult guidance or in collaboration with more capable peers" (Vygotsky, 1978, p. 86).

By describing the zone as proximal (next to, close to), he meant that the zone is limited by those behaviors that will develop in the *near* future. *Proximal* refers not to all possible behaviors that will eventually emerge, but to those closest to emergence at any given time: "What the child is able to do in collaboration today he will be able to do independently tomorrow" (Vygotsky, 1987, p. 211).

Independent Performance and Assisted Performance

For Vygotsky, development of a behavior occurs on two levels that form the boundaries of the ZPD. The lower level is the child's *independent performance*—what the child knows and can do alone. The higher level is the maximum the child can reach with help and is called *assisted performance.* Between maximally assisted performance and independent performance lie varying degrees of partially assisted performances (see Figure 4.1).

The skills and behaviors represented in the ZPD are dynamic and constantly changing. What a child does with some assistance today is what the child will do independently tomorrow. What requires maximum support and assistance today will be something the child can do with minimal help tomorrow. Thus, the assisted performance level will change as the child develops.

In education and psychology, we have traditionally focused on what is developed or achieved by independent performance only. For example, we say that if 5-year-old Susan correctly adds $2 + 2$ by herself, then she can add. Similarly, we say that Frank has learned to make the letter *n* only when he can write it on his own. If there is a prompt by an adult, for instance, if the teacher reminds Frank that "an *n* has one hump," then we say that the child has not developed this particular skill or doesn't know the information yet. Vygotsky maintains that the level of independent performance is an important index of development, but he argues that it is not sufficient to completely describe development.

The level of assisted performance includes behaviors performed with the help of, or in interaction with, another person, either an adult or a peer. This interaction may involve giving hints and clues, rephrasing questions, asking the child to restate what has been said, asking the child what he understands, demonstrating the task or a portion

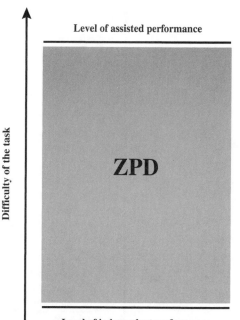

Figure 4.1   The zone of proximal development

of it, and so on. The interaction can also take the form of indirect help, such as setting up the environment to facilitate practicing a specific set of skills. For example, a teacher might provide labeled sorting trays to encourage classification. Assisted performance also includes interaction and talking to others who are present or imaginary, such as explaining something to a peer. Therefore, a child's level of assisted performance includes any situation in which there are improvements in the child's mental activities as a result of social interaction. The specific kinds of social interactions that result in advances in mental development are described in Chapters 5, 6, and 7.

Dynamics of the ZPD

The ZPD is not static but shifts as the child attains a higher level of thinking and knowledge (see Figure 4.2). Thus, development involves a sequence of constantly changing zones. With each shift, the child becomes capable of learning more and more complex concepts and skills. What the child did only with assistance yesterday becomes the level of independent performance today. Then, as the child tackles more difficult tasks, a new level of assisted performance emerges. This cycle is repeated over and over again, as the child climbs his way to complete acquisition of a body of knowledge, skill, strategy, discipline, or behavior.

The ZPD is different for different children. Some children require all possible assistance to make even small gains in the learning. Other children make huge leaps with much less assistance.

At the same time, the size of the ZPD for one child may vary from one area to another, or at different times in the learning process. A highly verbal child may not have trouble

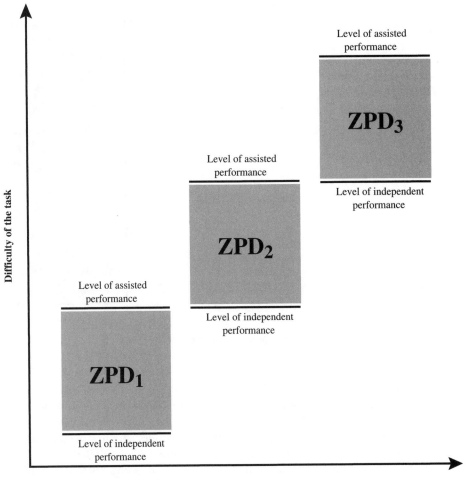

Figure 4.2   The dynamic nature of the ZPD

acquiring concepts in reading comprehension, for example, but have great difficulty with long division. Vygotskians would say that the child needs more assistance in one area than another. In addition, at various times in the process of learning, children respond to different types of assistance. If Mary has been counting for only a few weeks, she may need more assistance that is closer to her level of independent performance than she will 3 months later, after she has been counting for several months. At that time, the ZPD will be larger and the number of activities that she can do with assistance will be greater.

Using the ZPD to Study Development

Vygotsky's approach focuses on the child "to be" or "the future child," rather than on the "present child" or what she is like at this moment. As Leont'ev stated after Vygotsky's death, "American researchers are constantly seeking to discover how the child came to be what he is; we in the USSR are striving to discover not how the child came to be what he is, but how he can become what he not yet is" (Bronfenbrenner, p. 528, 1977). Because of this focus, the emphasis in the Vygotskian paradigm is on the higher level of the ZPD or what the child will be in time. But how can we study something that doesn't yet exist? If we wait until a certain concept or skill emerges, we will be studying today's child, not tomorrow's! What we need is a way to study the process that occurs between the current state and tomorrow's state.

One of the innovations of the Vygotskian approach is the research method of *double stimulation,* or *microgenetic method,* as it is better known in American psychology (Valsiner, 1989). In this method, the researcher studies the child as new concepts or skills emerge (Vygotsky, 1999). The researcher designs the hints, clues, and other assistance to reveal not just what the child learns but *how* the child learns. A child is given a novel learning task, and the researcher monitors which elements of the context (hints, prompts, materials, clues, and interactions) are used by the child. Thus, the researcher provides assistance at the higher level of the ZPD and monitors the child's progress within the ZPD (Gal'perin, 1969). The results from these microgenetic studies are then verified using standard traditional methods. Adaptations of the microgenetic method have led to the idea of dynamic assessment (See Chapter 14), which is gaining popularity in psychological laboratories as well as in the classrooms.

Vygotsky insisted that the entire ZPD be used to determine the child's developmental level because it reveals (a) skills on the edge of emergence, and (b) the limits of the child's development at this specific time.

The child's behavior in assisted performance reveals the behaviors that are on the verge of emergence. However, if we use only independent performance to find out where a child is—what she knows and what she can do—then the skills that are on the edge of emergence will not be apparent. Two children whose independent performance is on the same level may have very different developmental characteristics because their ZPDs differ. For example, neither Teresa nor Linda can walk across a balance beam. Both of them stand on the end and stare down the beam. The teacher holds out his hand to assist each girl's performance. Although each is given the same teacher support, Teresa can only stand on the balance beam holding the teacher's hand tightly, but Linda walks across the beam easily. Independent performance alone is misleading in this example. When we see how the two girls respond to assistance, we can tell that they are at very different levels.

The ZPD is not limitless; a child cannot always be taught any given thing at any given time. Assisted performance is the *maximum* level at which a child can perform today. Children cannot be taught skills or behaviors that exceed their ZPD. In the previous example, no matter what support the teacher gave that day, Teresa and Linda could not be taught to do a handstand on the beam.

When a skill is outside of the ZPD, children generally ignore, fail to use, or incorrectly use that skill. By observing children's reactions, teachers will know if the assistance provided falls within the ZPD. Teachers must carefully note which prompts, clues, hints, books, activities, or peer cooperative activities have a desired effect on the child's learning. Teachers should not be afraid to try a higher level, but they need to pay attention to the child's reaction to attempts at the higher level of the ZPD. Knowing which prompts and hints don't help gives the teacher just as much information as knowing the ones that do help.

Implications for Learning/Teaching

The term *learning/teaching* is currently used as a translation of the Russian word *obucheniye*. *Obucheniye* describes both a child's learning and the teacher's teaching of knowledge and skills. It includes the contribution of both the learner and the teacher and implies that both are active in this process. In contrast, in Western conceptions of education, learning tends to describe only what the pupil does, and words like *teaching, training,* and *educating* describe primarily the teacher's role. Thus, the term *learning/teaching* more accurately represents Vygotsky's meaning than either the words *learning* or *teaching* alone.

The ZPD has three important implications for learning/teaching:

1. How to assist a child in performing a task
2. How to assess children
3. How to determine what is developmentally appropriate

Assisting Performance

It is common to think of the assisted performance level of the ZPD in terms of expert-novice interactions, in which one person has more knowledge than the other. In this type of interaction, most commonly occurring in direct teaching, it is the expert's responsibility to provide support and direct the interaction so that the novice can acquire the necessary behavior. These expert-novice interactions can be informal, as when children interact with parents or siblings (Rogoff, 1990).

Vygotsky's conception of ZPD, however, is much broader than the expert-novice interaction, extending to all socially shared activities. Also, not all of the assistance used by the child is intentionally provided by an adult. Vygotsky believed that the child can start performing on a higher level of a ZPD through any type of social interaction: interaction with peers as equals, with imaginary partners, or with children at other developmental levels (Newman & Holzman, 1993). For example, 3-year-old Benny cannot sit still during a story. The teacher tries to provide different types of assistance to help him focus. She calls out his name, places her hand on his shoulder, and signals to him nonverbally. In spite of these efforts, Benny continues to wiggle and look around the room. Later that day, Benny is playing school with a group of friends. Tony sits in a chair and "reads" the book just like the teacher, while Benny and several other children pretend to be students and listen. Benny sits and listens, focusing his attention for 4 to 5 minutes. Benny is practicing the same behavior that the teacher desired—focused attention. The ability to concentrate for a short time is within his ZPD, but we can see that he requires a particular type of assistance, that of play and peers. With the assistance of his peers, he is able to perform at the higher levels of his ZPD, but with the teacher he is not able to do so. We will discuss in Chapter 10 why play is so useful in helping children to move through a ZPD.

Assessing Children's Abilities

The idea of ZPD has direct implications for assessing what children know and can do. Instead of limiting assessment only to what children can do independently, we should include what they can do with different levels of assistance. Teachers should note how children use their help as well as what hints are the most useful. This technique, often called "dynamic assessment," has great potential for improving and expanding authentic classroom assessment and is discussed in detail in Chapter 14 (Cronbach, 1990; McAfee & Leong, 2006; Spector, 1992).

By using the ZPD in assessment, not only do we have a more accurate estimate of the child's abilities, but we have a more flexible way of assessing children. Teachers can rephrase a question, pose it differently, or encourage the child to show what she knows. Using the ZPD, we get at the child's best understanding.

Defining Developmentally Appropriate Practice

The idea of Developmentally Appropriate Practice (DAP) does include the idea of the ZPD, although it is not explained in those terms. Because of misunderstandings about the meaning of DAP, the National Association for the Education of Young Children published the *Basics of Developmentally Appropriate Practice: An Introduction for Teachers of Children 3–6* to explain the tenets of the approach (Copple & Bredekamp, 2005). Copple and Bredekamp encourage teachers to meet learners "where they are, taking into account their physical, emotional, social, and cognitive development and characteristics" but at the same time to "identify goals for children that are both challenging and achievable—a stretch but not a leap" (p. 7). There is a recognition that teaching must identify both the independent level of performance that marks the lowest level of the ZPD as well as goals that are beyond what the child can do independently, reaching into the ZPD.

The concept of ZPD expands the idea of what is developmentally appropriate to include things the child can learn with assistance. Vygotsky argues that the most effective teaching is aimed at the higher level of a child's ZPD. Teachers should provide activities just beyond what the child can do on his own but within what the child can do with assistance. Thus, the learning/teaching dialogue proceeds slightly ahead of the child's status at any given time. For example, if adults only provided language stimulation geared to the child's actual speech and not at a level slightly higher, then they would only use baby talk with toddlers and never speak in full sentences. In actual practice, of course, both parents and teachers intuitively add more information and use more complex grammar than the toddler is currently capable of producing. As a result, the child learns more complex grammar and expands her vocabulary.

Another example of how we intuitively use the level of assisted performance is when we deal with the conflicts that naturally arise between young children. When $2\frac{1}{2}$ year-olds are fighting, the teacher points out each child's feelings even though the children may not yet be able to take another person's perspective. Few teachers would want to wait until perspective-taking skills emerge naturally when children are 4 and 5 years of age before asking students to use them.

Vygotsky emphasizes that the child should practice what he can do independently and, at the same time, be exposed to things at the higher levels of the ZPD. Both levels are developmentally appropriate. Teachers must be sensitive to the child's reaction to the support and assistance provided in the ZPD. If the child accepts the teacher's support, then the teacher has hit within the ZPD. If a child ignores help, and still cannot perform at the higher level of the ZPD as expected, then the teacher needs to rethink the support. Perhaps the skill is outside this child's zone or the type of assistance provided is not useful and should be modified. The ZPD helps teachers look, in a more sensitive way, at what support to provide and how the child reacts.

Using the ZPD to Teach

Several researchers have taken the idea of the ZPD and tried to delineate more specifically what goes on within it. Vygotsky was rather vague about exactly how the child reaches the upper limit of the zone. From among the many psychologists who have discussed the ZPD, we have chosen a few who present more detail and whose works help teachers in the practical job of teaching children. Zaporozhets (1978, 1986); Wood, Bruner, and Ross (1976); Newman, Griffin, and Cole (1989); Tharp and Gallimore (1988); Cazden (1981); and Rogoff (1986) have all described what goes on within the ZPD in slightly different ways. Each conception adds to our understanding of the ZPD and how it works, giving guidance to teachers who want to use the ZPD to improve their teaching. More in-depth analysis of theoretical issues associated with the idea of the ZPD, as well as discussion of the implications of this idea for learning in teaching, can be found in the works of such Vygotskian scholars as S. Chaiklin (Chaiklin, 2003) and G. Wells (Wells, 1999).

Amplification

Zaporozhets (1978, 1986) has coined the term *amplification* to describe how to use the child's entire current ZPD to the fullest. The idea of amplification is the opposite of acceleration or speeding up a child's development. "Optimal educational opportunities for a young child to reach his or her potential and to develop in a harmonious fashion are not created by accelerated ultra-early instruction aimed at shortening the childhood period—that would prematurely turn a toddler into a preschooler and a preschooler into a first-grader" (Zaporozhets, 1978, p. 88). Acceleration, Zaporozhets maintains, does not lead to optimum development; it teaches skills that the child is not prepared to learn, because they lie far outside her ZPD. You can teach children some things outside of their ZPD, but this skill or content knowledge will exist as an isolated bit of information that will not be integrated into their world view. Consequently, acceleration does not have a positive impact on developmental accomplishments of the next period. For example, after much training, children as young as 3 years old can be taught to locate the letters on a computer keyboard. This learning, however, does not lead to the development of written speech because it is outside the child's ZPD. Another example can be seen when children memorize the multiplication table before they understand addition. They can be taught to do this, but they will not be able to use it meaningfully to solve problems.

Amplification, on the other hand, builds upon strengths and increases development but does not reach outside the ZPD. Amplification assists behaviors on the edge of emergence, using the tools and assisted performance within the child's ZPD. For example, preschool children learn many things by manipulating objects. Manipulatives can be used to teach concepts such as number or classification, which forms a part of theoretical reasoning at the next stage. Children can use manipulatives to understand a physical relationship, such as that between distance and speed. Children can use this knowledge when they are 9 or 10 and begin to reason about distance and speed in a more abstract way. Therefore, teaching preschoolers the abstract formula for the relationship between speed and distance would not be appropriate.

Scaffolding

Wood, Bruner, and Ross (1976) propose that the expert provide *scaffolding* within the ZPD to enable the novice to perform at a higher level. With scaffolding, the task itself is not changed, but what the learner initially does is made easier with assistance. Gradually, the level of assistance decreases as the learner takes more responsibility for performance of the task (Wood, Bruner, & Ross, 1976). For example, if a child is to count 10 objects, the initial task asked of the child is to count 10 objects (not 3 or 5 or 7). At the level of maximum scaffolding, the teacher counts out loud with the child, holding her finger as she points to each object. At this point, the teacher has most of the responsibility for counting, while the child follows his action. The teacher then gradually begins to withdraw support, just as the scaffolding of a building is taken away as the walls are capable of standing alone. The next time the child counts, the teacher does not say the numbers but still helps her point. Then the teacher may stop pointing at the objects, allowing the child to both point and count on her own.

Wood, Bruner, and Ross (1976) suggest that what the expert does when providing scaffolding may vary. Sometimes the adult might direct attention to an aspect that was forgotten; at other times the adult might actually model the correct manner of doing something. For scaffolding to be effective, however, the expert must enlist the child's interest:

> Reduce or simplify the number of steps required to solve the problem so the child can manage them, maintain the child's interest in pursuing the goal, point out the critical features that show the difference between the child's performance and the ideal performance, control frustration, and demonstrate the idealized version of what the child is doing. (Wood, Bruner, & Ross, 1976, p. 60)

Bruner studied scaffolding primarily in the area of language acquisition. He points out that when young children are learning language, parents present the child with mature speech. Not all sentences are reduced to baby talk. However, parents vary the amount of contextual support they give. They restate, repeat the important words that have meaning, use gestures, and respond to the child's utterances by focusing on the meaning of the child's utterances and not the grammatical form. Adults maintain a dialogue with the child as if the child is another adult who understands everything. Parents act as if the child can understand, thus responding to the ZPD and not to the child's actual level of speech production. This is what Garvey called talking with "the future child" (Garvey, 1986). Say that a child points to a tiger at the zoo and says, "Rrrrr," and the parent responds by saying, "Yes, that's a tiger. See her babies? She has three babies." The parent responds as if the child has produced the sentence "Look at the tiger." After repeated exposures to more mature language forms within the ZPD, children begin to acquire grammar. Bruner gave this support a specific name—the *Language Acquisition Support System,* or LASS.

At the beginning of the learning process, the adult provides more active interventions and greater amounts of scaffolding, directing more of the child's behavior than he will later in the process. As the child or novice learns, responsibility for the performance shifts as the learner takes a greater role in producing the behavior. The task of the adult or teacher then becomes one of timing the removal of the scaffolding to enhance the child's successful independent performance of the final behavior. This shift in responsibility is what Bruner has called the "hand over principle" by which the child who was at first the spectator becomes a participant (Bruner, 1983). The adult or expert hands over the task to the child. In summary, the idea of scaffolding clarifies that the following occurs within the ZPD:

1. The task is not made easier, but the amount of assistance is varied.
2. Responsibility for performances is transferred, or handed over, to the child as the child learns.
3. The support provided is temporary, and supports are removed gradually leading to independence.

The ZPD as Construction Zone

Michael Cole and his colleagues (Newman, Griffin, & Cole, 1989), who worked with children in elementary school classrooms in California, describe the ZPD as a "construction zone." They point out that co-construction is more than the teacher just telling the child what to do. The teacher must be as active in the process as the child. While the child constructs the concept, the teacher is constructing the child's unfolding understanding through questions, probes, and actions. So the teacher strives to understand how and what the child understands. They placed emphasis on the fact that the child does not have a full understanding of the goal or final performance until she has appropriated the concept. Their work helps highlight the importance of both participants in co-construction.

Performance and Competence

Another idea that helps clarify the ZPD is what Cazden (1981) terms "performance comes before competence." Children do not need full knowledge or full understanding of a task before it is taught to them. Competence and understanding are acquired after the task has been performed a number of times. Linda is learning how to add numbers using the Cuisenaire rods. She can correctly line up the correct number of 1s and 5s to make 10, but she can't explain the process. Even when she repeats the teacher's explanation, it appears that she is just repeating the words with little understanding. After a few more practices, the teacher's explanation dawns on her, and she says, "I get it!" As long as the behavior is within the child's ZPD, the lack of complete understanding is not a problem. That understanding will come with continued dialogue and interaction with others.

Structuring Situations

Rogoff studied assisted performance in informal settings, including mother-toddler interactions and interactions between weaving teachers and apprentices in Mexico (Rogoff, 1986, 1990; Rogoff & Wertsch, 1984). Rogoff argues that the adult or expert will grade or structure tasks into different levels or subgoals. These subgoals are then broken down further or are changed, recombined, and redefined as the ZPD is explored in the interaction between the participants. By choosing toys, equipment, materials, or tools, the expert limits and structures the task even before the learner appears. Later, as the ZPD is explored, the expert adjusts the task, breaking it into smaller, more manageable tasks that the learner can do. In addition, the expert might build redundancy into the interaction, repeating directions or modeling actions several times. Structuring aids the learner in performing at the highest level of the ZPD. Rogoff emphasizes the importance of the changes the expert must make to assist performance. The changes in adult structuring and support follow the learner's lead and are not arbitrarily imposed based on the content of the material or an abstract idea of how the information should be taught. Even in apprenticeship situations, although different from those found in the classroom, the expert still breaks goals into subgoals that are redefined and recombined as the student's performance improves.

Dynamics of Scaffolding within the ZPD

Tharp and Gallimore (1988) directed the Kamehameha Elementary Education Program (KEEP) in Hawaii and worked with elementary-aged children. They have proposed a four-stage description of the ZPD that goes beyond the definition commonly used by most researchers in the Vygotskian framework. The most distinctive aspect of their approach is the concept of performance in the ZPD as a circular, recursive process, rather than a linear one. Their concept of the ZPD is similar to the one mentioned previously with the added idea that once a concept or skill is appropriated, there are conditions under which the child may need scaffolding anew. When confronted with new and different contexts, the child may need support in transferring the skills to a new situation.

The idea of the ZPD has important implications for education. It provides alternative perspectives on the way we assist children in the learning/teaching process, how we assess children, and how we define developmentally appropriate practice. In the chapters that follow, we will discuss how to apply these ideas in different classroom situations.

For Further Reading

Chaiklin, S. (2003). The zone of proximal development in Vygotsky's analysis of learning and instruction. In A. Kozulin, B. Gindis, V. Ageyev, & S. Miller (Eds.), *Vygotsky's educational theory in cultural context.* New York: Cambridge University Press.

Rogoff, B., & Wertsch, J. (Eds.). (1984). *Children's learning in the "zone of proximal development."* San Francisco: Jossey-Bass.

Wells, G. (1999). The zone of proximal development and its implications for learning and teaching. In *Dialogic inquiry: Towards a sociocultural practice and theory of education.* New York: Cambridge University Press.

CHAPTER 5

Tactics: Using Mediators

 Teachers can promote development and help children move from assisted to independent performance. The Vygotskian paradigm suggests that one way to do this is to have children use such simple mental tools as mediators. Mediators facilitate the handing over of responsibility to the child. Developed with adult assistance, they can be used by the child without the teacher's physical presence. In this chapter, we describe mediators and suggest ways in which they can be used in an early childhood classroom.

Mediators as Mental Tools

In Vygotsky's work, a *mediator* is something that stands as an intermediary between an environmental stimulus and an individual response to that stimulus (See chapter 3, Figure 3.1). We create mediators to prompt a specific response. For example, when we draw an arrow pointing to a specific place on a map, we do it so that we can find this spot faster next time we consult the map. The arrow mediator prompts us to attend to one particular spot and to not waste time scanning the entire map. Mediators can assist a number of mental processes—perception, attention, memory—as well as specific social behaviors.

Adults are capable of creating and using complex, abstract mediators—including signs, symbols, graphic models, plans, and maps—suitable for a variety of tasks. These mediators may be visible to others, such as a list of things to do, or they may be internal, such as a mnemonic technique. Most of the time, adults use these mediators in an integrated fashion and often automatically, without consciously thinking about it. Sometimes, however, adults are faced with situations in which the automatic use of mediators is interrupted or made difficult in some way. In such situations, adults resort to using external, overt mediators instead of their internal ones. For example, an adult who is using an unfamiliar stove must look at the dials on the control panel (the external mediator) and figure out which burner is which. When using a familiar stove, the adult has an internal pattern relating the burners to the dials. Another example is an adult who is driving a car with a shifting pattern that is new to her. She will look at the diagram on the handle of the gear shift to make sure that she is in first gear and not in reverse!

Unlike adults and older children, young children can only use mediators that are external and overt, because the use of mediation is not yet integrated into their thought patterns. External, overt mediators are visible to others and to the child, and can even be tangible. Sophie wants to write the word "make." She says the word slowly and isolates the "mm." She looks on an alphabet chart and finds the picture that starts with the same sound. She thinks "moon" starts like "make" so she writes the letter that is next to the picture of the "moon"—the letter "*M*." Tony is learning to add numbers. He uses his fingers to help him calculate. His fingers act as a mediator, making his adding more accurate. In each case, the child uses the mediator to expedite behavior. External mediators are among the first mental tools young children learn to use.

The Function of Mediators

As is the case with all mental tools, mediators have two functions. Their first, immediate function is to help children solve problems at hand and make it possible for them to perform independently in situations that previously required direct adult guidance. Ms. Martinez wants to limit the number of children who can play in the block-building area at one time. To rely on the children themselves to remember that only four can enter the area would not be effective because some of the children cannot count meaningfully or use counting as a way to regulate their actions. This means that Ms. Martinez has to act as the "center police"—a role she does not like. To encourage children to take responsibility for monitoring the number of children in a center, she places a box at the entrance of each center and a coffee can. The box contains pictures of four chairs and the coffee can has a picture of the center. When Michael enters the block area, he takes one of the chair pictures and puts it in the coffee can. Johannes, Morgan, and Erika do the same. When all of the chair pictures are gone, it signals to everyone that a new child cannot enter. By providing the chair pictures, Ms. Martinez provides a tangible mediator to help the children remember the limit.

The second function of mediators is a long-term one—to contribute to the restructuring of children's minds by promoting the transformation of lower mental functions into higher mental functions (see Chapter 2). Describing the effects of the use of mediators on a child's mental functioning Vygotsky (1978) writes:

> [T]he child who formerly solved the problem impulsively now solves it through an internally established connection between the stimulus and the corresponding auxiliary sign [i.e., mediator—EB, DL]. . . . The system of signs restructures the whole psychological process. (p. 35)

We can illustrate this "restructuring of the whole psychological process" using an example of memory. When asked about his favorite book, 4-year-old Trevor first recalls one episode, then another, then somehow switches to talking about a completely different book. In recalling the story, Trevor acts "impulsively" meaning that he uses his associative memory (Chapter 2) and not his deliberate memory. Four years later, Trevor has much better control over his recall. By now, he has several mediators he can choose from when retelling a story: he can mark beginning, middle, and end of the story with different colored stickers; draw pictures of the most important events; or write an outline of the story. Not only can his memory hold more information now, its entire structure has changed as a result of Trevor's learning to use mediators.

Developmental Path of Mediators

In the Vygotskian framework, mediators become mental tools when the child incorporates them into his own activity. Like other cultural tools, mediators first exist in shared activity and then are appropriated by the child. Vygotsky (1994) identified four stages in children's learning to use mediators. These stages can be applied to a child's learning of a specific mediator (such as learning to use an alphabet chart or to count on fingers), but they also can be applied to the overall transformation of a child's learning processes that takes place as a result of acquiring mental tools.

In the first stage, children's behavior is governed by lower mental functions and any mediators, even if introduced by an adult, have no effect on this behavior. In the second stage, children can use mediators but only with adults' help and only in situations similar to the ones in which these mediators were initially introduced. The third stage is where children begin using mediators independently with increased deliberateness. However, at this stage, similar to the previous one, the mediator remains external to a child, thus limiting the range of its usage. Finally, in the fourth stage, the tool is internalized. At this point, external tools are no longer needed and new behavior that is now mediated by a more sophisticated mental tool often reaches a qualitatively new level.

In his studies of the development of attention, memory, and other mental functions, Leont'ev (1981, 1994) was able to demonstrate the existence of these stages experimentally and to identify the age ranges where qualitative changes in the use of mediators take place. In one of his experiments, subjects were asked to play a game of "forbidden colors." In this game, the subject has to answer a series of questions without using the name of a certain color (e.g., black and white) and without using the same color twice. The experimenter meanwhile tries to "trick" the subject into naming the forbidden color by asking such questions as, "What is the color of snow?" or "What is the color of coal?" The accuracy of the answers increased with the age of the subjects: preschoolers were easily "tricked" by the experimenter and made many errors, in contrast high school students and adults were able to pay attention to all of the questions and to remember the colors they had named earlier.

In a different series of this experiment, subjects were given a stack of color cards (mediators) and told that they could use these cards to help them play the game. For the 4-year-old children, the introduction of cards did not change their behavior—they did not attempt to use the cards as external mediators. Six- and seven-year-olds attempted to make a connection between the color of a card and a color they named, but they were unable to use the cards as a tool in a systematic fashion. Eight- to ten-year-olds, on the other hand, significantly improved their game score by methodically rearranging the cards after each new answer so that only the allowed colors stayed visible. Interestingly, older children and adults did not seem to need the cards to assist in their game—Leont'ev hypothesized that by now their internal strategies for remembering were good enough to yield a high score without a visual reminder.

Leont'ev described the results of this experiment—as well as the results of similar experiments that focused on other mediated behaviors—in a graph that he labeled "developmental parallelogram" (see Figure 5.1). On this graph, the lines of nonmediated and mediated mental behaviors have two points of convergence: one in younger preschoolers who have not yet started to use mediators and the other in adults who have abandoned the use of external mediators in favor of more advanced internal strategies.

Mediation of Social and Emotional Behaviors

Vygotsky points out that people have a long history of using mediators to control their emotions. He uses an example of a person casting lots instead of forever agonizing over what would be the best course of action (Vygotsky, 1997). In Vygotsky's example, this person "delegates" the process of decision making to a die—an external mediator. Tossing a coin or drawing a straw are ways to resolve an argument using an external mediator to control one's emotions—this time in a situation that involves social interactions. Children use rhymes or finger plays ("one potato, two potato"; "scissors, paper, stone") to settle arguments about who goes first or how long each child gets to have a toy.

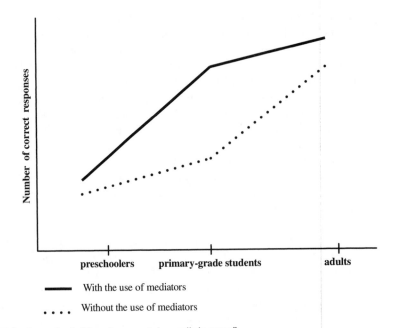

Figure 5.1   Leont'ev's "developmental parallelogram"

A common way to control emotions is "counting to 10" before reacting, as a way to avoid becoming angry. The act of counting serves as an external mediator. Children chant rhymes like "Sticks and stones may break my bones, but words will never hurt me" instead of hitting. By chanting, they gain control over their urge to fight.

Some external mediators are passed from one generation of children to another in the playgrounds of the world. Without older children around, it is unlikely that preschool children would know about these things. In some cases, teachers may have to give children the external mediators they would otherwise get from older children, for example how to use a rhyme or spin a spinner to resolve a dispute. Children can also be taught to use more "grown-up" mediators such as counting to 10 or taking 10 deep breaths to help overcome their angry feelings.

External Mediation of Cognition

The idea of using mediation to amplify and support cognitive development has been applied in a variety of classrooms in Russia and in the United States. In early childhood education, mediators are most useful in assisting children within their ZPD in the areas of perception, attention, memory, and thinking.

Perception

Alexander Zaporozhets, Vygotsky's student and colleague, suggests that children learn perceptual categories through external mediation (Zaporozhets, 1977). Everyday objects become sensory standards that help children perceive differences in color, size, shape, and even sound. For example, children learn the difference between orange and red when they compare an orange with a tomato. If 2-year-olds are just given color cards with no contextual clues and then asked which is red and which is orange, they may have a hard time answering. When the everyday object is included as a contextual clue, toddlers answer at a much higher level. Asking "Is it the color of a tomato or the color of an orange?" will elicit more correct answers. Zaporozhets argues that exposure to everyday objects in which the perceptual characteristics are identified helps in the development of perceptual categories.

Attention

Children use mediators to attend to, or focus on, objects, events, and behaviors. Vygotskians are interested in deliberate attention—when the child consciously focuses his mind. This higher mental function is different from the spontaneous attention that children display for bright-colored objects, loud noises, and perceptually distinctive events. The ability to attend deliberately is a necessary skill for learning because the thing that is most attention-grabbing may not be the most important characteristic of what the child is learning about. Children have to learn to ignore competing or distracting information and to focus on specific characteristics that are important to solving a problem or learning a task. In reading, it may not be important that the letter *b* is red, but the orientation of the letter—which side of the line has the bulge—is critical.

Actual mediators that can help in focusing attention differ depending on the nature of the task and the age of the child. A first grader learning to read uses her own finger as a mediator as she points to the words. Pointing helps her to focus on one word at a time and to not be distracted by other words on the page or by the bright pictures. A high school student studying for a test highlights the essential definitions in the textbook so he can later review the most important information at a glance and not waste time on lengthy examples and detailed explanations. In this later case, the student mediates his attention by highlighting some words and not the others.

Vygotskians argue that children cannot attend deliberately without the support of mediators, especially when the demands on their attention increase. As Leont'ev (1981; 1994) has found in his "forbidden colors" experiment and in other experiments, young children would not discover how to use external mediators on their own but would master their use in the context of meaningful activity shared with adults.

Memory

Another higher mental function that can be assisted through mediation is deliberate memory. With an ever-increasing amount of information to remember, memory definitely can use some help! Using external mediators to support memory is not a new idea; in fact, adults use them all the time. We use calendars, make lists of things to do, and set up electronic reminders for appointments. Many time-management techniques incorporate clever external mediators to help us stay on task and on target.

Teachers and parents agree that young children have very good memories for certain things, but most of them also note that this skill seems to disappear when children need to remember something on demand. The kindergartner, who has no trouble memorizing 150-something Pokémon characters in a week, can spend several months memorizing a mere 26 letters of the alphabet! Vygotskians make a distinction between *associative* memory that is increased by such things as multiple repetitions and *deliberate* memory (see Chapter 2). The latter is a higher mental function that emerges as a result of a child's aquisition and continuous use of mental tools.

In his research on memory, Leont'ev (1981) found that its developmental trajectory follows the same paralellogram as attention (see Figure 5.1). When asked to memorize a list of isolated words with and without pictures, preschoolers as well as adults demonstrated very little difference in their recall for a nonmediated and a mediated condition. In contrast, children of school age demonstrated much better recall when they were able to choose a picture to remind them of a word they were memorizing. In more recent research, it was confirmed that older preschoolers and primary grade students can be trained to use external mediators to increase their memory capacities (e.g., Fletcher & Bray, 1997). At the same time, research indicates that young children have difficulties, both with generating their own mediators and with the systematic use of existing mediators without substantial adult help. (See Pressley & Harris, in press, for the review of the research.)

Thinking

According to the Vygotskians, external mediation helps children make the transition from sensorimotor thinking to visual-representational thinking (Poddyakov, 1977) and facilitates their problem solving in situations that require logical reasoning (Pick, 1980; Venger, 1988). Mediators also help children to monitor and reflect on their own thinking and prompt metacognitive skills.

In younger children, mediation occurs in the context of "uniquely preschool" activities such as drawing and building with blocks:

> Development of . . . mediation in preschool period is connected with productive forms
> of activity, for example, drawing, construction, etc. (Zaporozhets, 1978, p. 149)

The value of these activities for Vygotskians lies in the fact that children use material objects (such as blocks) or materialized representations (such as pictures) to model real-life relationships. Block structures and pictures become mediators that assist young children in understanding these real-life relationships in a more abstract way. For example, using blocks to build two garages, one for a large car and one for a small car, helps preschoolers explore the idea of size.

In older children, similar modeling can be used to represent more complex relationships including the relationships between abstract concepts. These include social roles, musical patterns, sound-letter correspondences, elements of stories (story grammar), union and intersection of sets, projections of three-dimensional objects into two-dimensional space, speed and distance, and money value (Venger, 1988, 1986). In this case, teaching specific external mediators (such as Venn diagrams or graphs) requires a greater degree of adult support and monitoring.

Using Mediators in the Classroom

In an early childhood classroom, the mediators that children can be taught to use are primarily external. In later grades, as children master written language and develop higher mental functions, they will start using more and more internal mediators such as mnemonic techniques, while continuing to use some that are external such as tables or diagrams.

Mediators as Scaffolding

Mediators function as scaffolding, helping children make the transition from maximum assisted performance to independent performance (see Chapter 4). As the children move through the ZPD, what children can do with assistance becomes what children can do independently. How does this movement occur? First, an adult introduces new mediators and then assists children in practicing the use of these mediators in shared activity. Finally, mediators are appropriated by children and are applied in new situations. As children internalize mediators introduced by an adult, they are able to maintain the same high level of performance independently that was initially assisted by the adult.

As is the case with any type of scaffolding, most mediators are only needed temporarily and should no longer be used after they have outlived their utility. Children usually stop using mediators on their own once they have mastered a new skill or concept; you will not find a high school student still using his fingers to count. Other mediators evolve or become absorbed by the new, more advanced ones. For example, while preschool children turn over icons on their picture schedule to keep track of their daily routines, second graders use a written schedule and a clock for the same purpose.

Therefore teachers need to plan not only how to introduce an external mediator and how to monitor its use by children, but also how and when this external mediator will be removed and whether a new, more advanced mediator will be needed to replace the old one. The appropriate time for removing a mediator cannot be determined exactly. Sometimes children will forget the external mediator and need to use it again for a short time. Sometimes a few successes are enough, and you can begin weaning the child from the overt mediator very quickly.

External mediators lose their value if they are used after the children have developed an appropriate internal representation or strategy—in fact they may even become detrimental to learning because they distract children from the task. For example, after preschoolers begin to recognize (even not perfectly) their names in print, any pictures or symbols used earlier to label their chairs, cubbies, etc. should be removed in favor of the printed name alone. Using the printed name at this stage encourages children to pay better attention to print.

What Mediators Are Not

If you ask a teacher to point to a child who is or is not using a mediator, most teachers have no problem identifying the case of mediator use. They would correctly point to a child who moves a "word window" along the line of print while reading or to one who uses a calendar to count the days before a break. However, when trying to introduce a new mediator to children, teachers often become confused about what mediators are and what they are not. Here we will discuss the two most common confusions.

1. *Mediators are not the same as reinforcement.* Vygotskians make a distinction between giving children stickers for good behavior and mediation for self-regulation. Giving children stickers for behavior means that the teacher controls the sticker and that the sticker is given *after the fact.* This is "teacher-regulation." Mediation for self-regulation means that the child uses the mediator to self-prompt behavior *before* it happens so that he acts in a certain way. It occurs *prior to the behavior* and is regulated by the children themselves.

2. *Mediators are not the same as discriminative stimuli.* Used as a part of behavior modification strategy called "cueing" these stimuli are *initiated by the teacher* to indicate whether a certain behavior is appropriate and therefore will be reinforced. An example would be a teacher ringing the bell to signal the end of center time. Again, this is a case of "teacher-regulation" and not self-regulation: the teacher does not hand over responsibility to the child for using the mediator (the bell) to initiate a behavior. To be a mediator in the Vygotskian sense, the child must use it without prompting on his own accord. For example, if the teacher turns a timer on when two children have a dispute over computer time, this is "teacher-regulation." However, when a child turns the timer on by herself to limit her own computer time, the timer becomes the child's mediator for her own behavior.

Examples of Using External Mediators in a Classroom

In our work with teachers, we are often asked what makes a good external mediator. We have found that pretty much anything will work as long as it is salient and doesn't blend into the background. Colored pens and pencils, stick-on notes, and menus (lists of things to do) help to remind children about directions or to make aspects of the reading or writing process more salient. Tangible, movable objects such as rings, bracelets, clothespins, or stuffed animals on pins or bracelets work best for social behaviors and for attention and memory activities where children move around the room. To help children control physical behaviors, such as leaning on others during circle time, the mediator has to give the child a physical or kinesthetic boundary, such as a chair or a carpet square. We even used the teacher's picture as an external mediator to help a child who had trouble keeping on task doing his homework. When he put the teacher's picture on his desk, he was able to get his homework done much more quickly.

Mediators exist in shared activity first. This means that adults provide the mediators when the child begins to learn. Initially, adults may find that they have to provide many different mediators. Teachers should not assume that one mediator will work for all the children. Lani is very distractable during group meeting time and requires maximum mediation before he is able to attend through a story. He does best when he sits on a carpet square with his name on it, with a stuffed animal on his lap, between two children who hold his hands during the story, and in front of the teacher (four mediators!). With this much mediation, he is able to sit through the story. After successfully doing this for a week, the teacher begins to remove the mediators one by one. First, Lani sits alone in front of the teacher on his carpet square with the stuffed animal. The next week he sits on his carpet square alone. Then 4 weeks later, the teacher takes his name tag off the carpet square and Lani puts it on his arm; he no longer needs the physical reminder of the carpet square. Finally, in 5 weeks he no longer needs the name tag. The teacher carefully plans how she will take the scaffolding away.

In first and second grade, teachers typically give many directions to children orally without mediational support to help them remember what to do. Ms. Margolis expects her children to remember that there are three centers they must visit during center learning time. Many of the children have no trouble remembering, but Ida, Joseph, and Dionnia never get past the first center. No matter what Ms. Margolis does, these three children go through parts of the first center and then become wanderers around the room. Ms. Margolis decides to give them an external mediator in the form of a ticket with the numbers 1, 2, and 3 written on it. After she sends the other children to the centers, she sits down with her wandering threesome and has them write down in their own way something that will remind them of the centers they are supposed to go to. Ida writes a word after each number, Joseph writes letters, and Dionnia draws a picture. Ms. Margolis pins the notes to their clothes with clothespins. "When you have finished at the center," she tells them, "check it off on your ticket. Then the ticket will help you remember where to go next." By the end of the first week, only Ida and Dionnia need to use the tickets. By the end of the third week, all three children have begun to remember the routine.

Mediators such as Venn diagrams can illustrate how two categories of objects are similar and different. Two circles that completely overlap indicate that the categories are the same. Two distinct circles mean that the categories have no characteristics in common. When the two circles partially overlap, it means that some characteristics are shared and some are not. By using this visual mediator, children are able to classify objects at a much more abstract level than if they are merely asked to put the objects into piles. This mediator can be used first for real objects and then for ideas, as in asking second graders how two stories are the same or different (see Figure 5.2).

Some teachers use word maps or concept webs to help children see the relationship between different concepts, ideas, or words (see Figure 5.3). In a web, major categories can be written in larger print than subcategories. Developing the web as the children contribute ideas helps to crystallize and sharpen their understanding of the relationships.

External mediators like songs, rhymes, or a timer can be used to signal activities that have a short duration, such as cleanup time or other transition times. Make sure

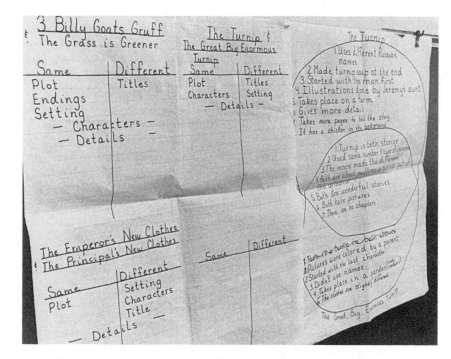

Figure 5.2 Using a Venn diagram as a mediator for story analysis

Figure 5.3   Using a word map as an external mediator

the song or rhyme is long enough so that when it is finished, the children have finished the activity and are ready for the next thing. If you use a timer, make sure it visibly shows how much time is left. Digital timers do not usually work well, but an analog timer with a dial or a three-minute egg timer in the shape of an old-fashioned hour glass would be useful. For a preschool child, the idea of being ready for the next activity in 3 minutes makes no sense. Three minutes may seem like a lifetime or a moment, depending on what the child is doing. Children need an external reminder to help them tell when the time is coming to an end. Thus, a song with a predictable melody and ending will signal "I have one song's worth of time to finish." They will then be better able to gauge how fast to move than they would be with just a verbal reminder.

Older children can use self-generated or teacher-given lists and menus to regulate their own behavior. One teacher in a mixed-age class (K–2) uses menus for reading, language arts, and math. The menu has a choice of activities the child can choose from during literacy block. For example, the children can read books and write their own versions, they can act out a flannel board version, or they can make a diorama. The menu reminds the children of what they are supposed to do during reading time (see Figure 5.4).

At the beginning of the year, the teacher and the child fill in the plan together. By the end of the year, the child fills in more and more of the plan himself. Each week, the teacher also asks the children a reflection question designed to get them to think about their own mental processes. This has been helpful in producing more self-regulatory behavior. Once when the teacher was late coming in from recess, she was shocked to see the entire class, including the kindergartners, fast at work without her. They had taken out their menus and were working furiously at their tasks unprompted. The room was hushed except for several children who were working in pairs. The idea of menus can be adapted to projects and many other areas of the primary classroom.

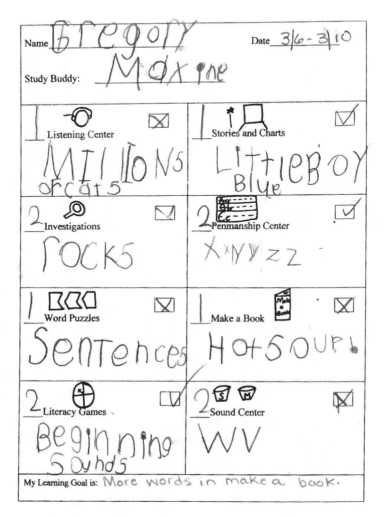

Figure 5.4   An example of a child's menu or learning plan

Guidelines for Using External Mediators

After Vygotsky introduced the idea of external mediation and its effects on child development, his students expanded the idea and applied it to teaching and learning. In
particular, Zaporozhets (1977), Venger (1977, 1986), Elkonin (1977), Gal'perin
(1969), and their students and colleagues elaborated on the uses of external mediation. The following recommendations are distilled and adapted from their work.

To be effective, the external mediator must initiate the behavior at the right time.
It must have the following characteristics.

1. *The mediator must have special meaning for the young child and be able to invoke that
meaning.* The child must be able to touch or see the mediator, and it must elicit specific thoughts or behaviors. The child must be able to say, for example, "When I put
a yellow sticker on my backpack, I am supposed to remember to go to my recorder

lesson today," "When I hear the last verse about the llamas wearing their pajamas in the clean-up song I am supposed to finish cleaning up and go to sit on the carpet," or "When the snack picture is taken off the schedule, the next thing we do is get dressed and go outside." The mediator must have meaning to the child; it will not be useful if it has meaning only to the adult. The child may choose the mediator with adult help, but she may need coaching and practice in using it before it takes on the intended meaning. Once it has, the child should take some action to evoke the mediator. For example, the child must pick up the carpet square, take the picture of a chair out of the box, or get the ticket. The act of mediation must be incorporated into the actions that occur as part of the activity.

2. *The mediator must be attached to an object that the child will use before or while performing the task.* If the goal is to remember to take home boots, the mediator must be attached to something the child looks at just before starting for home. It cannot be attached to something the child uses in the morning. If the child must remember something after lunch, then the mediator should be attached to the lunch box. If it is time to put toys away, a special kind of music can be played that is only used during cleanup time. If the alphabet line is to help children form letters as they write in their journals, the letters must be contained on a card the children have at their desks. The alphabet line on the bulletin board is too far removed from the child's activity to be a meaningful mediator for most children.

3. *The mediator must remain salient to the child.* Mediators will lose their distinctiveness and will no longer prompt appropriate behavior if they are used too much or for too long a time. Pick a specific time when the mediator will be most likely to stay salient. Do not have the child pick up the carpet square first thing in the morning and carry it with him all day and don't tape it to the carpet. Instead, have the child use the mediator for a short period of time during which she has trouble with a particular skill—for example only during the circle time. Make the purpose of the mediator explicit, as in, "This carpet square will help you remember not to lean on other people when you are sitting in the circle. If your foot sticks outside of the square it may bother your neighbor." Once the child succeeds in remembering successfully a number of times, the mediator should be removed.

4. *Combine mediation with language and other behavioral cues.* With the mediator, use a set of behaviors that can become a habit and words that can become private speech to self-coach. For example, you might put up a picture of a lightbulb right by the classroom door at the beginning of the school day to prompt focused attention. The lightbulb is a symbol for a routine of pausing and saying in a whisper before entering, "What am I supposed to remember to do today? I'm supposed to remember to listen and concentrate." Prompt the use of memory strategies by using a graphic picture of a child pointing to her temple. Bring the picture out when the children are supposed to remember something, such as bringing a book from home. Use the picture with words like "Let's put it in our memory bank by saying what we need to remember three times." Then both you and the children point at your temples and say "Bring a book from home to share." Soon the picture will prompt the strategy of repeating to oneself to remember.

5. *Choose a mediator that is within the child's ZPD.* For a mediator to work, it must be within the child's ZPD and used by the child to direct his actions. Using the

number *4* outside a center to remind students that only 4 children can go there would not be within the ZPD of a child who cannot count. For young children, usually one mediator relates to one behavior or action. Only when children are older can mediators remind them of several things to do.

6. *Always use the mediator to represent what you want the child to do.* Mediators prompt specific behaviors and actions. Be sure to coach the children on what you want them to *do* and not just what you want them to stop doing. It is easier to replace a behavior than to inhibit one. Having children highlight only the most important idea in a paragraph is a more effective way to teach summarization than to constantly remind them that they are not supposed to copy the entire paragraph.

7. *When introducing a new mediator, have a plan for how the child will use it independently.* It is critical that the child be able to use a mediator to prompt his own behavior without the teacher's reminder. The teacher must make a concerted effort to hand over this responsibility to the child, because it will not happen naturally. If after some time the child still has to be reminded of a specific behavior, it probably means that the mediator does not work. Review guidelines 1 through 6 and choose another mediator.

For Further Reading

Bodrova, E., & Leong, D. J. (2003). Learning and development of preschool children from the Vygotskian perspective. In A. Kozulin, B. Gindis, V. Ageyev, & S. Miller (Eds.), *Vygotsky's educational theory in cultural context* (pp. 156–176). New York: Cambridge University Press.

Karpov, Y. V. (2005). *The neo-Vygotskian approach to child development.* New York: Cambridge University Press.

Kozulin, A. (1990). *Vygotsky's psychology: A biography of ideas.* Cambridge: Harvard University Press.

Stetsenko, A. (2004). Section introduction: Scientific legacy. In R. W. Rieber & D. K. Robinson (Eds.), *The essential Vygotsky* (pp. 501–512). New York: Kluwer.

Van der Veer, R., & Valsiner, J. (1991). *Understanding Vygotsky, a quest for synthesis.* Cambridge: Blackwell.

Venger, L. A. (1977). The emergence of perceptual actions. In M. Cole (Ed.), *Soviet developmental psychology: An anthology.* White Plains, NY: Sharpe. (Original work published in 1969)

Venger, L. A. (1988). The origin and development of cognitive abilities in preschool children. *International Journal of Behavioral Development, 11*(2), 147–153.

CHAPTER 6

Tactics: Using Language

 Three-year-old Joe is baking pizza with the teacher but can't roll out the dough, so Mr. Sanchez says, "Roll the pin to you and away, to . . . and away . . . ," as he helps Joe move the rolling back and forth toward himself and then away from his body. He is helping Joe feel the rolling pin moving back and forth. With this aid, Joe is immediately able to roll out the dough. As Mr. Sanchez moves away to help another child, he hears Joe sing "To . . . away . . . to . . . away . . ." over and over again to himself as he rolls the pin over the dough.

Five-year-old Maura is counting objects. "There are eight of them," she says. The teacher adds one more to the pile and says, "I'm adding one. How many are there now?" Maura looks at the pile and then begins to count: "One, two, three, four, five, six, seven, eight, nine. There are nine now." The teacher adds another object, and Maura again starts counting from 1.

Six-year-old Jason is doing a movement exercise pattern of one jump and two hops. Jason says the pattern out loud, "Jump, hop, hop," as he does each step. He is so loud that the teacher asks him to stop talking because he is mixing everyone else up. The minute he stops, he cannot move. Only when all the other children finish and the teacher lets Jason resume his chant can he finish.

In all of these situations, children are using language to help them perform a behavior and to think. Language plays a central role in mental development. This is one of the four major principles of the Vygotskian paradigm. Language is a major cultural tool that enables us to think logically and to learn new behaviors. It facilitates the conversion of external experience into internal representations of that experience. It influences more than just the content that we know; it also impacts thinking and the acquisition of new knowledge. In this chapter, we discuss how language develops and how teachers can use language to promote development and to assist learning in the classroom.

Language as a Cultural Tool

Language is a universal cultural tool that is applied in many contexts to solve a myriad of problems. Vygotsky and many other theorists argue that language separates humans from animals, making humans more efficient and effective problem solvers. All humans in all cultures have developed language. Because humans possess language, they can solve much more complex problems than primates, who do not possess language. In studies comparing problem-solving skills, researchers found that young toddlers and chimpanzees were similar in solving sensorimotor problems (Kozulin, 1990). However, once the toddlers acquired language, their problem-solving ability improved dramatically. Thereafter, the chimpanzees were not able to solve problems at the same level as the toddlers.

We use language in speaking, writing, drawing, and thinking. These manifestations of language are different, but they have some common features. Speech directed outward enables us to communicate with other people, while speech directed inward allows us to communicate to ourselves, to regulate our own behavior and thinking. We use writing to communicate with others, and to externalize and make our own thought processes tangible. Drawing and other graphic representations of our thinking serve a function similar to writing. Thinking is an inner dialogue in which we play out different perspectives, ideas, or concepts in the mind.

As a cultural tool, language is a distillation of the categories, concepts, and modes of thinking of a culture. Like some Western anthropologists and psycholinguists (Sapir, 1921; Wells, 1981; Whorf, 1956), Vygotskians believe that language shapes the mind to function in the most efficient way for a particular culture. Therefore, Eskimo people have many words for snow, Guatemalan Indians who are weavers have many words for textures of yarn, and Asian cultures have many words to define familial relationships and kinships. Language reflects the importance of certain elements of the physical and social environment.

Language allows the acquisition of new information: content, skills, strategies, and processes. While not all learning involves language, complex ideas and processes can only be appropriated with the help of language. The idea of number is only internalized with the help of language. Through language, strategies for solving social conflicts are also taught.

Since language is a universal cultural tool, delays in its development have severe consequences. Language delays impact other areas of development, including motor, social, and cognitive. Luria presents the case of twins who had severe language delays because they had little interaction with others (Luria, 1979). These 5-year-olds also had significant delays in social and problem-solving skills. Once their language abilities improved, the twins showed similar gains in other areas of development. Research in special education also shows possible connections between language delays and problems in school.

The Functions of Speech

In the Vygotskian paradigm, speech has two different functions (Zivin, 1979). *Public speech,* the term used for language directed at others, has a social, communicative function. It is spoken aloud and directs or communicates with others. Public speech can be formal, such as a lecture, or informal, such as a discussion over the dinner table. *Private speech* describes self-directed speech that is audible but not intended for others. This type of speech has a self-regulatory function.

Public speech and private speech emerge at different times. In infancy, speech has a primarily public function and is vital for adaptation to the social environment and learning (Vygotsky, 1987). As the child grows, speech acquires a new function; it is not used solely for communication but also for helping the child to master his own behavior and acquire new knowledge. Not every concept the child learns proceeds through private speech, but most of them do. Young children establish relationships between concepts by trying different combinations of objects and ideas through private speech, because they cannot silently consider these relationships.

Developmental Path of Speech

Vygotsky believed that the origins of speech are social, even from the very beginning in infancy (Vygotsky, 1987). Both receptive and productive language have their roots in the social exchanges that occur between a child and her caregiver. Practically any infant vocalization is interpreted as a social, communicative event as if the baby is "saying" something. A parent engages in conversations with a baby even though the baby only responds with babbling and cooing sounds. Walk down a supermarket aisle behind a parent with a 6-month-old and you might hear a discussion like this: "Should we buy rice or oatmeal?" "Ababaa." "Oh, sure, let's buy the oatmeal!" "Abaaasajaa."

This interpreting of all vocalizations and gestures as social is a uniquely human trait. Even deaf parents treat infant gestures as conveying a message. However, studies of chimpanzees taught American Sign Language found that the chimpanzee mothers never try to interpret the random behaviors and gestures of their babies as having communicative value (Kozulin, 1990).

Interpreting language as social is a view that is different from that of Piaget, who believed that speech reflects the child's present level of mental processing and is based on the child's schemas and internal representations (Piaget, 1926). Using speech in social interactions follows these internal representations. In his early writings, Piaget argued that speech begins by being extremely egocentric or even autistic, reflecting the general egocentrism of the preschool child's mind. Piaget's later views on the role of social interaction in the development of cognitive processes were modified to accommodate Vygotsky's ideas. Also, current theories of language development acknowledge the contributions of the social context (John-Steiner, Panofsky, & Smith, 1994).

The Emergence of Speech and Thinking

Vygotsky believed that there is a time in infancy and toddlerhood when thinking proceeds without language and language is used only for communication. Other psychologists, such as Piaget (1926, 1951) and Bruner (1968), seem to concur that children go through a stage in which language is not essential to thinking or problem solving. Children solve problems with sensorimotor actions or by manipulating images rather than concepts or words (Bruner, 1968). Language at this stage communicates wants and needs to others. For example, the word *Baba* may mean "I want my bottle." *Baba* is not used to stand for all bottles, as it may when the child is older. Vygotsky used the terms *preverbal thought* and *preintellectual speech* to describe this stage (Vygotsky, 1987).

Between 2 and 3 years of age, thinking and speech merge. From this point on, so Vygotsky believed, neither speech nor thinking would ever be the same. When thinking and speech merge, thinking acquires a verbal basis and speech becomes intellectual, because it is used in thinking. Speech is then employed for purposes other than communication. After studying children using speech to solve problems, Vygotsky and Luria (1994) drew this conclusion:

> 1. A child's speech is an inalienable and internally necessary part of the operation [of problem solving], its role being as important as that of action in the attaining of a goal. The experimenter's impression is that the child not only speaks about what he is doing, but that for him speech and action are in this case *one and the same complex psychological function* directed toward the solution of the given problem.
> 2. The more complex the action demanded by the situation and the less directed its solution, the greater the importance played by speech in the operation as a whole.

Sometimes speech becomes of such vital importance that without it the child proves to be positively unable to accomplish the given task.(Vygotsky & Luria, 1994, p. 109)

To put this into simpler language, children become capable of thinking *as* they talk. The child can think aloud. This idea is very different from talking *after* we think. Vygotsky believed that for young children thinking and speaking occur simultaneously. He argues that in some cases, our external speech helps us form ideas that may exist only vaguely. Have you ever found yourself understanding your own thinking better when you talk it out with someone else? We may even say, "Can I talk to you about this so I can clarify what I think?"

When children become capable of thinking as they talk, speech actually becomes a tool for understanding, clarifying, and focusing what is in their minds. After listening to a string of directions for the next activity, Juan turns to Sue and says, "She said to start with the red book." He confirms the teacher's directions and focuses his own attention. Thinking while talking makes shared activity doubly powerful. When children talk to each other as they work, their language supports shared learning, but the verbal interaction also helps each child to think while talking.

Private Speech

When speech and thinking merge, a special kind of speech emerges. This speech is what Vygotsky called *private speech*: Private speech is audible but directed to the self rather than to other people. It contains information, as well as self-regulatory comments. It is the kind of thing that grown-ups do when faced with a difficult multistep task. We talk aloud to ourselves: "The first thing is to put the red rod into the red socket. Then the green rod fits into the spot marked with the green dot . . . ." Young children do this too, though more often than grown-ups. For example, Suzanne is playing at the computer and she says, "Need to move it here, then here—oops—then up. . . ." as she maneuvers the mouse to move a small truck through an on-screen maze. Two-year-old Harold says to himself, "more, more, more," as he fills up his dump truck to the very top.

Private speech is often abbreviated and condensed, unlike public speech, which communicates with others. Private speech sounds egocentric, as if the child doesn't care if she is understood by anyone else. Vygotsky points out that this egocentrism is not a deficiency of speech but an indicator of another function of speech at this age (Vygotsky, 1987). It is not necessary for private speech to be completely explicit since it must only be intelligible to the child. The child has an intuitive sense of internal audience.

Piaget (1926) calls such speech egocentric speech, and mostly focuses on its occurrence during *collective monologues* when several children are playing together. To Piaget, egocentric speech reflects the preoperational level of thinking, when the child has one worldview and cannot simultaneously take other perspectives. In collective monologues, each child holds a self-directed conversation at the same time, not caring whether the utterances are understood by others. With maturation, this type of speech disappears and is replaced by normal social speech when the child reaches the stage of concrete operations. For Piaget, there is no relationship between egocentric speech and self-regulation (Zivin, 1979).

In a series of experiments, Vygotsky showed that the collective monologue was not totally egocentric but social in nature (Vygotsky, 1987). The rate of speech was greater in group situations than when children were alone. If speech were totally egocentric, the rate would remain the same regardless of how many children were near. Vygotsky argues that collective monologues and seemingly egocentric speech are an emerging form of private speech. This early private speech has external manifestations and is self-directed, but it may appear similar to communicative speech. For Vygotsky, private speech does not disappear with age, as Piaget suggested, but becomes less audible, gradually moving inside the mind, and turns into verbal thinking. In young children, the speech used for communication and for private speech is not easily distinguished and occurs simultaneously in the same context. Public and private speech gradually separate into two distinct strands in older children and adults.

Alexander Luria, a colleague of Vygotsky, argues that private speech actually helps children make their behavior more deliberate (Luria, 1969). In a series of experiments, Luria found that general directions, such as "Squeeze two times," did not have an effect on the behavior of young children 3 to 3½ years of age. Children would squeeze any number of times. However, when children were taught to say "Squeeze, squeeze" and this private speech was directly paired with action, the private speech helped the children to control their behavior.

Here is another example. Mr. Smith raises his hand and says, "When I lower my hand, you jump." All of the preschool children start jumping up and down even before he gets his hand ready. The result is different, however, when Mr. Smith says, "Let's say, all together, 'One, two, three, jump,' and we'll jump on 'jump.'" The class says the four words together, and they all jump only on the word *jump*. Repeating the words rhythmically helps children to inhibit jumping at the wrong time.

A teacher might also use private speech to help a child with temper tantrums. Four-year-old Eric has a temper tantrum in the lunch line almost every day because he cannot wait his turn. As he walks to the lunchroom, his teacher rehearses what will happen. "You will *stand in line*, we will *count down* to your turn, you will get a *spoon, fork, food, and sit down*." The teacher coaches Eric and prompts him to repeat what they will do, holding out one finger, then two, and then three for the three actions he must remember. When they get to the lunch line, the teacher and Eric both signal "one" with their index fingers, and the teacher listens to Eric say, "Stand in line." Then they give the signal "two" as Eric says, "Count down." They proceed to count together: "Two more people till Eric's turn. One more person till Eric's turn. Eric's turn." Then they signal "three" as Eric says, "Get my fork and spoon and food and sit." After a week, Eric needs few prompts except the finger signals, and there are no tantrums in the lunchroom. Three weeks later, the teacher no longer prompts him at all. Sometimes Eric holds onto his fingers to prompt himself and sometimes he does not.

Inner Speech and Verbal Thinking

Once speech separates into two distinct strands, private speech goes "underground" and becomes inner speech and then verbal thinking. The concepts of inner speech and verbal thinking describe different internal mental processes. *Inner speech* is totally internal, nonaudible, and self-directed, and retains some of the characteristics of external speech. When people use inner speech to talk to themselves, they hear the words but do not say them aloud. For instance, when preparing for an important telephone call, you might mentally rehearse what you will say. Inner speech contains all of the things you might actually say, but it is an abbreviated version of the conversation. Inner speech in adults is similar to the private speech of preschoolers, because it is distilled, non-grammatical, and logical primarily to oneself.

After something exists as inner speech, it becomes *verbal thinking*, which is speech in an even more distilled form. It is described by Vygotsky as being *"folded."* When thinking is folded, you can think of several things simultaneously, and you may not be conscious of all that you are thinking (Vygotsky, 1987). Although you may be aware of the final product, it takes a concerted mental effort to "unfold" or draw the ideas back into consciousness. Strategies, concepts, and ideas that exist in verbal thinking have been *automatized* (Gal'perin, 1969); that is, they have been learned so well that they are automatic, not needing any conscious concentration to enact them. An adult immediately answers $2 + 2 = 4$. There is no thinking about the mental operation of addition. Automatization is not unique to verbal ideas: when a mother teaches her teenager to drive a car with a manual transmission, shifting is so automatic to her that she has to sit in the driver's seat and go through the actions slowly to figure out the order in which the clutch and gas pedals are used.

Once something has been automatized, it can still be unfolded and reexamined. At times children and adults who have already developed verbal thinking may need to return to previous levels and engage in private and public speech (Tharp & Gallimore, 1988). Sometimes, what has been automatized is not correct, such as when you learn someone's name incorrectly and when you see that person you automatically say the wrong name. When children are having trouble understanding something, it is particularly helpful to induce the reexamination of verbal thinking by having them explain things to others. Induced public speech helps the child think while talking, drawing out the folded ideas into a sequence. We have found that talking about Vygotsky often clarifies our understandings of complex concepts. By talking to each other, we actually understand our own individual thoughts better.

In verbal thinking, we may be unaware of flaws and gaps in our understanding. Have you ever read the definition of a word and thought you understood it, only to find out you cannot explain it in your own words to another person? Most of the time, an adult is able to sense a gap in understanding without having to discover it by talking aloud. Because children lack higher mental functions, they are less likely to sense when they do not know or understand something. Without higher mental functions, they are not able to monitor their understanding unassisted. This is why teachers need to draw out children's thinking from its folded state. When teachers do this, they provide the assistance necessary for the child to reexamine his own thinking. Asking children to explain their thinking, to think while talking to peers, and to write or draw their understandings are ways that teachers can assist the process of unfolding verbal thinking.

The Development of Meaning

Vygotsky also examined how children learn semantics, or the meaning of language. He believed that children construct meaning through shared activity. Meaning is a convergence between the adult's meaning and the child's inferences about what the adult means. Since meaning exists first in a shared state, contextual cues and the adult's strategies for interpreting the child's actions support meaning. When the teacher asks a toddler to point to the bird on a page containing a limited number of pictures, the context cues the child as to what a bird is. The child understands "bird" in that context but may not possess the same meaning for the word that the teacher does. For example, the child may point to a leaping frog as a bird on the next page.

As long as the child uses a word in familiar contexts while communicating with familiar adults, her understanding is sufficient to maintain conversation. Only when children try to apply meaning to different contexts and with different people does the difference between the child's meaning and the adult's become visible. Five-year-old Tamara uses the word *aunt* to describe all of her aunts correctly. However, she becomes confused when she meets a relative who is her niece and is actually older than she is. When her niece calls her "Auntie Tamara," she bursts into tears, saying, "I'm not an aunt, I'm a little girl."

Children and adults use the same words, but a child's meaning for a word will often be different from the adult's meaning. The younger the child, the more different is the meaning. As the child interacts with different people, in different contexts, over different tasks, he restructures his initial personal meaning over and over again. Eventually, the meaning becomes similar to the culturally adopted or conventional meaning. Generally, the older the child, the more similar her meanings for everyday concepts will be to the adult's meanings. For example, 4-year-old Juan says, "Day is when I play, and night is for sleeping." As he grows older, his conceptions of day and night will become less personal and eventually will be similar to the conventional definitions of day and night.

The Development of Written Speech

The central element of Vygotsky's approach to writing is the idea that humans employ it as a tool to expand their mental capacities:

> The development of written language belongs to the . . . most obvious line of cultural development because it is connected with the mastery of an external system of means developed and created in the process of cultural development of humanity. (Vygotsky, 1997, p. 133)

Vygotsky thus reserves a special place for written speech in the development of higher mental functions. Written speech is not just oral speech on paper but represents a higher level of thinking. It has a profound influence on development because

1. it makes thinking more explicit
2. it makes thinking and the use of symbols more deliberate
3. it makes the child aware of the elements of language

How Writing Promotes Thinking

Written speech makes thinking more explicit. Like spoken speech, written speech forces inner thoughts into a sequence because you can say or write only one idea at a time.

Forced to be sequential, you can no longer think about several things simultaneously. Written speech also forces you to unfold inner speech, but unlike the spoken word, writing allows you to literally "look at your thoughts." When we speak, our thoughts exist for the moment we say them. When we write, our thoughts are recorded and can be revisited and reflected upon. Gaps in understanding become more apparent when you reread your thoughts. Another characteristic of written speech is that it is more elaborated and therefore more context-free than spoken speech. Written speech must contain more information because there are no contextual cues to rely on when interpreting it. You cannot assume any common knowledge with your reader, and gesture and tone of voice cannot help you convey your meaning. As a child learns to write, he learns to take on the role of the reader, to see his thoughts as if for the first time. This gives the child even greater ability to see any gaps in his thinking and to notice any points of confusion in communicating those thoughts to others. After writing, our ideas are more explicit and elaborate than they were before. We see the flaws in our ideas more clearly and more objectively. Thus, for Vygotskians, writing improves thinking in a way that talking cannot.

Advocates of his perspective encourage the use of writing to help children structure and clarify new ideas. They make writing an integral part of the learning of all new content and skills. Children are encouraged to write about their understanding of a math problem as well as to solve the problem. Children write about their observations of a caterpillar in addition to making drawings and talking about what they see. By revisiting our thoughts on paper with others and by ourselves, we come to a deeper understanding of those thoughts.

Written speech also makes thinking and the use of symbols more deliberate. Because the child chooses the symbols she uses and must record them according to the laws of syntax, writing is a more deliberate process than talking (Vygotsky, 1987). In the Vygotskian view, the choice of the symbols we use when we talk can be unconscious and we might give minimal consideration to their effect on the listener (the proverbial foot in the mouth!). The decontextualized nature of writing means that symbols must be chosen carefully. In oral speech, the tone of voice, gestures, and common context can fill in the gaps. When listeners don't understand something, the speaker keeps adding information until they get it. In written speech, only what is on paper communicates, so one's words must be chosen more deliberately. Therefore, you are much more likely to play with different ways of saying the same thing when communicating on paper than when talking to someone.

Finally, written speech makes the child aware of the elements of the language. There are uniform rules governing relationships between sounds and symbols, between different kinds of words, and between ideas in a paragraph. While children may form some rudimentary ideas about the structure of language as they acquire metalinguistic awareness, these ideas become crystallized as the child learns to read and write. Meili has a vague understanding that words make up sentences, but when she sees sentences on a page, the idea of "word" becomes even clearer.

From the Vygotskian perspective, drawing serves a function similar to oral and written speech allowing children to communicate to others and to themselves (Stetsenko, 1995). There are many parallels between how children learn to say their first words and how they learn to draw: similar to how adults interpret infant's vocalizations as meaningful words they assign meaning to the toddler's scribbles. Josh is making repetitive motions with his marker leaving a series of spirals on paper. "Is it your car going round and round?—"asks his mother pointing to the spirals. Josh nods and goes on to make more spirals now accompanying his drawing with making vrroom-vrroom sounds.

Drawing plays an especially important role in helping children master one of the most complex tools of the mind–written speech. Vygotsky considered young children's drawings a direct prerequisite to writing, "a unique graphic speech, a graphic story about something . . . more speech than representation" (Vygotsky, 1997, p. 138). He argued that learning letters does not initiate children's writing but instead supplies the final component to move the child from idiosyncratic forms of "drawing speech" to a conventional way of recording speech in written words.

Early representational forms of drawing and scribbling are no less a tool to promote thinking and remembering than actual writing (Luria, 1979, 1983). This idea was tested in two early childhood programs, one in Russia and one in Italy. Vygotskian scholar Leonid Venger created an experimental curriculum for Russian preschools that emphasized the development of representational skills (Venger, 1986, 1994). Another early childhood educator, Loris Malaguzzi, came up with his own interpretation of Vygotskian ideas that were successfully applied in preschools in Reggio Emilia in northern Italy (Edwards, Gandini, & Forman, 1994).

Like Piaget (1926), Venger (Venger, 1986, 1996) argues that drawing is a representation of the child's thinking. Building on Vygotsky's idea of mental tools, Venger (Venger, 1986, 1996) argues that early drawings act as nonverbal tools that help a young child analyze objects into their essential and nonessential parts. Venger asserts that the lack of specificity in the child's representation, which makes the pictures look "primitive" and "undeveloped," occurs because the child produces a *model* of the object which includes only its essential parts (Venger, 1988, 1986, 1996). As the child learns more about the object, his drawings of it will change, reflecting his newfound understanding.

According to Venger, drawings can be used in the same way as writing. Children can use drawing to help them remember something. Although they look like scribbles, 2-year-old Jeremy can tell you 3 days later that his "drawing" on the sticky note on the refrigerator door means "Mommy buy candy." Asking 4-year-old Kanisha to draw a picture of what she is going to do in the house center will help her remember what she plans to do. Drawing can increase a child's awareness of her own thinking. Having the child add details or redraw models will help him think while drawing, thus increasing his understanding (Brofman, 1993). A similar technique has been used by teachers at Reggio Emilia to deepen children's understandings of space, time, and measurement (Edwards et al., 1994). American educators who have visited this program have been impressed not only with the quality of the children's drawings but also with the children's understanding of the subject matter.

Venger also suggests that drawing teaches children other cultural tools, such as how to express perspective in two-dimensional space. There are cultural conventions for how to draw objects that are near or far away and objects that are three-dimensional. This varies by culture. For example, in Western art, objects that are far away are drawn smaller than the ones that are nearer in space to the viewer. In Mongolian art, objects near and far are drawn the same size, but those far away are placed higher up on the page. By drawing and looking at drawings in books, children acquire these conventions and begin to apply them to their own work by 8 years of age.

As with drawing, scribbling and early attempts at writing have benefits that are similar to full-blown writing. Luria (1979, 1983) found that preschool children as young as 3 years of age begin to use prewritten speech in the same ways that adults use written speech. Three-year-olds used their scribbles to help them remember something or to label an object. These scribbles contained no real letters, nor were they understood by anyone but the child. Luria found that the children, nevertheless, gave these scribbles meaning and could remember the meaning several days later. Children thus begin to master the purpose of written speech long before they actually learn to write. Luria's ideas in this area influenced research on early writing in the West (e.g., Clay, 1991; Ferreiro & Teberosky, 1982) as well as the development of the whole language movement for teaching reading (e.g., Schickedanz & Casbergue, 2003; Schickendanz, 1982; Teale & Sulzby, 1986).

Using Language in the Classroom

From the Vygotskian approach, we can identify several ways to enhance children's use of language when we are teaching in the classroom.

Support the Development of Private Speech

Model the Use of Private Speech as a Tool for Thinking.   As you solve a problem, talk about what you are thinking about. Ms. Kaplan asks, "Which of these objects is bigger?" The children look puzzled. None of them responds. Ms. Kaplan then says, "Gee, I wonder how I might figure this out. Oh, I could put them together." She puts the objects next to each other and says, "If I look across, I can see that this one is bigger. What do you see?" Talking about strategies and giving several options will help children appropriate "hidden" thinking strategies.

Encourage Children to "Talk as They Think."   Have children talk when you want them to process new information or solidify old information. As Ms. Schlesinger finished explaining a new activity to her kindergarten class, she asked them to take time and "think in their heads" before telling her how they plan to build a boat. These directions would be appropriate for older students who, in fact, are capable of thinking before talking. However, Ms. Schlesinger is risking losing some of her young thinkers who might forget their ideas by the time the teacher is ready to listen to them. A better way would be to ask the children to turn to their friends and tell them what they thought might work for the boat. Some children need to talk things through with their peers as they complete a task, even before they do it alone. This strategy provides the assistance some children need to help them look at their own thinking. Seven-year-old Jolinda cannot identify grammar mistakes in her daily language-conversations activity. No matter how many times she reads it to herself, "he wented" sounds just fine. Only when she reads it aloud to her grammar buddy does she discover the mistake.

Encourage the Use of Private Speech.   Encourage children to use private speech to help them learn. Children can whisper to themselves or sit in a place where private speech will not bother others. Private speech may sometimes seem to be unrelated to the task at hand. However, if the child is able to perform the task with the speech, she should be allowed to continue. For example, Josie is sitting at her desk talking and humming to herself, but she is staying on task. This type of self-talk has meaning for the child and should not be discouraged. If the humming doesn't assist with task completion, then you might try prompting appropriate private speech. Private speech is abbreviated, so children may translate directions into a one- or two-word prompt for themselves.

Use Mediators to Facilitate Private Speech.   For some children, having an external mediator encourages private speech. Coach the child on what he might say to himself as he does something. If the child abbreviates this but is able to do the task, then let him continue to use the speech. For Alexei, having a card on his table with the numbers 1, 2, and 3 written on it helps him to remember which learning center he is to go to first, second, and third. The note prompts him to say to himself, "First I go to reading, then the listening center, then to the water table." One teacher uses the idea of having a place in your head called a memory bank. When children need to remember something, she says "We have to put this in our memory bank (pointing to her forehead). Let's say it three times and put it in. Ready? 'Bring a book to school tomorrow' (pointing to her forehead). 'Bring a book to school tomorrow' (pointing to her forehead). 'Bring a book to school tomorrow'" (pointing to her forehead). A very high percentage of her children remember to bring the book.

Support the Development of Meaning

Make Your Actions and the Children's Actions Verbally Explicit.   Label your own actions as you carry them out. Label the child's actions for him as they occur. The more you tie language to action, the more you will help children use language to facilitate learning. Avoid vague relational terms such as "these things" or "those." Use explicit terms, as in, "Hand me the blue blocks" or "See the small, furry squirrel puppet?" Teachers must also help children label their own behavior. Don't be afraid to say, "You're not paying attention" or "I can see your mind is wandering." If children don't seem to know what you mean by "paying attention," you will have to describe it more fully or even practice it. You might say, "When you pay attention, your mind is like a beam of light and it shines only here" or "When you pay attention your body is still and does not wiggle, your eyes are here, and you are thinking about this book."

When Introducing a New Concept, Be Sure to Tie It to Actions.   It helps the child when you introduce a concept in context and demonstrate the action of the object or your action upon the object. Include as many cues as you can. For example, when introducing a ruler, Ms. Brady says, "When we want to measure something to see how long it is, we put the ruler at the end of the object and read the numbers here." As she speaks, she models how to do this by placing the ruler at the very edge of the object.

Use Different Contexts and Different Tasks as You Check Whether or Not Children Understand a Concept or Strategy.   When you teach a concept or strategy, it is always embedded in a specific social context. It is difficult to know whether or not a child understands the concept because there are so many contextual clues that the child can reuse. For example, you say, "I like how Adrienne is paying attention," and you see that Morgan looks at Adrienne and stops wiggling. You do not know if Morgan truly understands what it means to pay attention or whether she thinks that "attention" is when you are seated cross-legged with your hands on your lap. To assess whether or not a child understands something, you must change contexts so that a new facet of the concept is exposed. You can do this by having the child interact with a peer (real or imaginary) or by changing tasks (counting cookies instead of bears).

Use Children's Own Public and Private Speech to Check Their Understanding of Concepts and Strategies.   Get children used to talking about what they think and how they solve problems. Have them repeat ideas back to you or show you how they understand an idea. As one teacher puts it, "I need to know how you think about things." Have children talk to each other; then listen to what they say to each other. Not only is your listening motivating for children, it gives you wonderful insights into what they understand.

Support the Development of Written Speech

Encourage the Use of Written Speech in a Variety of Contexts.   Don't confine writing to journals or a writer's workshop. In the primary classroom, use writing for math, science, reading, and art. Have children write about what they have learned, even if it is just a word or a letter. These reflections will help you understand what the child knows and will help the child look at his own thinking.

The more activities in which children use writing to help them remember or think, the better. Place the tools for writing in the dramatic play area and suggest ways that children might use writing in their play. Children can write out the orders for their play restaurant, write in a journal as they play school, or draw out the plans for a city as they play with blocks. Acting out stories with peers will also encourage the use of language and writing. Encourage writing during math and science activities to help children think about concepts.

Encourage Children to Use All Kinds of Written Speech Including Drawing and Scribbling. Encourage children to "write" and then "read" their messages, even if they do not use real letters. Invite a child to draw or scribble and then write notes for yourself about what the child says her writing means. You can label the child's representations. (More ideas are discussed in Chapters 11 and 13.) A few days later, ask the child again what her message says. If she remembers the message, encourage her to elaborate by pointing to different parts of the picture or scribble to prompt her to remember more.

Have Children Revisit Their Writing and Reprocess Their Ideas.   Revisit the child's writings, even if they are pictures with scribbles and dictated information. Talk about what the child might add to his writing or drawing after further thinking or studying. Use peers to reprocess the ideas represented. Have the child share the writing with a peer, such as during an "author's chair" activity. Coach the peers on what to say and on what questions to ask about the story. Write the responses down and use these to rediscuss the story. Ask children to redraw a picture of an object after they have examined it with a magnifying glass.

For Further Reading

Berk, L. E., & Winsler, A. (1995). *Scaffolding children's learning: Vygotsky and early childhood education.* NAEYC Research and Practice Series, 7. Washington DC: National Association for the Education of Young Children.

Bodrova, E., & Leong, D. (2005). Vygotskian perspectives on teaching and learning early literacy. In D. Dickinson & S. Neuman (Eds.), *Handbook of early literacy research* (Vol. 2). New York: Guilford Publications.

Luria, A. R. (1976). *Cognitive development: Its cultural and social foundations* (M. Lopez-Morillas & L. Solotaroff, Trans.). Cambridge, MA: Harvard University Press.

Luria, A. R. (1979). *The making of mind: A personal account of Soviet psychology* (M. Cole & S. Cole, Trans.). Cambridge, MA: Harvard University Press.

Vygotsky, L. S. (1962). *Thought and language* (E. Hanfmann & G. Vakar, Trans.). Cambridge, MA: MIT Press. (Original work published in 1934)

Vygotsky, L. S., & Luria, A. (1994). Tool and symbol in child development. In R. van der Veer & J. Valsiner (Eds.), *The Vygotsky reader* (T. Prout & R. van der Veer, Trans.). Oxford: Blackwell. (Original work published in 1984)

CHAPTER **7**

Tactics: Using Shared Activities

Zoe and Arlene are playing at the water table filling up different-size jugs with water. As they play, the teacher says, "I wonder how many smaller jugs of water it will take to fill up this large jug?" Zoe says, "I think three." Arlene shouts, "No, only one!" The teacher says, "Let's see. Let's use these blocks to stand for each bottle we measure. Zoe, you pour into the small jug, and Arlene, you put a block in this basket to stand for one small bottle. You'll do it each time, OK?" The teacher watches as the children empty water from the large, filled jug into the small jugs and put the blocks in the basket. The children count aloud as Arlene moves the block over. Once they pour until water spills out of a smaller jug, and the teacher says, "You have to fill it exactly and not spill or else we won't be measuring correctly." They refill the big jug and start over again. They gradually empty the large jug.

"There are three," Arlene says. "See." She points to the four blocks. The teacher pulls the basket closer and says, "Let's count these to make sure there are three." Arlene picks up the blocks and puts each one it in the teacher's open hand. "Oh, there are four," she says. "Yes," the teacher says, "sometimes it helps to point to the blocks or to pick them up when you count." Arlene says to Zoe, "Now I want to pour and you measure." After another cycle, Zoe looks at the basket of blocks, picks each one up as she counts and hands them to Arlene. "There are still four," Zoe says to Arlene and the teacher. "Yes," the teacher says, "it doesn't seem to matter who does the pouring. There are still four. Let's draw what we have learned about the difference between the big jug and the small jug." After they make the drawing, the teacher hangs it over the water table. The teacher encourages other children to "read" the drawing and "test out" what Zoe and Arlene have discovered.

It is within everyday exchanges such as this that learning occurs. We can easily recognize when such learning has occurred, but it is difficult to know what to do to make it happen. What can teachers do to increase the learning/teaching dialogue? This question is one that many American and Russian researchers have focused on. In this chapter, we will describe some of the recommendations derived from their applied research.

Interaction During Shared Activity

In Chapters 1 and 2, we explained Vygotsky's idea that mental functions can be shared; that is, they exist in shared activity. A mental function exists, or is distributed, between two people before it is appropriated and internalized.

There are a variety of ways in which an activity can be shared by two or more people. A child might use the strategy or concept with the support of another person. Two children might work together to solve a problem. One child might ask questions and another answer. In the earlier example of filling jugs with water, Zoe and Arlene shared the strategy with the teacher as a trio.

The word *assistance* is an essential part of the definition of the zone of proximal development, or ZPD (see Chapter 4). Thus, shared activity is a means of providing the assistance children need at the higher levels of the ZPD. To promote learning, teachers must create different types of assistance and consequently different types of shared activity.

Because so many examples of shared activity consist of adult-child exchanges, there are several misconceptions about what shared activity means. First, shared activities are not limited to adult-child interactions but include child interactions with peers and other partners. Vygotsky's ideas about shared activity and its role in development go for beyond the adult-directed learning (Tharp & Gallimore, 1988). The social context includes many kinds of interactions between more knowledgeable and less knowledgeable participants, participants with equal knowledge, and even imaginary participants (Newman, Griffin, & Cole, 1989; Salomon, 1993). Each type of shared activity supports a different facet of development. In this chapter, we will show how each type of shared activity can contribute to learning.

A second misconception is that the adult directs the child and the child is relatively passive—just following the adult's directions. No learning occurs if the learner is not mentally active. All participants, whether they are equal or unequal in knowledge, must be mentally engaged, or the activity will not be shared.

Finally, there must be a medium of sharing. Playing or working next to each other is not enough. The participants must communicate with each other by speaking, drawing, writing, or using another medium. Without rich verbal, written, or other kinds of exchanges, sharing will not produce the highest level of assistance possible. Language and interaction create the shared experience.

How Shared Activity Promotes Learning

Shared activity provides a meaningful social context for learning. When a child is first learning a skill, the social context may be the only thing that makes the learning meaningful. The child might try to learn simply because interacting with the teacher is very enjoyable. At the later stages of learning, teaching someone else a newly acquired concept can provide the child with a context that is meaningful in a similar way. A beginning reader might resist reading two pages when it is assigned by the teacher but be willing to read an entire book to a younger sister. Thus, the shared activity of reading to someone else supports the emerging skills in a way that the reading assignment by itself cannot. The child's motivation is much stronger and the interaction provides actual practice and an appropriate social context for the acquisition of the skill.

Through talking and communicating with another person, the gaps and flaws in one's thinking become explicit and accessible to correction. Once concepts are internalized, they may exist in a folded state so that mistakes are not easily revealed (see Chapter 6). Children may be able to come up with an answer but have only a vague understanding of how they got it. In talking, writing, or drawing for someone else, thought becomes sequential and visible to the thinker. For example, after making butter in class, Steven can only vaguely describe what happened. However, as he plays house with Ty, he begins to pretend to make butter using actions in the same order that they occurred in class. The ensuing argument with Ty over whether to shake the jar first or look at the directions in the recipe helps both children to clarify the steps in the process.

Children in a preschool class who observed a building being constructed in the lot across from the school try to explain to a new child what has happened. As they talk, the children clarify the sequence of events. When a child has solved a math problem and explains the answer to the teacher, she realizes that she made a mistake in the calculation.

Shared activity forces the participants to clarify and elaborate their thinking and to use language. To communicate with another person, you must be clear and explicit. You have to turn your idea into words and talk until you believe the other person understands you. You are forced to look at different aspects of an idea or task and to take another person's perspective. As a result, more and more sides or characteristics of an object or idea are exposed.

Shared Activity, Other-Regulation, and Self-Regulation

In shared activities with peers, or activities in which the child is performing at an independent level, being regulated by others and regulating others will occur more evenly. In preparing a dramatic play, for example, children will discuss and argue about what roles they will play and how the play situation will develop. Sometimes a child will agree to a role or scenario that was suggested by another child; then the same child may insist on the role or scenario that she has suggested.

The Importance of Other-Regulation

Vygotskians coined the term *other-regulation* to describe a situation in which a person is regulating another person or being regulated by someone else. This is distinguished from self-regulation in which one regulates oneself.

Much of post-Vygotskian research on shared activity has been done in the context of adult-child or expert-novice interactions. It is natural, then, that most attention was initially paid to "other-regulation" by an adult as a precursor to a child's self-regulation. This approach was taken, for example, by James Wertsch (Wertsch, 1979, 1985) who has identified several stages in children's learning of self-directed behaviors. In this progression, the first stages are characterized by an adult structuring the task, guiding children through a series of explicit steps, and providing detailed feedback. At the later stages, adult guidance diminishes until finally children are capable of planning, monitoring, and evaluating the correctness of their actions independently (Wertsch, 1985). The way children proceed to regulate their own behaviors reflects the shared nature of regulation that existed at the earlier stages: for example, in their private speech, children continue to use the same language they used in the past when communicating to the adult about the task.

When looking at shared activity that exists outside of expert-novice interaction, we can see, however, that other-regulation cannot be limited to the child being merely the recipient of an adult's regulation. The other element of other-regulation is the child's ability to regulate other people's behaviors—and learning to be both the regulator and the object of regulation are equally important for the development of self-regulation. The idea of this second aspect of other-regulation picks up on the fact that people are better able to see the mistakes in other people's behaviors than in their own. Vygotskians noted that often this is the first step in being able to do this for yourself, arguing that other-regulation precedes self-regulation (Leont'ev, 1978; Vygotsky, 1983). Because of this, other-regulation can be used as part of the learning process.

As is the case for all higher mental functions, for Vygotskians, the origins of self-regulation can be found in the child's social interactions with other people. We can even say that when it comes to learning a new behavior, children can regulate this behavior in other people before they are capable of regulating it in themselves. Many examples of this can be seen in preschool classrooms. Children who are about 3 or 4 years of age seem to be obsessed with rules and spend a great deal of their time telling the teacher when other people are not following the rules. Being a tattletale is a symptom of the desire to regulate others. The tattler usually does not apply the rule to himself but will be the first one to shout when someone else does wrong. The child wants to reaffirm the rule. For young children, the rule and the person who enforces it are the same: "I take just one cookie because the teacher said so." "I am quiet because the teacher said to be quiet." What children learn by using the rule to regulate others is the idea that the rule is abstract and exists apart from the person who enforces it. Once there is a rule, it can be applied in other situations. Then the child begins to internalize the rule or develop a standard. Instead of having to be reminded each time there are cookies that you take only one, the child now has a rule: "When there are cookies or any food, you take only one at a time." Likewise, the internalized rule about being quiet might be, "I need to use a quieter voice when I am inside."

The idea that other-regulation precedes and prepares the way for self-regulation is not limited to social interactions but can also be applied to the regulation of cognitive processes. Such post-Vygotskians as Zuckerman and others (Rubtsov, 1981; Zuckerman, 2003) argue that other-regulation is a precursor to the reflective thinking found in adults and older children. Many theorists, including Piaget and information processing theorists, argue that self-reflection is part of the problem-solving processes at the highest levels (Flavell, 1979; Piaget, 1977). Adults are not only able to solve a problem, but to reflect on the solution. In these perspectives, children in preschool and elementary school are not able to be reflective about their own thinking or are minimally reflective. In contrast, Zuckerman argued that other-regulation serves the same function as reflective thinking because it evaluates and considers the actions that have been taken. At this point, however, the reflection lies outside the child and is being carried out by another child, or by an entire group of peers. Eventually, the child who was other-regulating his or her classmates' actions will be able to "self-critique" and apply the same reflective procedures on his/her own actions. By the same token, the child who was previously on the receiving end of other-regulation will internalize the strategies used by his or her peers and will be able to use these independently. Having children engage in other-regulation is very helpful in developing their thought processes. We will discuss this further in Chapters 12 and 13.

Using Other-Regulation to Promote Self-Regulation

Much of what children learn is rule-based; some of these rules are explicit, like the rules of classroom behavior, and some are not obvious, like the rules of play. Addition, spelling, reading—almost everything taught in school—involves using rules. In school we learn rules and standards as well as concepts and strategies.

Because children engage in other-regulation first, they often can see a rule more easily by looking at the mistakes of another person, such as a classmate, than by trying to apply the same rule to their own actions. When children are doing something themselves, they may lose sight of the rule, but the rule jumps out at them when they see someone else's work. Have you ever noticed how easy it is to edit another person's work? The typos and flaws in thinking are obvious. When you read your own writing, problems and mistakes are much harder to catch.

Teachers can encourage the development of self-regulation by placing children in the position of regulating others. Some specific recommendations follow.

1. *Plan exercises in which children have to identify mistakes in the teacher's work or in written exercises.* Presenting written sentences that contain one or two grammatical or punctuation mistakes is useful in first and second grade. It is important to tell the children how many mistakes are in the sentence. Teachers can also make mistakes on purpose as they write sentences on the board for the children to correct. At first children might have to be prompted to see the mistake because they think that teachers don't make mistakes.

2. *Plan activities in which the child who has problems self-regulating regulates other people's use of the target behavior.* Give a child the responsibility for regulating the behavior you want him to learn. In Mr. Timothy's classroom, Jason's loud voice can be heard above all the other children, and it seems to increase the noise level to the point that some children hold their ears! Attempts to correct him by saying "Lower your voice" seem to have absolutely no effect on Jason. Mr. Timothy has even tried using a video recording to show Jason how much louder his voice is than those of the other children. None of his attempts has worked. Then Mr. Timothy puts a "noise meter" on the board (see Figure 7.1) and encourages Jason to identify when any person's noise level is too loud. Jason picks on everyone, including Mr. Timothy, mercilessly, pointing out when anyone speaks in a slightly raised voice. After 3 days, Mr. Timothy notices that when he asks Jason to lower his voice, he actually responds by lowering his voice! Vygotskians would argue that Jason has begun to internalize a standard for what a lower voice is. Before, he responded to Mr. Timothy as if his request were just a whim. After regulating everyone else, Jason began to see that "lowering your voice" meant something specific.

3. *Pair other-regulation and self-regulation with an external mediator and private or public speech.* Use external mediators as the reminders of the behavior you want the children to use to regulate others or themselves. In the previous example, the teacher used a picture of a noise meter to help the children remember what they were supposed to do with their voices. Having Jason say when someone's voice was "too loud" or "just right" helped him better distinguish between appropriate and inappropriate noise levels.

The Role of the Teacher in Shared Activity

A teacher may take part in a shared activity in two different ways: as a direct participant and as the person who promotes, plans, and creates the opportunities for shared activity to develop between children and their partners. In classroom activities, teachers may assume both of these roles depending on the goals, contexts, and content of what is being taught. Sometimes only adults can guide and direct learning, but there are times when working with peers is more beneficial for the young learners. Whether the

Figure 7.1   Jason's noise meter

teacher should directly participate in the activity depends on a number of factors such as where in the learning cycle the children are, the characteristics of specific children, the children's ages, and the group and its dynamics. For example, a peer discussion among a group of 5-year-olds might make them want to know more and to ask questions that can be answered on their own or only by the teacher (Palincsar, Brown, & Campione, 1993). In this situation, the teacher plays the role of both planner and participant. At other times, direct teacher questions can prompt the same interest and learning, so direct participation produces the best motivation. Astute teachers know that they must use a variety of techniques and constantly change the form of presentation and amount of guidance as learning emerges in different children.

Teachers as Partners

One way that teachers participate in shared activity is by engaging in what Vygotskians call *educational dialogue* (Newman et al., 1989). The word *dialogue* implies give and take among all participants. Therefore, a lecture given to students is not an example of an educational dialogue. In an educational dialogue, the children express their own understandings of what the teacher says and of the concept presented. This dialogue can involve written and drawn representations as well as speech.

An idea of educational dialogue is similar to the notion of *Socratic dialogue,* which is more commonly discussed in the context of teaching older students. In both kinds of dialogue, the teacher has a goal in mind and uses questions to guide the students toward that goal (Saran & Neisser, 2004). It is not a free-flowing discussion but a teacher-guided journey of discovery. The children must discover the meaning, but the teacher gently leads them to it, helping them correct misconceptions and avoid dead-end lines of thinking.

To engage in an educational dialogue, the teacher must have a concept or goal in mind and must be able to anticipate the possible misunderstandings that will emerge. She must guide, but the child must act and construct her own understanding. An analogy would be driving to a new destination. You drive at your own speed and make your own decisions about where to turn, but the road signs along the way provide useful information and anticipate your possible wrong turns. Along the road of learning, the teacher is the one who places the signs at the most useful and important points, and makes sure that students do not miss an important turn.

By asking questions, the teacher models the logic of learning, or the strategies that children can use to reach a solution next time. Put another way, the teacher constructs a template for learning that can be used in other situations. Ms. Osborne is looking at a new science book with her children. Winona asks, "Does it talk about bears?" Ms. Osborne says, "Let's see. Where can we look?" Sam says, "Let's look at the pictures." Ms. Osborne says, "We could look at pictures—that would tell us if it has bears in it—but I know a quicker way. We can look for the word *bears* in the index at the back of the book." Pointing to the columns she says, "The index tells you all of the topics covered. See how it's alphabetized? Where could we find bears?" "Under *B,*" several children say. "Right. Where is the *B* section?" she asks as she turns the book so that one child can turn the page. "Yes, I see *B*'s now," she says as the child successfully finds the *B* section. Ms. Osborne turns the book toward another child and says, "Can you find *bears?*" The child points to the correct line. "Follow along with your finger and you'll see a page number. Bears are discussed on page 78." If Ms. Osborne had simply said "yes" or turned to the page without leading the children through the process, they would not have been exposed to a strategy for finding information in a book.

Although the teacher has a goal in mind, the actual questions and steps used in the educational dialogue must be chosen anew with each child or group of children. Each child comes to the dialogue with a unique background and understandings, so the questions that lead to understanding for one child may not work with another. The teacher must keep in mind that children must participate in the dialogue for it to teach them anything, because they must construct their own meaning (see Chapter 1).

One purpose of the educational dialogue is for the teacher to discover what the child understands and what assistance will work best. Because the learner does not really understand the final goal until she has mastered the skill or concept (Wertsch, 1985), it is difficult for the learner to articulate what part of the final concept she understands. This is something that only the teacher, who knows the final goal, can tell the child.

In monitoring a child's engagement in an educational dialogue, the teacher must answer two questions about the child's thought process: (a) how did the child arrive at this answer? and (b) will the child's answer ultimately fit into the system of concepts for this area? First, for Vygotskians learning is as much about mastering the new "tools of the mind" as it is about acquiring specific knowledge, so it is not enough just to reach the right answer; the child must use the tools that are most relevant to finding the answer. For example, it is more important for the child to be able to describe the pattern in a series of objects than to predict the next object. Knowing only which object comes next does not tell the teacher whether or how the child understands the pattern.

The second thing the teacher must discover in the educational dialogue is whether the child's answer will ultimately fit into the system of concepts for a specific area. The teacher has to keep in mind the entire system of learning. She must make sure that each new concept builds toward understanding the entire system and does not create problems later. Ms. Berk goes over the elements of the calendar every school day. Most of her students can answer correctly when she asks them what day yesterday was or what day tomorrow will be. However, when she asks the children how many days there are in a week, she discovers that some of the children think there are 5 days. She asks the children to show her how there are 5 days. The children name the 5 days—from Monday through Friday—that she usually mentions during her opening circle time. Through her dialogue with the children, Ms. Berk discovers that they define the days of the week by the days they are in school. She then revises her calendar routine to make sure that children understand that there are 7 days in a week because she knows that their current misconception will lead to problems later.

As teachers participate in the educational dialogue, they need to keep these points in mind.

1. *Help the child distinguish between essential and nonessential properties.* For example, when showing children objects of different shapes, the teacher should demonstrate that color and size are irrelevant. She would ask the child, "If we paint this object red, is it still a circle?" "If we paint the circle blue, is it now a triangle?" "What if we make it bigger? Is it still a circle?"

2. *Help the child make connections with the larger system of concepts.* Susan points to the number *2* and says, "It's the letter two." The teacher engages her in a dialogue by asking, "Is this a letter or a number?" Susan says, "It's a letter like this" (pointing to an *A*). The teacher then says, "We write both letters and numbers, but we use them differently. How many fingers do I have up?" Susan says, "Two." The teacher says, "Yes, we would write that with a number because we use numbers to tell 'how many.' We use letters to make words."

3. *Look for clues about the child's thinking process.* Using the child's responses, try to identify the properties that are salient. The teacher asks the children, "What rhymes with *ball*?" She hears the following answers: *fall, tall, ball,* and *box*. From the children's answers, she knows that at least some of them define rhyme as the same beginning sound. Her original definition of rhyming, "sounds the same," has led to some misunderstanding. She then modifies the definition so that children know which part of the words has to "sound the same" for them to rhyme. By detecting what the child is thinking, the teacher can begin to reconstruct the child's meaning.

4. *Decide how much support should be given.* Because the amount of support each child needs depends on her ZPD, children who are equally unable to perform

a certain task may need different supports. Lisa and Fred both have trouble sounding out the word *balloon*. Lisa requires only the first sound to be able to say the word. Fred needs to have each syllable said slowly in a slurred manner before he can pronounce *balloon*. In deciding how to support a child's learning, ask questions like these: Should I vary the amount of support given to a particular child? Does the child need more verbal cues or does she need manipulatives? Do I need to change the context and try the activity in a smaller group (or larger group)? Do I need to have the child draw or represent his thinking or tell somebody else how he did it? Does this child need several cues or just one? Using the special kind of assessment described in Chapter 14 of this book will help you to better determine how much support should be given to different children.

5. *Generate a number of possible ways of handing over the responsibility for learning to the child.* Have in mind a number of ways that you will provide scaffolding and then withdraw support in a gradual way. Keep track of the child's reaction to your hints and clues, as well as the way the child responds as you withdraw support. These will give you clues as to what works.

6. *Plan the size of the groups you will work with so that the educational dialogue is meaningful and effective.* Organize your classroom so that you have time to work with children individually and in small groups of up to eight children. Although you can have a dialogue with the entire class, some children will dominate in larger groups. These will usually be the children at the upper and lower ends of the learning continuum. To maximize the number of dialogues you can have, use peers and prepared materials to provide scaffolding and assistance to other students at those times when you want to interact with just part of the class.

Teachers as the Planners

Teachers also engage in shared activity indirectly by modifying and planning the learning environment. By choosing manipulatives, objects, books, videos, computer programs, audiotapes, and play props, the teacher provides assistance to support independent performance. The teacher may create mediators to facilitate the process (see Chapter 5). These supports are withdrawn as the child masters the skill. For example, when the child can solve a particular math problem with manipulatives, the next step is to have him draw or write, and then to solve the problem in the mind. (Of course, for some concepts it will take longer than a school year for a child to progress through all the steps.) The goal of using manipulatives is not just to solve the math problem but to provide a stepping-stone toward internalization of the concept of "number." Therefore, the teacher needs to plan not only how to use these aids but also how the child will make the transition from using them to more advanced forms of thinking. The use of materials is also very helpful in consolidating learning, when the child is at the independent level of the ZPD. Confirming his understanding helps the child become confident and strengthens understanding.

Teachers also orchestrate the activities shared by others in the classroom, primarily peers. We engage in teaching not only when we directly interact with children but also when we organize different peer activities to encourage learning. In the next section, we discuss the many ways peers can support each other's learning.

The Role of Peers in Shared Activity

Just interacting with another peer is not sufficient to promote a child's development. Sometimes casual interaction does help children to learn, but this learning can be haphazard, and children can be misled by each other's misunderstandings. Important attributes or concepts may not emerge in peer interaction. When children interact with each other, the social situation is full of complex pieces of information relating to friendships, past interactions, the content, and the goal of the group. It is very difficult for children to figure out on their own what the group is trying to accomplish in different social situations. However, by structuring the situation, the teacher can use peer interaction to further learning goals. Both the goal of the group and the type of interaction that will occur must be carefully spelled out.

In the early stages of the learning process, interaction with the teacher may be more beneficial than sharing activities with peers. This is particularly true when the child has not used a skill or strategy correctly or when a concept is still very vague in the child's mind. If the misunderstandings of others would confuse the child, then this is not the time for peer interaction. Cassie is just learning the concept of regrouping, and she is not sure what place value is. This is not the time for her to interact with Joseph, who is also confused and thinks that you write the *10* in the answer next to the tens place. Cassie might benefit from interacting with a more knowledgeable peer, one who is not confused; however, the teacher will probably need to clarify things for her first. Once the child has learned the skill, practice with a peer is very beneficial.

To promote learning, children must engage in very specific types of interaction with each other. Vygotskians describe the following peer interactions as the most beneficial for development:

1. *Cooperating with more (less) capable peers on the same task.* When a peer expert helps a novice, or gives peer tutoring, there are double benefits for learning. First, peer tutoring helps the novice, who is at the lower level of understanding, by providing individualized support. Second, it helps the expert by requiring that child to be more explicit and consistent. It supports the learning of metacognitive skills for the expert as well as a deeper understanding of content (Cohen, Kulik, & Kulik, 1982; Palincsar, Brown, & Martin, 1987).

To make peer tutoring work in the early childhood setting, the activity must be carefully planned. The tutor needs extensive training about how to help another person learn. The young Tutor is likely to tell the answer rather than model strategies, which is not helpful for the novice. Show the Tutor exactly how to act—what to do if the answer is partly correct or wrong, and how to praise and encourage the child being tutored. If a child never gets the chance to be tutor, then this kind of pairing can be very discouraging. Make sure that every child gets a chance to be the tutor. Pair lower-functioning children with children in a lower grade; for example, first graders can read a familiar book to preschoolers or kindergartners who cannot read.
2. *Cooperating with equally capable peers on the same task.* The idea that the beneficial effects of peer interactions are limited to novice-expert situations has been one of the most prevalent misinterpretations of the Vygotskian principle of shared activity (Zuckerman, 2003). In fact, research done both within (Wells, 1999) and outside of

the Vygotskian approach (Johnson & Johnson, 1994; Slavin, 1994) provide evidence of positive effects of cooperation between peers at the same level of expertise.

One of the mechanisms responsible for cognitive outcomes of peer cooperation is the creation and subsequent resolution of cognitive conflict (Zuckerman, 2003). Sometimes children in a group will have different opinions or perspectives. A natural outgrowth of these disagreements is cognitive conflict, which can be conducive to growth. Both Piagetians and Vygotskians believe that encountering incompatible or different views of the same situation improves the individual child's ability to experiment mentally. For example, 8-year-old Donna learns that the earth revolves around the sun, but in a discussion she finds out that other children believe the sun revolves around the earth. Until she has to explain her ideas to another child, she will not understand the internal logic of her own belief or the conclusions that this would lead to. In older children, this external discussion can occur internally. An example of this would be when a student in preparing to write an essay tries to conceive of the counter arguments presented by an imaginary opponent.

Another way for peers of the same levels of expertise to positively affect each other's learning is by taking on different roles that represent different cognitive processes (e.g., planning, monitoring) necessary for completing a task (Zuckerman, 2003). For example, in creating a block structure, one child draws a plan for the block building, another child builds it, and a third child checks to see whether the plan matches the final building (Brofman, 1993). Each child has a distinct role, but they share the plan and the blocks. The roles played by each individual child change as the group moves on to a new construction project. This kind of shared activity helps children to develop all the skills needed to complete a process: to plan, monitor, and evaluate their behavior.

Another example of how different roles can be coordinated in a shared activity is a preliteracy activity for preschoolers in which children take turns "reading" a book to their partners. To facilitate this shared activity, the teacher assigns the roles of storyteller and listener to children in pairs by giving the storyteller a card with a picture of a mouth and the listener a card with a picture of an ear. These cards help the children keep their roles straight.

Peer editing is another illustration of a shared activity where children assume complementary roles. In peer editing, one child writes and the other edits and checks the writer's work. When assigning a checking, directing, or editing role, it is important to be explicit about the standards for evaluating the peer's work. Children should not just say whether they like the story. Shared activity is a vehicle for children to learn concepts, skills, and strategies; these must be made explicit or the children will not learn them. The more specific you can be about what you want them to do, the better. A second-grade teacher asks editors to comment on the flow of the story, the main character, and simple grammar (use of sentences and periods). To support children in playing the role of editor, the teacher has them put on their "editor's eyes," a pair of eyeglasses without lenses, or use a magnifying glass. By taking the role of editor, the child will appropriate the ideas of flow, character, and grammar as the child regulates his partner. This type of activity uses the principle that other-regulation precedes self-regulation. If you try using "editor's eyes" in your classroom, do not be surprised when children begin asking for them even when working individually! These children will use the glasses as a reminder (an external mediator) so they can apply the same editing processes to their own writing that they used with a peer.

In the previous examples, there were two types of learning situations. In one, the child is practicing a process in which his performance is compared with a standard. In other words, there is a "correct answer." In the other, the goal is for the child to just practice; the outcome is not specified. It is important in situations where children are practicing something specific that the teacher makes the activity self-correcting or provides an example that the child can use for comparison. Without this step, children may lead each other astray.

3. *Cooperating with peers on interrelated tasks.* This type of cooperation tends to motivate children, encourages them to coordinate roles, and provides the missing components in an individual child's skills. An example is when children have complementary pieces of information and have to share and coordinate this information to solve a problem or create a whole. Each member has an essential piece of information, like a piece of a puzzle. This kind of shared activity is used in reading instruction when a story is divided into several pieces and each child is given one piece to read. The entire story line cannot be reconstructed without all of the pieces. Each child must read and summarize her own piece and present it to others in the right order.

Cooperation on interrelated tasks can be combined with assigning children different roles. For example, while working on different pieces of text in small groups, children in each group can also be assigned different roles, such as "the person who asks about the words that are hard to say" or "the person who asks about the main idea." As a result, children engage in cooperation both at the level of content and at the level of reading strategies (Cole, 1989).

4. *Cooperating with virtual peers.* Children do not always have to engage in face-to-face interaction with their peers to participate in shared activity. What matters is the entire context of the activity where interacting with a virtual peer has the same meaning for a child as interacting with one who is physically present. For example, drawing a map for a newcomer to campus leads kindergartners to produce highly detailed maps of the school campus. The same kindergartners might be less likely to produce as many details when drawing the map as a class assignment since they expect the teacher (obviously familiar with the campus layout) to fill in the missing details.

When designing an activity to engage children in interactions with virtual peers, it is important to keep in mind that these activities will result in more positive learning outcomes only when they are truly meaningful for the participants. For example, writing letters has been a meaningful activity for many in the past. However, today's second graders, faced with many alternative means of communication, may not demonstrate their highest levels of writing when asked to write letters to each other. By contrast, putting their best effort into writing directions for a complicated game will ensure that they will be able to later enjoy playing the game with their friends. Therefore, this second activity provides a more meaningful context for cooperating with virtual peers.

5. *Engaging in make-believe play and games.* Another way teachers can use peers to scaffold each child's learning and development is to initiate a game or to facilitate dramatic play. For more information on these specific kinds of shared activity, see Chapters 10 and 11.

Even when not engaged in full-blown make-believe play, young children can benefit from the elements of play in specifically designed shared activity. For example, instead of sharing with a real partner, children can share with an imaginary partner or with the one to whom they attribute the characteristics of a real one. Reading to a stuffed animal or to their pet prompts the same kinds of reading behavior in beginning readers as reading to a real person. In another example, a preschool teacher who had a hamster in her classroom encouraged more detailed dictated stories after the teacher-as-hamster wrote the children a "letter."

As we can see, children benefit from all types of shared activities with adults, peers, and materials. Ways of implementing the principle of shared activity in specific activities will be discussed in Section III.

For Further Reading

Newman D., Griffin P., & Cole, M. (1989). *The construction zone: Working for cognitive change in school.* Cambridge: Cambridge University Press.

Rogoff, B. (1990). *Apprenticeship in thinking: Cognitive development in social context.* New York: Oxford University Press.

Rubtsov, V. V. (1991). *Learning in children: Organization and development of cooperative actions.* New York: Nova Science Publishers.

Zuckerman, G. (2003). The learning activity in the first years of schooling: The developmental path toward reflection. In A. Kozulin, B. Gindis, V. S. Ageev, & S. M. Miller (Eds.), *Vygotsky's educational theory in cultural context* (pp. 177–199). New York: Cambridge University Press.

Applying the Vygotskian Approach to Development and Learning in Early Childhood

This section will specify how the main principles of the Vygotskian approach apply to development of children of different ages: from infants and toddlers to primary-grade students. Although Vygotskians do not view child development as going through distinct stages, they do recognize the unique nature of children's social situation of development at different ages that affects these children's acquisition and use of their "tools of the mind." For each age period that is traditionally included in the definition of early childhood, specific examples of scaffolding are discussed. These scaffolds are a combination of various tactics discussed in Section II and can be used to promote development of children of this particular age. There are seven chapters in Section III:

Chapter 8   Developmental Accomplishments and Leading Activity:
Infants and Toddlers

Chapter 9   Supporting the Developmental Accomplishments
of Infants and Toddlers

Chapter 10   Developmental Accomplishments and Leading Activity:
Preschool and Kindergarten

Chapter 11   Supporting the Developmental Accomplishments
in Preschool and Kindergarten

Chapter 12   Developmental Accomplishments and Leading Activity:
Primary Grades

Chapter 13   Supporting the Developmental Accomplishments
in the Primary Grades

Chapter 14   Dynamic Assessment: Application of the Zone of Proximal Development

CHAPTER **8**

Developmental Accomplishments and Leading Activity: Infants and Toddlers

Vygotsky believed that development includes both qualitative and quantitative changes. Children go through periods of qualitative changes when there is a change in the very nature and form of the child's mind, or quality of thinking. Each phase heralds new cognitive and emotional structures. Likewise, there are periods when no new formations appear, but children still continue to develop their existing competencies. During these periods, growth occurs as a quantitative change in the number of things the child can remember and process.

The Concept of Developmental Accomplishment

We have coined the term *developmental accomplishments* to describe the cognitive and social-emotional "neo-formations" Vygotsky and his students identified as the indicators of each distinct period in child development. Not all of the abilities that are new to a child in a given age period are considered developmental accomplishments. Only those that are critical for the child's moving into the next period are so designated. For example, the ability to think in images, an outgrowth of sensorimotor thinking, is a developmental accomplishment of toddlerhood because it is necessary for the make-believe play that develops in preschoolers. Discussion of these developmental accomplishments is scattered within Vygotsky's writings, rather than presented as a coherent theory. After his death, his colleagues and students (Elkonin, 1977; Leont'ev, 1978) extended and consolidated these ideas into definitive stages that are currently used in child development studies in Russia (e.g., Karpov, 2005).

Social Situation of Development

In the Vygotskian framework, developmental accomplishments are considered outgrowths of the *social situation of development* that is specific for each age. The social situation of development is defined by Vygotsky as a "unique relation, specific to a given age, between the child and reality, mainly the social reality that surrounds him" (Vygotsky, 1998, p.198). It is a set of unique social and environmental factors that combine to create the context in which development will occur and be nurtured, as well as the competencies a child possesses to interact with this context.

The social situation of development is determined by two factors. First, there are cognitive and social-emotional competencies specific to a certain age: a 4-month-old obviously has different competencies than a 4-year-old.

Second, the way adults interact with the child changes as the child matures. Vygotsky argued that society changes its expectations and ways of treating the child as the child grows up. Therefore, the social context, or the child's social environment, is different at different ages. For example, many expectations for preschoolers are different from those for school-age children. School-age children are expected to do more for themselves and, therefore, many cultures emphasize the development of deliberate behaviors in children of this age. In addition, these social expectations have changed throughout history so that the expectations are different for children of a specific age today than they were 25 years ago. For example, more and more toddlers are in group care than previously, which has led to changing expectations of social competency. Toddlers are expected to interact socially with peers at an earlier age. Sometimes, even children of the same age find themselves in different social situations, such as when one child is the youngest sibling and another is the oldest, with many more responsibilities.

The Role of Social Situation of Development in Child Development

Vygotsky sees the changes in the social situation of development as the mechanism that propels development forward by providing new and more advanced mental tools that continue to shape their growing competencies: "Neo-formations that arise toward the end of a given age lead to a reconstruction of the whole structure of the child's consciousness and in this way change the whole system of relations to external reality and to himself" (Vygotsky, 1998, p.199). This means that as children's abilities grow, the social context itself adjusts to accommodate these new skills and needs. What we expect children to be able to learn and what we expect to teach them depends, in part, on what they are able to do. As children show they are able to act without assistance, parents and teachers begin to give them more responsibilities and expect them to be more independent. As adults' expectations change with the age of the children, so do the cultural tools that adults help children to acquire. Eventually, the very acquisition of these cultural tools shapes the children's further development.

When societal expectations do not match the children's actual and potential capacities, either underestimating or overestimating them, the optimal conditions for development will not be created. Therefore, the optimal conditions for development are dependent on the adults having expectations that are aligned with what the child can and will be able to do. If adults expect a 2-year-old to be able to identify all 26 letters of the alphabet, but the child does not have the capacity to do so, the adult's expectations will not be conducive to development. On the other hand, if parents do not expect the 2-year-old to know how to use words to express his wants and needs, this underestimation of what the child can do will also have a negative impact on development.

Developmental accomplishments are not the only capacities that children build during a particular age. Along with acquiring specific competencies for each period of life, children are constantly developing other skills and capacities, laying the groundwork for achieving the more complex competencies of the next period of their development. Thus, they are simultaneously practicing aspects of later developmental accomplishments all along. Although higher mental functions do not emerge until the primary grades, preschool children are practicing deliberate memory when they memorize a fingerplay during circle time, for instance.

The Concept of Leading Activity

It is important to remember that Vygotsky's original idea of developmental accomplishments is not a strict stage theory in which development manifests itself in certain behaviors during a particular period, as in Piaget's concept of stages. In the work of post-Vygotskians, however, this idea was refined and expanded to result in the theory of child development that contains well-defined stages along with the explanation of the mechanisms underlying children's transition from one stage to the next (Karpov,

2005). One of the major innovations contributed by the post-Vygotskians to his theory of child development was the introduction of the idea of leading activity that replaced Vygotsky's notion of social situation of development.

The Definition of Leading Activity

Leont'ev (1978, 1981) uses the concept of *leading activity* to specify the types of interactions between a child and the social environment that will lead to achievement of the developmental accomplishments in one period of life and prepare him for the next period. His ideas bring specificity to the idea of social situation of development by identifying the key elements required for optimum development. According to Leont'ev,

> Some types of activity are the leading ones at a given stage and are of greatest significance for the individual's subsequent development, and others are less important. We can say accordingly, that each stage of psychic development is characterized by a definite relation of the child to reality that is the leading one at that stage and by a definite, leading type of activity. (1981, p. 395)

Leont'ev defined the leading activity as the only type of interaction at a certain period of life that will

- produce major developmental accomplishments
- provide the basis for other activities (interactions)
- induce the creation of new mental processes and the restructuring of old ones

Produce Major Developmental Accomplishments.   Children engage in many types of activities, but only the leading activity is crucial for the emergence of the developmental accomplishments. When engaged in a leading activity, a child learns skills that make it possible for him to begin the transition to other types of interactions with the environment. Leading activities are unique in their ability to shape the mind; they enable the child to generate new mental functions and to restructure current ones.

Another contribution of the leading activity for any age period is that it creates a motivation for engaging in a new kind of activity that will become the leading activity for the next period of life. Thus, there is an overlapping nature to the concept of leading activities, each foreshadowing the next. For example, in the process of playing increasingly complex games, older preschoolers and kindergartners gradually become more interested in winning than in the make-believe playing that had been the leading activity for their age period. Games with winners motivate a child to try out, refine, and master the procedures and strategies necessary for success at that particular game. This kind of motivation, of working toward a goal, is a precedent for the motivation necessary for formal classroom learning.

Provide the Basis for Other Activities.   Leading activities are the optimal activities for development at any particular age period. Although children can, and do learn from other activities within their ZPD, leading activities are the most beneficial, since they have an impact not just on one or two areas but on the child's overall developmental status.

Induce the Creation of New Mental Processes and the Restructuring of Old Ones.   The outcome of the leading activity is that new mental processes will emerge as the child engages in it. As a 3-year-old engages in more and more mature make-believe play, which is the leading activity of preschool, he begins to acquire self-regulation, the ability to monitor and control his behavior. As this self-regulation grows, it will influence the way he remembers and learns. The capacities that he had as a toddler will become restructured.

How Children Begin to Engage in Leading Activity

In most cases, we can see the beginnings of a leading activity long before it begins to be THE leading activity in a child's life. Although an individual child is not yet capable of engaging in the activity by herself, she can participate in it as long as her participation is supported by an adult or by a group of peers. It is in this shared setting that children first acquire, and then start using the new cultural tools that are essential for later sustaining the leading activity independently.

Eighteen-month-old Tina will not engage in extended role-playing—the leading activity of 4- and 5-year-old children for several years. However, she can go beyond her current state of development and even "try on" an imaginary role if prompted by an adult. Seeing how Tina is trying to turn any knob in sight with her new toy wrench, Tina's mom supports her role-play by saying, "Oh, this is what I need now—a mechanic. Ms. Mechanic, my washing machine would not start. Would you fix it for me please?" Tina nods and starts applying her wrench to the knobs on the washing machine, periodically looking up at her mom.

When the development of a child's leading activity lags behind that of other children of the same age, the child may experience difficulties meeting the expectations of his current social context. For example, a school-aged child whose make-believe play has never reached an advanced level might have trouble performing academic tasks that require high levels of symbolic thought and self-regulation, competencies that are acquired from extensive role-playing. Reversing the clock is not an option; second-grade teachers can't send students back to preschool or even kindergarten. However, individual interventions for these "lagging" students will be more successful when teachers take into account not only the level of their current leading activity—in this case learning activity—but also the level they have reached in the preceding leading activity. Therefore, for a second grader with a "Play Deficit Disorder," playing games that combine academic content with some fantasy elements and structured rules will do more that completing extra worksheets.

Consistent with Vygotsky's stance on the role of the social context in child development, Leont'ev and Elkonin saw the leading activity as a cultural construct, determined by a specific society's expectations for children of a certain age. In other words, it specifies optimal activities within the social situation of development. The following leading activities (see Table 8.1), proposed by Leont'ev (1978) and Elkonin (1972), are specific to industrialized societies and may be different in other societies. Vygotskians recognize that the leading activity is closely associated with cultural tools and specific types of institutions, such as schools that are designed to pass on these tools to children.

The remainder of this chapter discusses the leading activities and developmental accomplishments for infancy and toddlerhood. Chapter 10 discusses the leading activities and developmental accomplishments for children in preschool and kindergarten, and Chapter 12 focuses on those emerging in the primary grades and culminating by the end of elementary school.

Table 8.1   Leading activities and developmental accomplishments in childhood

Age Period	Leading Activity	Developmental Accomplishments
Infancy	Emotional interactions with caregivers	Attachment Object-oriented sensorimotor actions
Toddlerhood	Object-oriented activity	Sensorimotor thinking Self-concept
Preschool and Kindergarten	Make-believe play	Imagination Symbolic function Ability to act on an internal mental plane Integration of thinking and emotions Self-regulation
Elementary Grades	Learning activity	Theoretical reasoning Higher mental functions Motivation to learn

Developmental Accomplishments of Infancy

Emotional communication is the context in which the developmental accomplishments of infancy occur. Therefore, Vygotskians acknowledge the importance of the children's one-on-one interactions with parents and caregivers—interactions that many other theories also identify as critical for development. Unlike theories that view these one-on-one interactions as primarily the outgrowth of the human species' drive to survive, Vygotsky saw these interactions as the foundation of the social context that would lead to learning and development in a uniquely human way (Karpov, 2005).

The word *emotional* in *emotional communication* is used to emphasize the fact that parents need to interact with their babies in a way that goes beyond caregiving—that is, the diapering and feeding routines. The purpose of the interactions is to establish emotional contact and a resulting emotional relationship, which in turn leads to the emergence of the developmental accomplishments of infancy: attachment and object-oriented sensorimotor actions.

Attachment

Although the term *attachment* was not used by Vygotskians, their concept of a fundamental emotional relationship was very similar to Western definitions of attachment (Bowlby, 1969; Bretherton, 1992). Attachment is a two-way emotional relationship involving the active participation of both child and caregiver, and is the blueprint for future relationships the child will develop.

Many Western psychologists have studied the relationship among different types of attachment, cognitive development, and later achievement (Frankel & Bates, 1990;

Grossman & Grossman, 1990). Western researchers have found that the quality of attachment affects a child's emotional state, which in turn affects his cognitive development. The poorly attached child suffers from a sense of insecurity, which impairs his ability to learn. The Vygotskian view of the role of attachment in cognitive development goes beyond this. A disordered attachment, they think, also deprives the child of cognitive interactions that are necessary for optimal mental growth. The interactions between a child and his early attachment figures shape the child's expectations for shared experience, and shared experience is basic to the acquisition of mental functions. The interactions of a baby and his caregiver provide crucial cognitive experiences.

Object-Oriented Sensorimotor Actions

Emotional communication also impacts the development of *sensorimotor object-oriented actions.* By shaking the rattle, the father does not just entertain the child but models what can be done with a rattle. He shows his child that a rattle can be shaken to produce a noise. He places the rattle in the baby's hands and encourages the baby to shake it. The father-child interaction with the rattle becomes a blueprint for interacting with rattles and with other objects. Shared experiences structure the child's perception, making the child focus on separate objects and their attributes. Caregivers use words like *big, small, far,* and *near* as they show objects to the baby. These descriptive words call the baby's attention to perceptual and relational characteristics.

Piaget believed that sensorimotor manipulations grow out of the baby's spontaneous body movements and actions. Babies, he felt, accidentally discover properties through random exploration (Ginsberg & Opper, 1988). Vygotsky thought that while children's manipulations are limited by their motor capabilities, the way to interact with objects is learned. A child learns to shake the rattle, not by his random movements when he is holding it, but because it has been demonstrated by another person. Some evidence for the Vygotskian perspective is found in the fact that children who had been severely deprived of emotional contact did not engage in much object manipulation, even though the objects were accessible to them in their cribs (Lisina, 1974; Spitz, 1946). Vygotskians argue that if object manipulation were a consequence of the baby's spontaneous actions, then object manipulation would develop independently of any social experience, and emotional deprivation would not affect it. However, because emotionally deprived children have been shown to have an almost complete absence of sensorimotor manipulation, there must be a link between emotional interactions and the development of exploratory behavior.

Leading Activity of Infants: Emotional Interactions with Caregivers

The leading activity for infancy is involvement in *emotional interactions,* which for Vygotskians means the establishment of an emotional dialogue between the infant and the primary caregiver (Elkonin, 1969; Lisina & Galiguzova, 1980). Western psychologists have found that this type of emotional dialogue is essential for the development of the child's social and emotional life, but Elkonin's and Lisina's further contribution is the idea that this dialogue has a direct influence on cognitive development.

Leont'ev (1978) argued that early emotional dialogue provides the motivation for later forms of shared activity. Because the infant can and wants to communicate with others, he is drawn into shared experience. Shared activity becomes a vital part of the infant's life. Vygotsky believed that during infancy all mental functions are shared, and only at the end of infancy do some of these processes become appropriated by the child. In the views of many Western psychologists, including Piaget, the end of infancy is also conceived the time when the "separation of self" occurs (Erikson, 1963; Piaget, 1952).

Emotional Exchanges

Infants' emotional interactions with caregivers evolve throughout infancy. They begin with purely emotional exchanges (e.g., smiling or cooing back and forth) and shift to include emotional exchanges or dialogues over objects (e.g., smiling after shaking a rattle). Purely emotional exchanges include the interactions that occur when a baby attends, smiles, or coos to a loving voice, and the more physical ones when a baby happily responds to hugging, bouncing, patting, or tickling. These interactions are highly positive exchanges with each responding to the other.

A detailed analysis of the evolution of infants' communicative behaviors carried out by Maya Lisina and her colleagues (Lisina, 1974; Lisina & Galiguzova, 1980) suggests that there are qualitative changes in these behaviors that mark the transition from the baby being a relatively passive recipient of adults' attention to taking an increasingly more active part in the dialogue. The first of these transitions takes place in the beginning of the second month, when babies start smiling in response to their caregivers' smile and voice:

> By the second month of a child's life, an adult's smile and words evoke positive responses: the child calms down and concentrates his attention on the adult; after some time, he smiles and coos and becomes more energetic in his motor activity. (Zaporozhets & Markova, 1983, p. 74)

First Child Initiations

The next milestone that Lisina and her colleagues identified in the development of infants' communicative behavior is the emergence of what Vygotskians refer to as the "kompleks ozhivleniia"—the way that 3-month-old babies become animated when greeting familiar adults (see Figure 8.1). This animation is not limited to smiles but also includes gesturing and vocalizations, such as when a baby throws her hands up and starts cooing at the sight of the approaching caregiver:

> By the age of two months, the child has formed a characteristic, complex reaction, which includes all the components enumerated and is known as the animation complex [kompleks ozhivleniia]. The animation complex forms as reactive education and soon becomes activity that is intended to arouse the attention of adults and to maintain contact with them. (Zaporozhets & Markova, 1983, pp. 74–75)

Between 3 and 6 months of age, babies begin to use smiles and vocalizations to invite the caregivers to engage in emotional exchanges. What Lisina and her colleagues described are the behaviors similar to the ones described by Tronick and others as part of

Figure 8.1   Infant engaged in an emotional exchange with his father

the "interactional synchrony" (Tronick, 1989). For the Vygotskians, the most important thing about this new communicative behavior is that now infants can initiate the dialogue with the adults, not just respond to the adults' overtures.

Exchanges Around Objects

During the second half of the first year, the purely emotional dialogue is supplemented with interactions between the caregiver and the child around objects, and actions upon objects. Now the father shakes a rattle in response to the baby's smile. Around this time, parents begin to label and talk about objects. Parents and others interpret the baby's actions as if the actions were communicating something. For example, 6-month-old Lisa gestures toward her teddy bear, and her sister says, "Oh, you want your bear. I'll get it for you." For infants, objects become interesting through the mediation of others. By modeling how to interact with objects and interacting by engaging the child in with older persons provides assistance that enables the child to acquire object-oriented actions. Object manipulation exists in a shared experience first, as do all other mental processes. It is a product of the child's emotional dialogue with her caregiver.

First Gestures and Words

It is in this new context of communication around objects that infants develop their first communication tools: gestures and words. When a baby attempts to reach for an attractive toy that is out of her range, an adult hands it to the baby. The action of reaching for an inaccessible toy in the presence of a caregiver evolves into a pointing gesture that signals the baby's desire for the toy to the adult (see Figure 8.2). Vygotsky describes

Figure 8.2 Child gesturing to her mother

the development of infants first gestures as an example of how mental tools emerge first in an inter-mental plane:

> Initially, the pointing gesture represents a simply unsuccessful grasping movement directed toward an object and denoting a future action. The child attempts to grasp an object that is somewhat too far away, his hands stretched toward the object are left hanging in the air, the fingers make pointing movements. (Vygotsky, 1997, p. 104)

It is the adult's behavior that assigns meaning to the pointing gesture; for some time the gesture exists as pointing only in the context of "shared activity." Only later is the gesture recognized to be a gesture by the child himself:

> When the mother comes to help the child and recognizes his movement as pointing, the situation changes substantially. The pointing gesture becomes a gesture for others. . . .
> In this way, others carry out the initial idea of the unsuccessful grasping movement.
> And only subsequently, on the basis of the fact that the unsuccessful grasping movement is connected by the child with the whole objective situation, does he himself begin to regard this movement as a direction. (Vygotsky, 1997, p. 105)

Like the first gestures, the first words infants utter are initially treated as meaningful by the adults who interact with them and only later are used by the infants to signify people, objects, and actions. Parents are pleased when a baby makes a random "da da" sound in the presence of the father and soon assign these sounds the meaning "Daddy," a meaning the baby learns from the parents. As with all mental tools, language first appears in its shared form with adults providing most of the conversation. Gradually, caregivers' monologues are transformed into true dialogues with babies who use their smiles, gestures, and vocalizations to actively participate. By the end of infancy, babies use language more independently, which signals the beginning of their appropriation of this essential tool.

By the end of the first year of life, children become interested in interacting with caregivers about objects and become interested in their own actions on these objects. Vygotskians hypothesize that the reason for this interest is that the positive attitude toward adults, which is an outgrowth of secure attachment, is transferred to everything that adults present to them or are doing in their presence (Karpov, 2005). In addition to being interested in interacting with the adults over objects, infants become increasingly competent in initiating and maintaining these interactions by expanding their repertoire of communication tools (verbal as well as nonverbal), which allows them to initiate and maintain these interactions. This prepares infants to make the transition to the leading activity of toddlerhood: object-oriented activity.

Developmental Accomplishments of Toddlers

As children make the transition from infancy to toddlerhood, their social situation of development changes. They become able to do more things independently, largely as a result of their advanced motor development. Children are now capable of walking, reaching for an increasingly wider variety of objects, and exploring new places. Because of progress in fine motor skill development, children can handle objects in more complex ways. The emergence of speech increases the child's independence even further by allowing her to ask for desired objects or actions, including ones that are not present. For example, a toddler might ask for more cookies after eating the last one. This greater independence leads to situations where parents must begin to limit children's behavior. Because babies cannot move or reach for objects without adult permission, adults regulate their behavior merely by not handing them forbidden objects. Toddlers are not limited in this way and can seek out situations and objects by themselves. One of the changes in the social situation of development is that children are expected to comply to adult restrictions and to internalize those restrictions. Parents expect children to keep their fingers out of the light socket and to remember to do that whenever they see a light socket. Toddlers' ability to use speech becomes a further asset as they begin to use private speech as a means to control their own behavior and to internalize the adult's restrictions (see Chapter 6).

This growing independence, however, is still limited by the toddler's existing repertoire of knowledge and skills, especially regarding the use of objects. Elkonin (1972) described toddlerhood as the age period when adults still have to be present (physically or virtually) in all of the child's object-oriented actions. Eloise has her baby doll in her hand walking around the house. Only when her dad says "Are you going to feed your baby?" does she begin to play with the doll like a baby, taking a spoon that is on the table and trying to feed the baby. As toddlers move from joint object-oriented actions to independent actions, they acquire tools for exploring and processing the properties of objects and situations. These tools bring about advances in their cognitive development. Through comparing the results of their actions with the models demonstrated by adults, toddlers' awareness of their own actions strengthens. This leads to the emergence of a self-concept.

Vygotsky thought that in toddlerhood, nonverbal (sensorimotor) thought begins to merge with spoken language. This, he argued, leads to the later emergence of verbal thinking (Vygotsky, 1987). However, toddlers themselves do not yet think in words. Their words are associated with certain actions but do not form the basis of thinking. Vygotsky believed that the child associates the word *spoon* when eating with a spoon, but does not think of the word to plan what to do with the spoon without having it present on the table. Words are integrated into thinking, but the child still depends on the physical manipulations of objects to support problem solving. When the child can think primarily in words, then language and thinking have merged. This takes place during the preschool and school years.

The object-oriented activity of toddlers along with their increasing mastery of language leads to the following developmental accomplishments: sensorimotor thinking and self-concept.

Sensorimotor Thinking

Like Piaget (1952), Vygotsky believed that young children use *sensory-motor thinking;* that is, they solve problems using motoric actions and perceptions. Unlike Piaget, Vygotsky (1987) argued that sensorimotor thinking was mediated by other people through shared activity and language, and was not the result of the maturation of sensorimotor schemas, as it was in Piaget's view.

Vygotskians consider sensorimotor thinking to be an important step in cognitive development. Alexander Zaporozhets, who studied the development of perception and thinking in young children, wrote:

> The visual representations of reality and the ability to manipulate these representations by young children constitute the ground floor of the multi-storey building of human thinking. Without this ground floor, it is impossible to later build the upper stories, or cognitive levels: those complex systems of abstract operations carried out with the help of special symbolic systems. (Zaporozhets, 1986, pp. 242–243)

An important characteristic of toddlers' sensorimotor thinking compared with the isolated sensorimotor actions of infants is that for toddlers the thinking becomes infused with speech. Being able to use words to describe the properties of objects and actions liberates toddlers from the limitations of the "here and now," allowing them to develop their first generalizations. Moreover, the use of words transforms perception itself, changing it from a series of isolated sensory images into a system of meaningful relationships between perceived objects:

> Nonverbal perception gradually is replaced by verbal perception. Objective perception develops in conjunction with naming an object . . . Speech changes the structure of perception due to generalization. It analyzes what is perceived and caterizes it, signifying a complex logical processing that is, dividing the object, action, quality, etc. into parts. (Vygotsky, 1998, p. 280)

As a result of engaging in adult-mediated actions with objects and learning the words that stand for these actions and objects, toddlers become capable of generalizing their actions from object to object and from one situation to another. One example of such generalization is when a toddler learns that different objects can serve the same function—you can drink from a cup, a mug, or a bottle. Another example is when a toddler starts using the same object in different situations: having learned to put her socks on, Trisha proceeds to put socks on her teddy bear and on the legs of the chair, and even attempts to put socks on her cat! In both of these examples, toddlers master one of their first generalized notions—that the same action can be performed with different objects, in different situations, and by different people. Separating actions from objects allows toddlers to start using actions in pretend ways, thus laying the foundation for the subsequent emergence of imagination and symbolic function.

Emerging Self-Concept

The second major developmental accomplishment of infancy is the *emergence of a self-concept,* or self-awareness (Elkonin, 1972; Leont'ev 1978). First, toddlers become aware that they do things differently than adults. Later they discover that they have thoughts and desires that are separate from those of their caregivers. Toddlers express this awareness by wanting to do things for themselves, asserting their own will, and acting independently from others. This independent behavior is similar to what Erikson (1963) labeled "autonomy" in children of this age. Infants, in contrast, participate in emotional dialogues unaware of their separateness.

As toddlers begin to see themselves as separate entities, they often have to prove it to themselves by opposing the will of others. We have all seen situations like this. Two-year-old Rick's mother tries to get him to drink a glass of milk, which he refuses to do. Finally, she says, "Okay, no milk for you." He immediately reaches for the milk and tries to grab it.

Becoming aware of one's wants and needs takes time, and toddlers often get confused if adults give in to their demands too easily: they are no longer sure if something they want to do is the same or different from what their caregivers want them to do. This phenomenon might lead to the tantrums and outbursts often associated with toddlerhood. For Vygotskians, these seemingly negative behaviors are an outward indication of an important restructuring that is taking place in the toddlers' social and emotional processes. Their growing awareness of their wishes, along with the realization that many of these wishes cannot be satisfied "for real," leads toddlers to attempt to fulfill some of their wishes in an imaginary way by engaging in make-believe play (Elkonin, 1978; Vygotsky, 1977).

Development of self-concept also gives rise to the development of self-regulation as children become aware of whether their own behaviors are similar to or different from the behaviors that adults model for them. Mark stands in front of the light socket and reaches for the socket. He looks at his mom as he inches closer and closer. He is aware of his mother's disapproval as she says, "No, Mark. Don't touch the light socket." While this seems more like a step in the direction of defiance, Vygotskians would argue that it is the first step in self-regulation as the child must first learn that his behavior is "different" from what his mother wishes him to do.

In late toddlerhood when self-concept is established, children are in the process of acquiring some of the underlying capacities that will help them to develop self-regulation. The toddlers' growing mastery of language that leads to the emergence of private speech will help them regulate their behavior. By 3 years of age, a child will use the speech he has heard modeled by the adults around him to regulate himself. For example, Nina has been using a crayon to draw on a piece of paper. When her mother leaves the room, she starts to draw on the wall next to her chair. Nina's mother has told her not to draw on the wall. Looking very serious, Nina says "no, don't" to herself as she proceeds to draw on the wall. The private speech she uses are the words she has heard her mother say to her. She repeats these to herself, although the admonitions are not strong enough to actually inhibit her behavior.

Numerous studies of the development of self-regulation done in the Vygotskian tradition (see Smirnova, 1998 for the review on this topic) reveal the limitations and fragility of self-regulatory mechanisms in toddlers. They indicate that the quality of adult-child interactions during the first years of life has a significant impact on children's self-regulatory behaviors.

Leading Activity of Toddlers: Object-Oriented Activity

For toddlers (ages 1 to 3 years), the leading activity is *object-oriented activity*. Unlike infants, who treat objects merely as physical bodies capable of rolling, bouncing, or rattling, toddlers learn about the culturally determined use of objects. They learn that one eats with a spoon, uses a brush to brush hair, and puts mittens on one's hands. The function of the objects cannot be discovered by simply manipulating these objects; it takes an adult to guide a youngster through a series of demonstrations and joint actions upon the objects to learn their use.

Adult Mediation of Object-Oriented Activity

When a toddler is first learning to perform an object-oriented action, adults have to actually hold the child's hand to complete the action, and the child's participation in the action is minimal. For example, in teaching self-feeding, the caregiver has to guide the child's hand holding the spoon toward her mouth. At this point, all components of the action—from planning to execution and feedback—are carried out by the adult. Soon, the adult is able to hand over some parts of the action to the child. The child can probably soon move the spoon toward her mouth, but will still need help with picking up the food from the dish and with the final movement of actually directing the spoon into her mouth. Eventually, the entire action can be carried out by the toddler herself. As toddlers develop generalized schemas of actions and associate them with specific words, adults become able to initiate new actions simply by demonstrating them or even by directing the child verbally. For example, a child who knows how to toss a ball might be directed to toss his dirty socks into the clothes basket.

Instrumental Activity

In the course of their adult-mediated actions with the objects, toddlers also discover that some objects can be used as tools or instruments. Elkonin (1969) called this *instrumental activity*. Instead of playing with one object at a time as infants do, toddlers play with several objects together. They put a block inside a bowl, or they stack blocks on top of each other. In contrast, infants tend to examine one block at a time, not considering how several blocks can be used together. Coordinated manipulation enables toddlers to look at relationships between objects and their attributes. Using object-instruments, toddlers begin to explore the hidden attributes of other objects, something that they cannot immediately access with their senses. As Toby plays in the sandbox, he makes mud pies with his little buckets and then crashes them with his shovel. However, when he presses the shovel against the bucket itself nothing happens. The concepts of "soft" and "hard" are the relevant ones in this situation, and Toby cannot know if a new object is softer or harder than his shovel until he tests it by touching it and banging the objects together.

The Role of Language in Object-Oriented Activity

The newly discovered properties of the objects become new concepts and will be used in new situations only if the child learns new words or phrases to label them. Therefore, for toddlers, language is no longer a tool used just for emotional communication, as it was in infancy. Now, language is intimately tied to object-oriented actions. Language facilitates the manipulation of objects because it enables the child to retain an understanding of the newly discovered attributes and relationships between objects. For example, the words *put inside* will trigger a whole set of associations between an object and other objects, such as a toy truck and a box.

In addition, Vygotskians showed that the way a toddler plays with an object is determined in part by that object's name. If the caregiver hands a toddler a stick and says "spoon," the child will pretend to eat with it. If she takes a stick and pretends to eat with it, the child will mimic her and say "spoon." On the other hand, if the caregiver takes the same stick and says "pen" the toddler will treat it like a pen and write with it. Clearly, the physical attributes of an object are not the only determinates of how a child plays with or uses an object; rather, it is its meaning as communicated by others (Elkonin, 1989; Karpov, 2005). Therefore, even when toddlers seem to be engaged in independent exploration, they are still participating in adult-mediated activity, because they are applying language to their actions that they have learned through interchanges with adults.

Restructuring of Perception Through Object-Oriented Activity

In addition to language-based mental tools, toddlers begin to acquire another category of tools—the one based on nonverbal images. Vygotsky considered perception to be the most dominant function in children of this age and the first one to start its transformation from lower mental function into a higher mental function (see Chapter 2). However, he did not specify the mechanisms of this transformation. This was done later by his students who studied the emergence of mediated perception in young children. Zaporozhets and Venger proposed the concept of "sensory standards" to describe specific mental tools responsible for elevating perception from the level of a natural, lower mental function to the level of a higher mental function. They coined the term *sensory standards* to describe the "representations corresponding to socially elaborated patterns of sensory characteristics of objects" (Venger, 1988, p. 148). An example of a sensory standard is referring to a shade of color by the name of a familiar object that has this color, such as persimmon red. Existence of these standards is demonstrated by the fact that we have such names for the colors as "turquoise," "violet," or "sea green." We also talk about something having a "minty" taste or a "fruity" smell. Among the first sensory standards to be acquired by young children are the colors of the spectrum, simple geometric shapes, and basic tastes.

Symbolic Substitution

Another way adults mediate the object-oriented activity of toddlers is by providing them with specific toys to play with. Just as toys designed for infants encourage their discovery of physical properties of objects that rattle, squeak, or roll, toys designed for toddlers encourage their imitation of adults' actions. A child who just learned to feed herself or brush her own hair now tries to use the same spoon to feed her toy bunny or brushes her doll's hair. At this point, although the toddler uses the toys, she is not yet "playing" with them in the same sense that she will be later. There is no imaginary situation, and she does not take on an imaginary role herself. Neither does she assign roles to her toys.

Later, following adults' demonstrations, toddlers are able to go beyond simple imitation and start using objects in a pretend way; the same action of feeding a baby can now be carried out using a stick or a pencil representing a spoon. This use of object substitutes can typically be observed in toddlers approaching 2 years of age depending on how much experience they have had with adults modeling these pretend actions (see Karpov, 2005, for the review of research connecting adult modeling with children's levels of play). By the end of their third year of life, children not only engage in pretend actions, but also start using language indicating the rudimentary role-playing in which they are engaged. Cheryl rocks her baby doll and says, "Cheryl-mommy."

The development of object substitution is the ability to use one object to stand for another, which signals the emergence of symbolic function, a competency that will continue to grow through preschool.

Language used while involved in object-oriented activity prepares toddlers for the transition to the leading activity of preschool years—make-believe play. Both adult mediation and communicating and playing with other children, facilitate the development of language. While children at this age are not skilled in dealing with same-age mates, toddlers benefit from contact with children of all ages.

For Further Reading

Elkonin, D. (1972). Toward the problem of stages in the mental development of the child. *Soviet Psychology, 10*, 225–251.

Elkonin, D. (1989). Izbrannye psychologicheskie trudy [Selected psychological works]. Moscow: Pedagogika.

Karpov, Y. V. (2005). *The neo-Vygotskian approach to child development.* New York: Cambridge University Press.

Leont'ev, A. (1978). *Activity, consciousness, and personality.* Englewood Cliffs, NJ: Prentice Hall.

Leont'ev, A. N. (1981). *Problems in the development of mind.* Moscow: Progress Publishers.

Zaporozhets, A., & Markova, T. A. (1983). Principles of preschool pedagogy: The psychological foundations of preschool education. *Soviet Education, 25*(3), 71–90.

CHAPTER **9**

Supporting the Developmental Accomplishments of Infants and Toddlers

According to Vygotsky, babies are born into this world as social beings and from the very first minutes of life, their development is shaped by interactions with caregivers. Even when children's actions with objects become increasingly important in their mental development during the second half of infancy and in toddlerhood, Vygotskians believe that it is not an object's physical characteristics that affect development but rather the object's cultural meaning. The cultural meaning of objects is not something that children can discover on their own but only through interactions with adults.

Supporting Infants from Birth to 6 Months

Scaffolding Emotional Communication

Caregivers support the development of emotional interactions as they respond to the emotional expressions of a baby. It is important to note that these interactions have to change as the baby grows. The caregiver should always take into account not just the current capacities of the baby, but also the emergent ones that exist within the baby's zone of proximal development (ZPD).

The most important thing adults can do for the cognitive and emotional development of young babies is to treat behaviors that are not yet truly communicative as if they are communicative. In the first months of life, babies do not express any emotional reactions to their caregivers; they are not yet capable of mutual interactions. However, it is critical at this time that caregivers take the initiative in establishing emotional contact with infants. Responding to a newborn's crying, sneezing, and facial expressions as if they are intentional attempts to communicate, as is characteristic of parents who are in tune with their babies, promotes the development of an infant's need for emotional communication with his caregivers. It is this emotional communication that builds the attachment so necessary for optimal development later on (see Chapter 8). In contrast, responding to a newborn's physical needs without attempting to enter into an emotional dialogue with her may result in problems with communication down the road.

Maya Lisina, who can be credited with developing the theory of infancy within the Vygotskian framework, characterizes the role of adults in the first months of the infant's life as "taking the lead" by using communication tools that will be appropriated and used by the child much later (Lisina, 1986). Therefore, caregivers should talk to young babies, sing to them, tell them stories and read them books long before the babies' own interest in these activities is detectable. By the same token, when a baby cries, caregivers should treat this cry as a message and respond to it with an appropriate verbal or *nonverbal* message of their own—instead of simply satisfying the infants presumed need for food or the desire to be picked up.

Scaffolding the First Child Initiations

Caregivers should continue taking the initiative in engaging infants in emotional dialogue until about the third month of age when babies develop "social smiles" and, soon after, other components of the "animation complex"—a reaction to an approaching caregiver. At first, this animation complex appears as a response to the caregivers' smiling and talking to the baby, and later babies start using the same behavior to initiate an emotional dialogue with the caregiver. Vygotskians emphasize the importance of direct interactions between a child and an adult. They see the adult as the carrier of the cultural tools necessary for the child's future development. No inanimate object, no matter how sophisticated, can replace an adult during this critical period of child development. Moreover, even the question of "if" or "to what extent" a baby might benefit from interacting with media or "smart toys" in the future, depends largely on the quality of human-to-human interactions formed in the early months and years of life.

As we discussed in Chapter 8, many of an infant's behaviors first appear in a shared state between him and the caregiver and only later are expressed independently by him. For the infant to be able to finally separate himself from an adult and to engage in independent actions, it is important that the baby be given an opportunity to initiate some actions on her own. Consider, for example, the very way the caregiver feeds the baby. If the caregiver puts the spoon in the baby's mouth without regard to the baby's need for food but because it is dinner time, the adult deprives the child of the opportunity to signal his needs. Vygotskians believe that it is important that the baby signal in some way the need for food. They counsel parents to wait until the baby opens his mouth or smacks his lips before putting the spoonful of food in it. The parent needs to wait for the baby to initiate the interaction, giving the baby control over the interaction. These first initiations later build into more complicated communications.

Even in the context of group care where the amount of time caregivers spend with each individual child is somewhat limited, it is possible to use routines such as feeding, bathing, or diapering to provide one-on-one attention and thus promote emotional interactions with all the children. An example of such an approach, which is highly consistent with Vygotskian ideas of the social situation of development for infants (Obukhova, 1996), is a system developed in the Lóczy Institute in Hungary by Emmi Pikler and later adapted in the United States by Magda Gerber (Gerber & Johnson, 1998). In this system, adults are encouraged to communicate about what they will be doing for the infants (e.g., "I am going to pick you up."), and to wait for the infant's response before proceeding. This makes the infant an active participant in caregiving routines and thus an active participant in the interactions with the adult. The adult's actions must be contingent on the child's response and should not overwhelm the child. Some parenting experts encourage the parent to talk nonstop to their child, describing everything the child is doing as well as describing what the parent is doing. This practice does not treat the child as an equal participant. When conversing with an adult, one would not talk nonstop. One gives the other person a chance to communicate and then responds. Pikler and Gerber argued that the same should be true with interactions with an infant even if the baby is communicating only with gestures, facial expressions, eye contact, and movements.

Vygotskians maintain that adults should always respond at a level higher than that of the child's current one. When babies start addressing their caregivers with gestures and vocalizations, adults need to extend these initiations to the next level. For example, when the baby coos or babbles, the caregiver should talk as if she were participating in a conversation. When the baby looks at something, the caregiver should act as if the baby had pointed at something. She should makes comments about the object or bring it closer. If the baby points or reaches, the caregiver should react as if the baby had described an aspect of an object or the object itself. The caregiver then comments on what the baby sees and touches. When the baby looks away or breaks gaze, the caregiver should step back and wait; the baby has signaled "stop" and the caregiver ideally responds by giving the baby a break from the interaction.

Supporting Infants from 6 to 12 Months Old

Scaffolding Exchanges Around Objects

Although adults usually begin introducing their baby to various objects earlier, it is only during the second half of infancy that the baby can really become interested in manipulating them. On one hand, this new interest in objects is driven by the infant's increased dexterity, and ability to reach and to grasp. On the other hand, it is driven by the infant's interest in everything his primary caregivers do. While warm and loving interactions between infants and their caregivers continue to scaffold the development of attachment, now they acquire a new focus: object-oriented actions. "Through manipulations of objects and drawing child attention to these manipulations, an adult can shift the child's interests and positive emotions from herself to these objects" (Karpov, 2005, p. 86; Zapozozhets & Lisina, 1974, p. 67).

In describing the evolution of communication needs in infancy, Lisina defines this period of later infancy in terms of communication that switches from the "emotional" to the "practical" (Lisina, 1986). Infants continue to seek adult attention, but they are no longer satisfied when this attention is limited to smiling and cooing. Now infants want adults to cooperate with them in the exploration and manipulation of objects. Sometimes this cooperation consists of helping the child to get a hold of an object; at other times the infant wants the adult to help her with a difficult manipulation. At another time, all the infant wants is the adult's encouragement and praise. Adults have become mediators for interactions with the world. The child starts using the adult as an extension of herself—both physically as her arms and legs, and as the carrier of knowledge about objects yet unknown to the child herself.

Caregivers therefore should introduce infants of this age to increasingly complex objects, and should model new operations and provide opportunities for the infants to practice these new operations and to apply them to new objects. Vygotskians suggest that adults can best support the development of babies from 6 to 12 months by choosing appropriate toys or everyday objects for their babies to manipulate and by modeling the use of these materials so the children can use them most effectively. The entire process of helping children manipulate objects consists of a sensitive interaction between determining the developing child's abilities and proceeding just ahead of what the child can do by himself. Adults must be sensitive to what the child is currently capable of, and provide assistance for what he is on the verge of achieving.

In later infancy, babies also begin to explore objects by themselves, so adults need to choose objects with different characteristics that can be experienced differently. For example, babies should be provided with toys of various sizes that are grasped differently. Objects with different characteristics—colors, textures, weight—are interesting, particularly when they are part of the same toy.

The development of reaching and grasping is dependent on the way adults interact with a child. Although these motoric actions seem like something babies do independently, in reality, adults shape these behaviors. By holding the rattle just out of reach, the adult causes the child to stretch his arm further and to lean forward to touch it. Adults demonstrate how to use different toys, such as a rattle, by shaking it or by holding the baby's hand around it to cause him to shake it. Vygotskians argue that these simple behaviors are not "discovered" by the baby but are socially engineered through adult input. Objects alone, such as a hanging mobile, no matter how colorful or technically sophisticated, do not engender the same development as an adult who varies his actions in response to the baby and keeps him engaged by changing objects and varying the distance of the object from his grasp. Only another human being can make the small, subtle adjustments necessary to increase engagement as a child learns to manipulate objects.

Scaffolding First Gestures

It is through these interactions over objects that a baby's gestures become linked to language. Language is initially learned through shared activity in which the caregiver provides the words and the baby contributes gestures. An adult says things like, "Do you want to hold your teddy?" as the baby waves his arm toward it. As time goes on, the child appropriates the words for the objects and actions that the adult used to supply. These become the first words that children learn. It is important that the language the adults use is in direct response to the child's gestures and interactions over objects.

The importance of the contingency, or connection, of language to the child's own actions cannot be overstressed in this age of baby media programs and interactive toys and videos. Listening to adults talking or to the radio or television where the speech is not interactive does not have the same positive effect on development as direct, face-to-face communication. For this reason, even videos and toys that are specifically designed for babies with slowed-down action and with interactions where the toy or character seems to be responding or talking to the child can never substitute for the real thing. The verbal interactions that are required are those that are truly responsive to a particular child's specific vocalizations. These very personal interactions extend the baby's own initiations and are relevant to the object that the baby is touching or seeing at that very second. General words from a video or toy that occur at the same time an image appears or the toy moves do not have the same impact, because the baby might be looking at another part of the screen or something else. The toy or video's words are not contingent on the baby's actions but are contingent on what appears visually. Lisina would not consider this electronic kind of mechanized dialogue to be nearly as valuable as the "true interaction" that can really only occur between a baby and a responsive, loving adult.

Supporting Toddlers from 12 to 24 Months Old

The transition from infancy to toddlerhood occurs when babies become mobile—when they crawl and walk. This mobility opens the child to new opportunities for interacting with people and exploring objects. But it also means that the baby can now get into situations that are unsafe or reach objects that before needed the adult's cooperation. Young toddlers often seem like they are acting in opposition to the adult, which made Vygotsky himself and many of his followers describe this age in the challenging terms that are often used in the West to describe the "terrible twos" (Vygotsky, 1998). At the same time, Vygotskians emphasize that in reality these seemingly oppositional behaviors are just an extension of the exploration children did when they were younger and adults brought them objects to interact with. A young toddler will not be able to follow the adult's directives to stop doing something. However, it is important that the caregiver not just move the child or object out of reach, but that she also use simple commands like "no" as she does so. The simultaneous use of language with the action is important because the adult is again acting as if the child is at the next level and is able to use private speech as self-direction.

Supporting Object-Oriented Activities

Armed with ever-expanding knowledge about the physical characteristics of various objects, toddlers begin to test the relationship between these objects. No longer content with exploring one object alone, children now look at the effect of one object on another, such as putting one object into another or banging one object against another. Therefore when interacting with toddlers, adults should give them objects that help them discover differences and similarities between things as well as hidden characteristics that are revealed only as a result of actions of one object upon another. For example, one cannot know if one object is softer than another without actually trying to fit it into another object, or hitting it with another.

Carmen's father gives her two plastic containers that fit into each other. He lets her manipulate them, but he also shows her how the objects fit together. At the beginning, she struggles to put one into the other, but soon figures out the way to turn the objects to make them fit. Next, he hands her a soft cube that can be squished. Carmen squeezes the object. Her father shows her how she can squeeze the object and put it into the big container. Carmen does this several times, as she turns the object over in her hand. Her father labels her actions as she does it. He says, "Squeeze it and put it inside." Carmen then discovers that she can put the soft block into the smaller container.

For Vygotskians, the child's exploratory behaviors result from an interplay between what the adult demonstrates and the child's own explorations. Appropriate scaffolding occurs when adults help the child discover one relationship and then step back and allow the child to take it to the next step. This shared activity cannot be dominated by the adult if the child is to eventually learn how to manipulate objects independently and find new ways of interacting with them. On the other hand, if the child plays with an object all alone without sharing this experience with another person, it will take much longer for her to discover all the potential of the object. Vygotskians continuously emphasize the importance of appropriate scaffolding in helping toddlers move to the next level of development.

Supporting Instrumental Activity

As toddlers discover the use of objects, they learn that they can use some of them as simple tools. In the beginning, children treat tools they hold as if they were merely an extension of their hands; later, they learn to adjust their hands to accommodate the specific characteristics of a tool, such as its shape or weight (Novoselova, 1978). For example, when young toddlers begin to use a spoon, they do not hold the spoon in a specific way. Consequently, they often miss their mouths or turn the spoon in the wrong direction, spilling the contents all over themselves. As they become more familiar with it, they begin to hold the spoon differently from other objects, twisting their hand in a specific way and mastering a specific grasp that enables them to get whatever is in the spoon into their mouths.

Adults provide guidance and support as children learn to use the many tools in the world around them. In this context, tools can range from feeding implements such as spoons and cups to brooms, brushes, and shovels. At first, tool use may occur with the adult actually placing her hand over the child's to form the correct hand position (or body position in the case of some larger tools) for holding the tool most efficiently. Next, the child and the adult begin together, but the child completes the action. Then, as the child begins to use the tool with an approximation of the adult use, the parent should step back, watching the child complete the action and providing support only when the child makes a mistake. At this point, the adult's role is to provide feedback and encouragement. Following the principle of scaffolding, the parent is handing over the responsibility of the tool use to the child.

Supporting the Development of "Sensorimotor Concepts"

As they learn to use objects, toddlers imitate the manner in which adults interact with them. Vygotskians argue that this imitation of a series of behaviors becomes internalized, and the child begins to develop a specific schema for interacting with a specific object or "sensorimotor concepts."

To help Lisa learn about the brush and brushing, Lisa's mother shows her how she brushes her own hair. Lisa watches her mother intently. She picks up the brush and tries to imitate her mother. Looking at her mother, she hits herself on the head with the back of the brush. Her mother adjusts the brush so that the soft bristles are on the side of the brush that will come in contact with Lisa's hair. She then makes the movements with her own hand that Lisa makes with the brush in her hand. She nods and says, "Let's brush your hair." Through this interaction, Lisa develops a sensorimotor schema or concept for the brush that not only combines visual, tactile, and kinesthetic representations of brushing, but is also associated with the specific words her mother used to explain the use of this new tool. Thus, the development of a child's use of the tools around her is essentially shaped by the interactions she has with her parent. If the parent were not around to demonstrate this use, it is unlikely that Lisa would even know what to do with the brush.

It is important that the adult model the use of a tool and the language associated with it when it is introduced. Without these models, children will not develop the important sensorimotor schemas that are the building blocks for other concepts. Adults should model tool use and also the language and the sensorimotor actions that go along with it. As with babies, the people in the toddler's world should always be reacting to her on a higher level than where the child actually is at that moment. The use of language during instructional episodes, such as Lisa's hairbrush example, ensures that children make the transition from purely sensorimotor concepts to symbolic-verbal ones as well. The word *brush* will bring to Lisa's mind more than just an image of the object, but also the action and feel of the brush in her hair. These early words are the basic building blocks of the many concepts the child will learn in the years to come.

Supporting the Acquisition of Sensory Standards

Another important focus of scaffolding at this age is making sure that toddlers not only learn the words to describe the characteristics of the objects, such as big, red, or sticky, but that they start to use these words as *mental tools* to explore both new and familiar objects. Vygotskians emphasize the instrumental value of descriptive words and their associated concepts, what they call "sensory standards" (see Chapter 8). When writing about scaffolding the acquisition of sensory standards, Vygotskians emphasize that learning fairly abstract words such as *red* or *square* does not help toddlers to structure their perception as well as using more familiar words that exemplify these sensory characteristics. Therefore, describing a color as "red as a tomato" or describing a shape as "round as a ball" would be a better way to help a toddler learn about colors and shapes.

Vygotskians also believe that learning color and shape words should be integrated into a meaningful activity, one in which these words affect the way children interact with certain objects. For example, merely asking a toddler to hand you a big ball or a red block may not teach the child to isolate the property of color or size from other characteristics of the ball or the block. On the other hand, demonstrating that a color can be a sign of some hidden characteristics that cannot be discovered by observation alone will make the child pay more attention to the absence or presence of a specific color. A good example would be to show the child that when a strawberry is ripe and sweet it is red all over, and that green strawberries are not ripe yet and do not taste that great! Thus, the red color has meaning that will make the child try to pay attention to it. Another example would be demonstrating different shapes by having the child try to roll various objects such as a ball, an apple, and a box while you tell the child the shape of the object. After discovering that only round objects roll, the child will pay more attention to the shape.

Supporting Symbolic Substitutions

To ensure that toddlers build the capacity to make symbolic substitutions, adults must demonstrate and provide verbal support for them. One way to do this is by playing with children as the substitution is modeled.

Ryan has a toy car, and as he rolls it on the ground his father says "Varrrooom." His father takes a block and says, "This is my car," as he pushes it forward. Ryan is immediately delighted. He reaches for the block. His father hands it to him and Ryan drops his toy car and imitates his father's movements saying "varoom," as if the block is the toy car. Ryan's father has shown him how to treat the block as if it were something else. In other exchanges, the block becomes a man who walks and talks to another block, then it becomes a telephone that they use to pretend to talk, and finally it becomes a pillow for Ryan's teddy bear. By demonstrating all the different things the block can become through his actions and language, Ryan's father helps him make symbolic substitutions.

The importance of such play exchanges cannot be underestimated in an age where toys have become more and more specific replicas of the real thing. Toddlers have little practice with symbolic substitution when most of the toys they own look exactly like the real thing. Adults can help model how toys can be used in different ways and how everyday objects can become toys, and thus foster this cognitive skill that will come to fruition in later years in symbolic play.

Supporting Toddlers from 24 to 36 Months Old: Transition from Toddlerhood to Preschool

Supporting the Toddler's Emerging Self-Concept

As children begin to move out of toddlerhood, they begin to behave independently from adults. As they now walk on their own and use objects when adults are not present, children discover that their own will and desires are not the same as their parents' or caregivers'. The transition from being a baby to being a toddler is based on the ability to physically separate from caregivers by crawling and walking. The transition out of toddlerhood is another step toward independence, but this time it is mental rather than physical. Late toddlerhood is when toddlers discover that they can say "no" and refuse to do what an adult wants.

Manny, who has in the past eaten whatever his mother put onto his plate, now refuses to eat spinach. His mother tries to feed him the spinach, but he closes his mouth and wrestles his body around as far away from the food as possible. When she leaves it on his high chair tray he drops it on the ground or grinds it up by smashing it into the tray.

Adults can support the emergence of a child's self-concept by recognizing that much of the seemingly contrary behavior at this age is not defiance but attempts for independence. Not getting emotionally upset about a child's behavior is admittedly difficult when the child is having a tantrum in the middle of the supermarket. It will help to ease the situation, however, if the tantrum is handled in a calm, reasoning way. When a toddler refuses something, it may not be for the same reasons that an older child does. The rejection of spinach, for example, may have more to do with the time and place than with the taste. Offering the spinach as a choice on the plate later may encourage the child to try it. Giving toddlers opportunities to assert their will in nondangerous situations goes a long way to prevent power struggles and to build their self-concept as an independent person.

Giving children real, reasonable, and limited choices helps to build their self-concept, but reasonable boundaries must be provided as well. Operating within these limits allows children to assert their independence, which is something that they must experience in order to develop normally.

Supporting the Beginnings of Make-Believe Play

Children begin to exhibit their first symbolic acts during toddlerhood, which will lead to the development of make-believe play (see Figure 9.1). Children begin by using the

Figure 9.1   Toddlers interacting over objects

tools they know how to use but in a context different from that in which the tool is routinely used. By removing the tool from its usual context, they begin their first steps toward abstraction.

Toby takes his spoon and pretends to feed his teddy bear. There is no food, but Toby still uses the actions that he would have used to feed himself if he had food. He has not yet reached the level of make-believe play of a year hence, when he will be able to use some other object like a stick to substitute for the spoon. He is only at the earliest level of symbolic substitution.

Make-believe play emerges out of the use of tools, but as with the child's other behaviors, Vygotskians believe that make-believe play is modeled first by someone in the child's social world (see Figure 9.2). The adult's role in fostering make-believe play is to demonstrate to the toddler how he can pretend to feed the bear. Again, using language to describe actions helps the child move into the pretend world.

Francesca's mom picks up the baby doll and says, "Oh, the baby is so hungry. I'm going to feed the baby." The mom picks up one of the spoons and says, "Here, yum yum" (she smacks her lips), and holds the spoon up to the baby doll's mouth. Francesca takes a spoon and says "Yum" and smacks her lips as she hits the baby doll's cheek with the spoon. Her mom adjusts her hand and Francesca repeats the motion, saying "yum," but this time puts the spoon in the vicinity of the doll's mouth. She looks at her mom. Her mom smiles and nods, "Yum, yum."

Sometimes a child will produce a behavior independently, such as sliding a car along the table. At this point, the adult's ability to provide the words that describe this action is very important. The adult should say, "Vroom, vroom. Are you driving your car?" By providing words that the toddler might be able to repeat and giving a verbal description of

Figure 9.2 Toddler engages in pretend actions with her mother

the situation, the adult helps the toddler move toward the realm of make-believe play that will occur in the next stage of development—that of the preschool child.

Supporting the Beginning of Self-Regulation

Vygotskians associate the beginnings of self-regulation in toddlers with their use of private speech (see Chapters 6 and 7). While the use of private speech varies from child to child and depends on the child's overall level of language development (Smirnova, 1998), certain recommendations for scaffolding private speech can be applied to all children of this age.

First, to be able to regulate their own actions, children need to learn the rules and standards they will use for this self-regulation along with the language that labels these rules and standards. It means that when telling toddlers what to do and what not to do, adults should use language that is simple but specific. Saying "Do not touch the stove," or "Turn off the TV," is better than saying "no" or "stop it." Saying "Don't touch the stove. It is too hot to touch and it's dangerous. You could hurt yourself. Ouch," would be too much for the child to remember. The speech the adult uses should model what the child will say to himself.

Second, before issuing "self-commands" in private speech, toddlers need to understand the relationship between their speech and its effect on the behavior of other people (see Chapter 7 for a discussion of other-regulation and self-regulation). A good way to practice this relationship would be playing games where the adult and child take turns telling each other what to do and then doing it. For example, you could take turns rolling a toy car down the ramp or placing one block on top of another as you take turns asking each other to do a simple action. The adult says, "You take a block," and the child takes a block. Then the child says, "You take a block," and the adult takes the block. These kinds of games establish the relationship between giving commands and obeying them.

Finally, adults can help children by reiterating and expanding the child's private speech while modeling the correct action. For the child who keeps saying "no" while reaching for a hot pot, it will mean holding the child's hand back, encouraging the child to keep saying "no" and saying, "That's right. No, don't touch the pot." The toddler's actions should not be interpreted the same as those of a 4- or 5-year old child. The toddler is not being purposefully disobedient or teasing because the child is not able to self-regulate yet. Private speech is just emerging. With proper adult support during the next several years, the child will be able to use private speech independently to regulate his behavior.

For Further Reading

Karpov, Y. V. (2005). *The neo-Vygotskian approach to child development.* New York: Cambridge University Press.

Venger, L. A. (1988). The origin and development of cognitive abilities in preschool children. *International Journal of Behavioral Development, 11*(2), 147–153.

Vygotsky, L. S. (1998). *Child psychology* (Vol. 5). New York: Plenum Press.

CHAPTER **10**

Developmental Accomplishments and Leading Activity: Preschool and Kindergarten

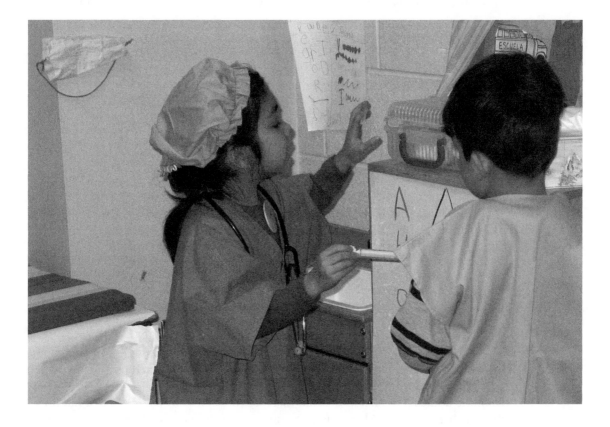

 In this chapter, we discuss the developmental accomplishments and the leading activity in preschool and kindergarten children (age 3 through 5). Definitions of the terms *developmental accomplishments* and the *leading activity* are found at the beginning of Chapter 8.

Developmental Accomplishments

The developmental accomplishments that emerge in kindergarten are imagination, symbolic function, the ability to act on an *internal mental plane*, the integration of thinking and emotions, and self-regulation. These developmental accomplishments will not emerge unless the child has had sufficient experience in the leading activity of this period. Unless the child has engaged in creative, imaginary, make-believe play, he or she will not attain this period's developmental accomplishments. As we explained in Chapter 8, the developmental accomplishments are not simply the result of maturation, but require participation in the leading activity and support from the social context to make sure that the participation is sufficiently intensive to acquire the accomplishments.

Symbolic Function

The first developmental accomplishment of early childhood is *symbolic function*, which should emerge by the end of kindergarten (Elkonin, 1972; Leont'ev, 1978). Children who have attained this accomplishment are able to use objects, actions, words, and people to stand for something else. For instance, using a box for a spaceship, waving arms to represent flying, and declaring "We're aliens" or pretending to be a tree are examples of the use of symbolic function. Vygotsky thought that this symbolic use of objects, actions, words, and people prepared the way for children to learn literacies based on the use of symbols like reading, writing, and drawing.

Another aspect of the development of the symbolic function is that children begin to use words as concepts. Vygotsky pointed out that children's first concepts are different from those of adults (see Chapter 6). Young children form what he called *complexes* in which the various attributes used to categorize objects are not differentiated from each other (Vygotsky, 1962). Thus, attributes are tied together in one complex; the block is "big-square-red." Only after many experiences with objects and with other people through shared activity can each attribute be recognized independently; the block is "big" and "square" and "red." Preschool children may use the word *red* when they mean "big-square-red." Adults may take the child's use of the word *red* as a sign that the child's concept of "red" is the same as theirs—one attribute describing color. In everyday conversations where children may rely on many contextual cues, it is not clear whether the meanings they assign to a word and the meaning adults assign to the same word are the same or different. However, when children are asked to use a particular word out of context, it often becomes obvious that the children's concept is different from the adults'. For example, when asked to sort blocks by color, a 4-year-old might place all big, red, square blocks together and leave out small, red blocks or rectangular, red blocks.

By the end of kindergarten, most of children refine their initial complexes through interactions with people and objects. Their complexes move closer and closer to those of adults to form what Vygotsky called *everyday concepts* (Vygotsky, 1962). These everyday concepts are based on intuition or naive observations, and are not dependent on strict definitions. They are integrated into a broad personal structure. For example, when a child uses the word *fish*, she could be referring to the object she has encountered that was labeled *fish* or to a generalized idea of fishiness, including anything that swims, from goldfish to whales. She does not yet have in mind the strict biological definition of *fish* as part of a scientific classification scheme.

Beginning to Act on an Internal Mental Plane

More mature than toddlers, preschool and kindergarten children should have now developed the ability to think on an *internal mental plane*, meaning that their thinking is no longer dependent on physically manipulating objects. One example is the ability to think in visual images, which is a stepping-stone between the sensorimotor thinking of toddlers and the conceptual abstract thought of older children (Zaporozhets, 2002). By kindergarten, children do not need to physically touch and manipulate objects in order to think about them; they can manipulate the images in their mind. At $2\frac{1}{2}$ years of age, Marcus cannot solve a puzzle unless he takes the pieces in his hand and turns them until they fit. By 5 years, he looks at the pieces in front of him, choosing the ones that fit and ignoring the ones that are too big, too small, or have the wrong shape. He no longer needs to touch the pieces; he can assess their fit mentally. Being able to think in visual images is an important competency and one not connected to language.

By the end of kindergarten, most children are able to move beyond thinking in discrete visual images to using generalized nonverbal representations, which Venger called "models" (Venger, 1986, 1996). Examples of models are schematic drawings, block constructions, and the play props children create to represent a role they are playing. These early models reveal much about young children's thinking processes. In young children's early schematic drawings of people, the most prominent feature is the head. Is it that children only see "heads" or is there something else involved? Venger argued that these early models were abbreviated and inexact because they represent what children take for the essential properties of an object. The head, for young children, carries the essence of personhood. Young children perceive objects much the same way as adults do, but they do not mentally focus on the same elements as being important. For instance, children see the wheels of a vehicle as important, so they often draw cars and buses with wheels but without people in them. As their ideas about vehicles change, they often add people prior to drawing the doors or the bumper of the car. In real life, children do see the people, the doors, and other details of cars, but their drawn model of a car represents only the elements that are essential to them.

Later, children will be able to identify essential properties of an object on an internal plane using abstractions such as written words or numerals; however, as preschoolers and kindergartners, they still need the support of visual images to perform the act of abstraction. Abbreviated and schematic drawings are a stepping-stone to the use of more advanced symbolic representations.

Imagination

Imagination is a generative mental activity; it allows children to invent new ways of thinking about all kinds of things. Joan and Tim play out the story of "Little Red Riding Hood." The first time, Tim is a mean loud wolf. The second time, Joan asks him to be a nice wolf that becomes her pet instead of the mean wolf. They try this out together, changing the characteristics of the make-believe roles. Children can imagine new buildings and constructions as they play with blocks. They dream up new ways of using objects as props during play, being able to change a piece of cloth into a magic carpet or the top of a tree as the play scenario requires. Imagination frees children from the restrictions of the real world; children can invent a new world—with words, symbols, and images—that exists in their minds (see Figure 10.1). In these new worlds, they can solve real problems and real issues. Imaginary thinking separates thought into two planes, the real plane and the imaginary plane. On the imaginary plane, the rules can be changed and manipulated at will to explore possible outcomes. Imaginary thinking helps us to create new combinations of ideas and to create new solutions to problems. It allows us to think outside the box to come up with creative solutions to old dilemmas (Dyachenko, 1996; Kravtsova, 1996).

Integration of Emotions and Thinking

The developmental accomplishment of the *integration of emotions and thinking* also should emerge at the end of kindergarten when children's emotions become "thoughtful" (Elkonin, 1972; Leont'ev, 1978; Vygotsky, 1998; Zaporozhets & Neverovich, 1986). Toddlers react emotionally to immediate situations: when they feel angry, they cry and

Figure 10.1 Preschool child playing alone

throw themselves on the ground. In contrast, most kindergartners moderate their emotions by using the memory of past experiences when faced with new ones. They anticipate possible outcomes. These past experiences color a child's perception and reaction to new events. Four-year-old Bridget wants to play with a group of older children, but when she goes outside, the children do not include her. This rejection is repeated every day, but Bridget does not seem to remember what happened the day before. Her 5-year-old sister, Mona, is also rejected by the older kids, but instead of going outside every day to attempt to join the group, she tells her mother that she would rather stay at home. She remembers her past rejection and the memory affects her decision to stay inside.

This developmental accomplishment of relating emotions and thinking explains why feelings of success and failure at school begin to influence kindergartners' motivation and their willingness to risk failure in taking on new learning tasks. This insight is supported by research findings that preschool children are learning optimists, believing they can learn anything at any time, a trait not universally found in older children (see, e.g., Nicholls, 1978). It also explains why children's positive and negative feelings toward each other become more entrenched and difficult to change by the end of kindergarten. The merging of thought and emotion creates strong opinions that are challenging to modify.

Development of Self-Regulation

At the end of kindergarten, young children should be capable of self-regulation—the ability to act in a deliberate, planned manner in governing much of their own behavior. They should be able to regulate their physical and emotional behaviors, and some of their cognitive behaviors. Young preschool children are reactive, meaning that their actions are spontaneous reactions to the environment. Fran sees a cookie, is hungry, and reaches for the cookie. Luis sees that Jon has a toy he wants, so he grabs the toy from Jon. Fran and Luis act without thinking about the consequences of their actions; their behavior is a pure reaction to the situation at hand. They are "slaves to the environment." Vygotsky argued that during the preschool and kindergarten years there is a change in the relationship between a child's intentions and the subsequent implementation of an action. Instead of having an immediate "thoughtless" response to a situation, usually the kindergartner is able to inhibit his initial reaction and act in a thoughtful, planned way. Instead of acting without thinking, the kindergartner can think before he acts. The self-regulated child acts deliberately and thus becomes the "master of his own behavior."

In the Vygotskian tradition, physical, cognitive, and social-emotional self-regulation are considered part of a whole. Children plan and think deliberately. They can focus attention on purpose, willfully ignoring distractions. They can remember deliberately, learning information that is not necessarily exciting but is required by the curriculum. They can delay gratification, stop aggressive behavior, and act in a positive way, controlling their emotions.

Self-regulation has often been delegated to the "touchy-feely" domain of social-emotional development, but increasingly Western psychologists are making the case that self-regulation involves the regulation of both cognitive processes and social-emotional ones (Blair, 2002). Although they are parts of a whole, physical, cognitive, and emotional self-regulation do not all develop at the same rate. Children first learn to regulate their physical behaviors, then their emotional ones. Cognitive self-regulation, involving such advanced processes as metacognition and reflective thinking, does not appear full-blown until the end of elementary school.

Several processes are responsible for the emergence of self-regulation during the preschool and kindergarten years. These include the use of private speech, engagement in other-regulation, and generalization of rules. As we discussed in Chapter 6, preschool and kindergarten are the years when children's use of self-talk or private speech peaks. Private speech provides children with a tool for self-regulation: The same words that adults used to regulate children's behaviors can now be appropriated by children to direct their own behaviors. Thus, adult directions become internalized, turning into rules for the child's own actions.

As with other higher mental functions, before self-regulation becomes part of a child's own mental processes, it exists in a shared or inter-mental form (see Chapters 2 and 7). Long before children become able to self-regulate their behaviors, they participate in "other-regulation," or interactions in which their behavior is guided by others (Wertsch, 1979). Children notice early on when other people are breaking the rules, even though they seem unaware that they are breaking the same rules. They apply the rules to others before applying them to themselves. This recognition of rules is a step toward generalizing rules across different situations. When regulation is performed by a more competent person, usually a parent or a teacher, it guides the child's behavior in the ways he is not yet capable of, but it also arms him with specific "mental tools" that eventually lead him to be self-regulated. However, this can be overdone; when an adult provides all the regulation, true self-regulation will not develop. In that case, children might be able to internalize some rules and expectations, but they will still lack the ability to self-initiate desired behaviors or to refrain from undesired ones on their own.

At the end of kindergarten, most children become able to create the generalized rules, based on experience, that form the basis of self-regulation. Three-year-old children might remember certain restrictions, but they are unable to generalize them to situations that seem similar to adults. Deana remembers being admonished by her mother for hitting Tommy, but she does not take the next step, which is to generalize the specific instance into a rule for hitting. She would be likely to hit Marsha, because there was no rule about hitting Marsha, only about hitting Tommy. By 5 years of age, children can generalize from the situation to the rule "don't hit other people."

It is important to note that self-regulation has two aspects: it includes both what the child should not do and what the child should do. Self-regulation should not be construed as just refraining from undesirable behaviors. In fact, it involves the inhibition of one behavior and the subsequent enactment of another. A truly self-regulated child is capable of intentional behaviors; she can think first and act later. By the end of kindergarten, Deana can not only resist hitting Marsha when she wants Marsha's toy, but she also knows that she should say, "Can I have a turn after you?" Deana can stop herself from hitting and also act in a prosocial way.

Make–Believe Play: The Leading Activity

For Vygotskians (Elkonin, 1972; Leont'ev, 1978; Vygotsky, 1998; Zaporozhets & Markova, 1983), make-believe play is the leading activity of the preschool and kindergarten period. Vygotsky and other educational theorists, such as Piaget (Piaget, 1951), stated that play promotes development of both mental and social abilities in children. Play is both a symbolic and social activity.

Conceptions of Play in Psychology and Education

Most people's idea of play is that it is the opposite of work. This common definition of play encompasses any situation in which people are not productive or engaged in specific activities. Play is often described as something that is enjoyable, free, and spontaneous. These views of play as rather mindless activity, however, undercut the importance of play in the development of young children.

Over the years, many psychological theorists have emphasized the importance of play in child development. They stress various aspects of play and how it influences specific psychological processes. Some well-known views of play include the psychoanalytic perspective (Erickson, 1963, 1977; Freud, 1966), play as social interaction (Howes, 1980; Howes & Matheson, 1992; Parten, 1932; Rubin, 1980), and the constructivist perspective (Piaget, 1951). Other theories of play discussed in the works of Vygotsky and Elkonin—such as the view of play as an instinctive behavior—are now of mostly historic interest (Elkonin, 2005).

Play in the Vygotskian Framework

Vygotsky believed that play promotes cognitive, emotional, and social development. This is a more integrated view of play than that of other theorists who only studied the benefits of one aspect of play's influence on development. In his writings, Vygotsky limited the definition of play to the dramatic or make-believe play of preschoolers and primary school-age children. The Vygotskian definition of play does not include activities such as games, movement activities, object manipulations, and explorations that were (and still are) referred to as play by most educators as well as noneducators. Real play, according to Vygotsky, has three components:

- children create an imaginary situation,
- take on and act out roles, and
- follow a set of rules determined by specific roles.

The creation of an imaginary situation and role-playing are commonly accepted features of make-believe play. However, added to these features is Vygotsky's idea that play is not totally spontaneous but is instead contingent on players abiding by a set of rules. The imaginary situation and role-playing are planned ahead of time and there are rules for participating in the play. This is a unique view of play and one that on the surface may seem counterintuitive.

Vygotsky pointed out that children who are engaged in dramatic play, act in a specific way that corresponds to the roles they are playing. As Vygotsky wrote,

> whenever there is an imaginary situation in play, there are rules—not rules that are formulated in advance and change during the course of the game, but rules stemming from the imaginary situation. Therefore, to imagine that a child can behave in an imaginary situation without rules, i.e., as he behaves in a real situation, is simply impossible. If the child is playing the role of a mother, then she has rules of maternal behavior. The role the child plays, and her relationship to the object if the object has changed its meaning, will always stem from the rules, i.e., the imaginary situation will always contain rules. In play the child is free. But this is an illusory freedom. (1967, p. 10)

The imaginary situations created in play are the first constraints for a child's independent behavior that channel and direct actions in specific ways. Unlike other activities where children comply with directives imposed from the outside, in play children place constraints on their own behavior. It is the first time that children engage in self-restraint—the beginning of self-regulation. Instead of producing totally spontaneous behavior, the child has to adhere to the actions required by the role. For instance, while acting like a truck driver, the child has to stay in "the cab" and cannot dash off to chase a friend unless she has "stopped" the truck and somehow incorporated the chase into the play scenario. To stay in the play, the child has to inhibit the desire to run off and look at an enticing toy in another center.

Each imaginary situation contains a set of roles and rules that surface naturally. Roles are the characters that the children play, such as pirate or teacher. Rules are the sets of behaviors allowed either by the role or by the pretend scenario. The roles and rules change as the theme for the imaginary situation changes. For instance, a group of children playing grocery store will have different roles from children who are playing at being a pride of lions. At first the rules are hidden in the play; later, these rules become explicit and are negotiated between children (see Figure 10.2).

Play, then, involves an explicit imaginary situation and roles with hidden or implicit rules. The imaginary situation is the pretend situation that children create. Although the situation is imaginary, it can be observed by others because children make the characteristics of the situation explicit. They say things like, "Let's pretend there is a chair here and a table here. We'll pretend there are six children in our class and we are the teachers." Children can also make the situation explicit by using gestures and noises, such as "vroom, vroom" as a truck pulls out of a gas station or "neiheyheyhey" as the child pulls on the reins of an imaginary horse.

Roles are also explicit. Sun-li is the mom so she dresses up like the mom, carries a baby doll, and acts like the mom by feeding the baby, going shopping, etc. She declares her role to the other children by explaining who she is, even though anyone watching would be able to guess who she is.

Rules, on the other hand, are considered implicit because they cannot be observed easily and can only be inferred from behavior. Rules are expressed as the pattern of behavior that is associated with a specific role. Each role in an imaginary play situation imposes its own rules on the child's behavior. The rules become apparent when a child

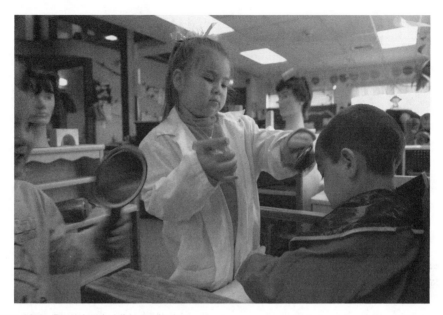

Figure 10.2 Preschool children playing

violates them. Children distinguish between playing mommy and playing teacher. There are different gestures, costumes, and even language that go with each role. Children at the early stages of play will not be aware of these differences. However, most 4-year-olds show that they are sensitive to mistakes in the carrying out of a role and often correct each other: "Mommies carry a briefcase!" "When you're the teacher, the children have to sit down." "The teacher reads the book this way." Children even enjoy violating the rules of the role as a joke. Three-year-old Toby says, "Now I'm the Daddy," as he climbs into his high chair and then bursts out laughing, "Daddy can't sit in the high chair!"

How Play Influences Development

Vygotskians argue that play influences development in several ways. The main effects of play are as follows:

1. Play creates a zone of proximal development for many areas of intellectual development.
2. Play facilitates the separation of thought from actions and objects.
3. Play facilitates the development of self-regulation.
4. Play impacts motivation.
5. Play facilitates decentration.

Creating the Zone of Proximal Development

For Vygotsky, play establishes a ZPD for the child by providing support for the skills that are on the edge of emergence. Not only can children act more socially mature, but they also show better cognitive skills—higher levels of self-regulation, and better ability to attend on purpose and remember deliberately.

> In play the child is always behaving beyond his age, above his usual everyday behavior; in play he is, as it were, a head above himself. Play contains in a concentrated form, as in the focus of a magnifying glass, all developmental tendencies; it is as if the child tries to jump above his usual level. The relationship of play to development should be compared to the relationship between instruction and development . . . . Play is a source of development and creates the zone of proximal development. (Vygotsky, 1978, p. 74)

It is not just the content of the play that defines the ZPD. The psychological processes that the child must use in order to play create support for emerging skills. The roles, rules, and motivational support provided by the imaginary situation provide the assistance necessary for the child to perform at a higher level of his ZPD.

Vygotskians have examined the mechanisms by which play influences development. For example, Manujlenko (Elkonin, 1978) and Istomina (Istomina, 1977) found that the young child employs mental skills that are more mature during play than during other activities, thereby operating at what Vygotsky identified as the higher level of the ZPD. Manujlenko also found higher levels of self-regulation during play than during other times of the day. For example, when a boy was asked to be the lookout, he remained at his post and concentrated for a longer period of time than he could when the teacher asked him to pay attention to something in her lesson.

Istomina compared the number of items children could deliberately remember during a dramatic play session involving a grocery store with those they could remember in a typical laboratory experiment. In the dramatic play situation, children were given a list of words describing items they could buy when they played grocery store. In the laboratory experiment, they were given the same list on a piece of paper. Istomina found that children remembered more items in the dramatic play condition.

If we compare the child's behavior in play and nonplay settings, we see examples of the higher and lower levels of the ZPD. In the nonplay, or real-life, situation in a grocery store, Louis wants candy, but his mother won't give it to him so he cries. He cannot control his behavior. He reacts automatically to wanting candy and even says, "I can't stop crying." While playing, Louis can control his behavior. He can pretend to go to the grocery store and not cry. He can pretend to cry and then make himself stop. Play allows him to act at a higher level than he can when he is in the actual situation.

In a classroom example, 5-year-old Jessica has trouble sitting at group circle time. She leans on other children and talks to her neighbor. In spite of the teacher's verbal cues and support, she cannot sit for more than 3 minutes. In contrast, when she is playing school with several of her friends, she can sit during the pretend group circle time. Pretending to be a good student, she can concentrate and act interested for 10 minutes. Play provides the roles, rules, and scenario that enable her to focus and attend at a higher level than she can without this scaffolding.

If a child has no play experience, it is likely that both his cognitive and social-emotional development will suffer. This led Vygotsky's students Leont'ev and Elkonin to the idea of suggesting play as the leading activity for children ages 3 to 6 (Elkonin, 1972; Leont'ev, 1978). Leont'ev and Elkonin believed that for this age group play has a unique role and cannot be replaced by any other activity, even though children also benefit from a variety of other experiences during this period. Their research on play as the leading activity during early childhood will be discussed later in this chapter.

By the "focus of a magnifying glass" in the earlier quotation, Vygotsky meant that new developmental accomplishments become apparent in play far earlier that they do in other activities, especially in more academic learning activities. Therefore, at age 4 academic-type activities, such as the recognition of letters, are not as good as play at predicting later scholastic abilities. In a 4-year-old's play, we can observe higher levels of such abilities as attention, symbolizing, and problem solving than in other situations. We are actually watching the child of tomorrow.

Facilitating the Separation of Thought from Actions and Objects

In play, children act in accordance with internal ideas rather than with external reality. The child sees one thing, but acts differently in relation to what she sees, such as when she uses a long block as a computer keyboard. In Vygotsky's words, "a condition is reached in which the child begins to act independently of what he perceives" (1978, p. 97).

Because play requires the substitution of one object for another, the child begins to separate the meaning or idea of the object from the object itself (Berk, 1994). When the child uses a block as a boat, the idea of "boatness" becomes separated from the actual boat. If the block is made to act like a boat, then it can stand for that boat. As preschoolers grow, their ability to make these substitutions becomes more flexible. Eventually objects can be symbolized by a simple gesture or by saying "Let's pretend. . . ."

This separation of the meaning from the object is preparation for the development of abstract ideas and abstract thinking (Berk, 1994). In abstract thinking, we evaluate, manipulate, and monitor thoughts and ideas without reference to the real world. This act of separating object and idea is also preparation for the transition to writing, where the word looks nothing like the object it stands for. And when behavior is no longer defined by the object, it is no longer reactive. Objects can be used as tools to understand other ideas. Instead of using blocks as blocks, a child can employ them to solve problems, such as using them as math manipulatives.

Role-playing an imaginary situation requires children to carry on two types of actions simultaneously—external and internal. In play, these internal actions—operations on the meanings—are still dependent on external operations on the objects. Children act out their internal ideas on real objects because they cannot yet operate entirely on an internal plane. However, the very emergence of the internal actions signals the beginning of a child's transition from the earlier forms of thought processes where thinking does not occur internally, as in the case of sensorimotor and visual-representational thinking. The use of internal actions is the first step to more advanced abstract thought:

> A child learns to consciously recognize his own actions and becomes aware that every object has a meaning. From the point of view of development, the fact of creating an imaginary situation can be regarded as a means of developing abstract thought. (Vygotsky, 1967, p. 17).

For example, when Marcella uses a toy block as a telephone to order pizza at the restaurant, she is aware that the block is being used as a pretend telephone as she holds it up to her ear and starts talking. By using the block in this way, she imposes another meaning on the object by her actions.

Facilitating the Development of Self-Regulation

The development of self-regulation in play becomes possible due to the child's need to follow the rules of the play and because play partners constantly monitor each other's compliance to these rules (i.e., engage in other-regulation). Vygotsky writes,

> At every step the child is faced with a conflict between the rule of the game and what he would do if he could suddenly act spontaneously. In the game he acts counter to what he wants . . . [achieving] the maximum display of willpower in the sense of renunciation of an immediate attraction in the game in the form of candy, which by the rules of the game the children are not allowed to eat because it represents something inedible. Ordinarily a child experiences subordination to a rule in the renunciation of something he wants, but here subordination to a rule and renunciation of acting on immediate impulse are the means to maximum pleasure. (1967, p. 10)

At first, a child's emerging ability to self-regulate is applied to physical actions (e.g., a child moving on all fours when playing a cat or staying still when playing a guard), social behaviors (waiting to be called on when playing student), and changing speech registers (using a deep voice when playing "daddy") in language use. Later, self-regulation extends to mental processes such as memory and attention.

Impacting the Child's Motivation

In play, children develop a complex hierarchical system of immediate and long-term goals where immediate goals can occasionally be forgone in order to reach long-term goals. Through the process of coordinating these short-term and long-term goals, children become aware of their own actions, which makes it possible for them to move from reactive behaviors to intentional ones. In order to play airplane, children have to first make tickets and passports, and set up a security line. They have to postpone the airplane play to make props and set up the environment.

Facilitating Cognitive "De-centering"

The ability to take other people's perspectives is critical for coordinating multiple roles and negotiating play scenarios. In addition, in play, children learn to look at objects through the eyes of their play partners—a form of cognitive de-centering. To act out his role as a patient who is about to be given a "shot" with a pencil, Vincent has to put himself in the shoes of Lilly, who is playing the doctor. Vincent reacts as the patient to the doctor's actions because he anticipates what the doctor means by her actions. He must think of his own actions and the actions of his play partners. These de-centering skills will eventually lead to the development of reflective thinking.

The Developmental Path of Play

Elkonin did research and experimented with interventions to show the connection between play and the development of learning activities in older children. He elaborated on Leont'ev's concept of leading activities and identified the properties that make play the leading activity for early childhood. In this section, we present the description of play derived from his research.

Play in Toddlers

According to Elkonin (Elkonin, 1972, 1978), the roots of play lie in the object-oriented or instrumental activities of toddlers, ages 1 to about 3 (see Chapters 8 and 9). During these manipulative activities, children explore the physical properties of objects and learn to use them in conventional ways. Later, when children begin to use everyday objects in imaginary situations, play emerges. For example, 2-year-old Leila picks up a spoon and tries to feed herself. She uses the spoon in a conventional way, not just to bang on the table. The first signs of play occur when 18-month-old John feeds his bear or pretends to feed himself. Play springs out of the child's exploration and use of common, everyday objects.

For the behavior to become play, the child must label the action with words. Thus, language plays an important role in transforming behavior from manipulation into play. When the teacher says, "Will you feed your bear?" he helps the toddler who has just picked up a spoon to make the transition to play. Twenty-month-old Jody rolls the toy truck back and forth and listens to the sounds it makes. Her teacher says, "Why don't you drive your truck over here and give it some gas?" Jody responds and drives her truck over to the teacher, who pretends to put some gas in it. Without the teacher's words and interaction, Jody would only continue to listen to the sounds of the wheels and explore the movement of the truck. The teacher's actions create a ZPD, propelling the child to a more sophisticated level, from physical manipulation to play.

In play, the child can pretend to be somebody else or use an object in a symbolic way. Like Piaget, Elkonin defined *symbolic function* as using objects, actions, words, and people to represent something else. To qualify as play, exploration of objects must include symbolic representation. When a child squeezes, drops, and bangs a soft plastic cup on the table, this is object manipulation, not play. When the child uses the cup as a duck and makes it swim on the table and peck bread crumbs, the actions become play.

Play in Preschoolers and Kindergartners

Elkonin describes play in preschool years as initially *object-oriented* (Elkonin, 1969, 1972, 1978). This play focuses on objects, while the roles of the players in the interaction are of secondary importance. When 3-year-olds Joann and Tomaso play house together, they say to each other, "We're playing house," but the roles of adults in the family are not enacted. They spend their time washing dishes and stirring pots on the stove, and they do not talk to each other very much.

Contrast this with the play of older preschoolers and kindergartners, which is much more socially oriented. For 5-year-old children, stirring the pots and washing dishes provide a context for the intricate social roles the children are enacting. The objects are not the focus of play. The actions of washing and stirring can even be abbreviated or just labeled verbally. In socially oriented play, roles are negotiated and enacted for an extended period of time. The child becomes the character she is playing. This kind of play is typical for children between the ages of 4 and 6, but continues in some forms through elementary school.

In the Vygotskian paradigm, socially oriented play does not have to occur with other children. The child can engage in what is called *director's play,* as when a child plays with pretend playmates or directs and acts out a scene with toys (Kravtsova, 1996). Isaac pretends to be the conductor of a symphony orchestra made up of stuffed animals and dolls. Maya plays school, at one moment pretending to be the teacher and at another talking for her teddy bear student. Unlike some Western researchers (Parten, 1932), Vygotskians do not consider all solitary play immature. If the child is playing alone but pretending that there are other people, then director's play is considered the equivalent of social pretend play.

In contrast to Piaget (Piaget, 1951), Vygotskians do not believe that socially oriented play disappears when children reach the age of 7 or 8. Children at 10 and 11 still play socially, but the importance of social play as the leading activity fades. As children get older, they develop more explicit rules for their socially oriented play. Six-year-old Frank says, "This one will be the bad guy, and bad guys always try to capture the good guy." Mary replies, "OK, but he won't be able to because good guys are faster and their planes are better, so they'll get away." The older the child, the more time is spent in negotiating roles and actions (rules) and the less time is spent on acting out the script (imaginary situation). In fact, 6-year-olds often spend several minutes discussing a scenario and only a few seconds acting out the situation.

Nonplay Activities in Preschool/Kindergarten

Although not leading, other activities are beneficial for development during this period:

- Games with rules
- Productive activities (drama and storytelling, block building, art and drawing)
- Preacademic activities (early literacy and mathematics)
- Motor activities (large-muscle activities)

Games with Rules

Game-playing is another type of play-like interaction that emerges at around 5 years of age. Games are similar to make-believe play in that the players abide by explicit and detailed rules, but the imaginary situation and the roles are hidden. For example, playing chess creates an imaginary situation. Why? Because the knight, king, queen, and so forth can only move in a specified way and because covering and taking pieces are unique chess concepts. Although in a chess game there is no direct substitute for real-life relationships, it is a kind of imaginary situation nevertheless (Vygotsky, 1978).

Another example of game-playing is soccer, a game in which players are not allowed to touch the ball with their hands. Soccer creates an imaginary situation, since in reality all of the players could use their hands to move the ball. However, all of the players agree that they will not use their hands. This is a similar phenomenon to children spelling out what they can or cannot do during dramatic play.

Games are also distinguished from make-believe play by the balance between roles and rules. In make-believe play, the roles are explicit and the rules are not. In social play, children discuss the roles and what is expected, but breaking the rules does not terminate it. A child can do something outside the agreed-upon sequence, but this will not materially upset the play. By contrast, games have explicit rules; if the rules are broken, then the game cannot continue.

Games with rules provide a ZPD for the development of a number of unique skills and act as a complement to make-believe play. Games help children learn to conform their actions to mandatory rules and norms. They voluntarily comply in order to play the game. Vygotskians argue that games provide an opportunity to develop resilience in the face of temporary setbacks. When children lose, they gain practice in dealing with temporary failures (Michailenko & Korotkova, 2002), such as when academic learning becomes difficult (see Figure 10.3).

Vygotskians think that playing games with rules prepares young children for a specific kind of learning activity frequently used in kindergarten and primary grades—*didactic games*. In didactic games, children engage in interactions that are playful, like

Figure 10.3 Kindergarten children playing a game

other games. The difference is that the content is academic. By playing properly designed didactic games, kindergartners learn important behaviors essential for their later engagement in *learning activity*, such as the ability to identify the *learning task* (see Chapters 12 and 13). In their kindergarten classroom, Lisa and Ariel are playing Alphabet Dominos, matching a card with an alligator with a card picturing an ant. Both girls can tell you that the purpose of the game is to find the pictures that start with the same first letter. They know what is being learned as they play the game. Later in the afternoon when Lisa tries to teach her 3-year-old brother, Jacob, how to play this game, it does not function as a learning task for him. Although Jacob knows many beginning sounds and letter names, he is yet unable to concentrate on the learning task aspect of the game—that of matching the beginning sounds. Instead, Jacob groups the pictures together based on how similar the pictures are. For a game to be a learning task, the child has to be able to state what is learned from it.

Productive Activities

Vygotskians identify several types of productive activities for young children that are also beneficial for development (Zaporozhets, 1978). In dramatizations, children act out familiar stories and fairy tales like Billy Goats Gruff. Like play, these provide roles and a similar pretend scenario. The difference in dramatization is that there is a previously created script, not one created by the children as in make-believe play. Creative teachers, however often use these dramatizations as a jumping off point for real play. In that way, dramatization can enrich play. An added benefit of dramatization is that it can be used to teach children about the underlying structure of stories. It can also help with literacy development by promoting the use of new vocabulary and providing opportunities for children to practice memory skills.

Block building and other constructive activities, particularly when done with others, promote the same kind of shared activity as play. When children are assigned or assign themselves roles and are required to communicate with another person during and after the creation of structures, constructive activities have the same beneficial effects as play (Brofman, 1993). In constructive activities, like building with blocks or interlocking plastic tubes, children learn to use a different set of symbols than those learned during play, such as reading diagrams or making maps.

Preacademic Activities

Like the authors of such books as *Engaging Children's Minds: The Project Approach* (Katz & Chard, 1989) or *Hundred Languages of Children* (Edwards, Gandini, & Forman, 1994), Vygotskians argue that preacademic skills should not be the main focus of preschool curriculum. Moreover, Vygotskians stress that preacademic activities can be beneficial in the early childhood classroom, but only if they emerge out of children's interests and only if they occur in a social context appropriate for young children, such as pretend play, painting, or building with blocks (Zaporozhets, 1978). Presenting academic activities in a teacher-led large group situation where children are drilled on phonics or counting is not appropriate. It does not promote the uniquely preschool developmental accomplishments and, in fact, does little to truly get children ready for school.

On the other hand, when preacademic activities are part of the child's interaction with materials, in construction or in play, they are appropriate. For example, writing should emerge out of the desire to write messages to friends or a note to Mom or Dad and not from children's attempts to form perfect letters. Discussing the issue of early literacy instruction, Vygotsky (1997) emphasized that "teaching must be set up so that reading and writing satisfy the child's need" and that the goal of the instruction should be "to teach a child written language and not writing the alphabet." Similarly, using numbers ideally emerges when children are engaged in activities such as dividing up the cups for snack time or measuring ingredients for a cooking recipe.

Motor Activities

Motor, or movement, activities are the third type of activity that promotes development at this age. Gal'perin (1992) and Leont'ev (1978) found that motor activities that required the inhibition of reactive responses were particularly useful for the development of attention and self-regulation. They suggest that there is a relationship between motor control and the later control of mental processes. For teachers, this means that children who cannot sit still and inhibit their bodies from wiggling usually also have trouble attending to formal instruction. Activities in which children are required to turn into statues or freeze are helpful in promoting self-regulation (Michailenko & Korotkova, 2002).

School Readiness

Vygotsky's view on school readiness stems from his theory that child development is driven by changes in the social situations in which the child participates. Therefore, the issue of school readiness has two aspects. The first one is the social situation itself as comprised of particular cultural practices of schooling and the expectations associated with the role of a student. The second aspect is the child's awareness of these expectations and his ability to meet them. To gain this awareness, a child has to actually participate in school activities and engage in specific social interactions with teachers and the other students. Therefore, Vygotsky thought school readiness was formed during the first months of elementary school through actual interactions in that environment and not prior to school entry.

However, certain accomplishments of the preschool years do make it easier for children to develop this readiness. Among these accomplishments are mastery of some mental tools, development of self-regulation, and the integration of emotions and cognition. Vygotskians argue that the quantity of skills and concepts is not as important as the level at which cognitive processes function. For example, the children's ability to conform their actions to a rule (Elkonin, 1989) or to learn intentionally are more important than being able to count to a hundred. Cognitive abilities like following rules or being able to memorize, facilitate later learning.

The social and emotional achievements of early childhood are extremely important for later school success. Children must have the motivation to learn formally; that is, to learn in a situation where the outcome of learning may not be directly tied to their immediate interests or desires. Motivation to learn in such situations requires curiosity and the desire to learn how to do new things and meet the expectations of school classrooms. These qualities are possible only if children can think about emotions. With these social-emotional prerequisites in place, a preschool child is able to make the necessary transition from learning that follows the child's own agenda to learning that follows the school agenda.

For Further Reading

Berk, L. E. (1994). Vygotsky's theory: The importance of make-believe play. *Young Children,* *50*(1), 30–39.

Berk, L. E., & Winsler, A. (1995). Scaffolding children's learning: Vygotsky and early childhood education. *NAEYC Research and Practice Series, 7.* Washington, DC: National Association for the Education of Young Children.

Elkonin, D. (1977). Toward the problem of stages in the mental development of the child. In M. Cole (Ed.), *Soviet developmental psychology.* White Plains, NY: M. E. Sharpe. (Original work published in 1971)

Elkonin, D. B. (2005). The psychology of play: Preface. *Journal of Russian and East European Psychology, 43*(1), (Original work published in 1978)

Karpov, Yu. V. (2005). The neo-Vygotskian approach to child development. New York: Cambridge University Press.

Vygotsky, L.S. (1977). Play and its role in the mental development of the child. In J. S. Bruner, A. Jolly, & K. Sylva (Eds.), *Play: Its role in development and evolution* (pp. 537–554). New York: Basic Books. (Original work published in 1966)

CHAPTER **11**

Supporting the Developmental Accomplishments in Preschool and Kindergarten

What should we be doing in the classroom with preschool and kindergarten children? Vygotskians argue that it should involve more than teaching discrete facts and skills. This is not to say that academic skills are not important or are incompatible with scaffolding development but rather, that early education should encompass much more and should not be reduced only to those skills. The focus of the preschool and kindergarten experience has to lay the groundwork, the underlying foundations for learning in the elementary grades. Early education must emphasize the underlying skills that will make later academic success possible. This should be accomplished, not by pushing down the curriculum goals and objectives of first grade, but by creating learning opportunities that will address the unique developmental accomplishments that ought to emerge in kindergarten.

> Optimal educational opportunities for a young child to reach his or her potential and to develop in a harmonious fashion are not created by accelerated ultra-early instruction aimed at shortening the childhood period—that would prematurely turn a toddler into a preschooler and a preschooler into a first-grader. What is needed is just the opposite—expansion and enrichment of the content in the activities that are uniquely "preschool": from play to painting to interactions with peers and adults. (Zaporozhets, 1978, p. 88)

This passage describes Zaporozhets's concept of *amplification*—the idea that teachers should use tools and tactics to cultivate the abilities that lie within the child's ZPD and that will foster experiences during which the developmental accomplishments can grow (see Chapter 4). The primary activity during which this will happen is the leading activity for that time, so for preschool- and kindergarten-aged children it is play.

In this chapter, we will discuss how to scaffold the kind of intentional, mature play that is the leading activity of this age and we will also discuss some of Vygotsky's ideas about how to scaffold other activities such as productive activities, preacademic activities, and motor activities.

Scaffolding Make-Believe Play as a Leading Activity

Characteristics of Mature Play

Not all play can be considered a leading activity because not all play-like behaviors promote development to the same extent. Elkonin used the terms *mature, developed* or *advanced* to describe the kind of play that provides maximum benefits for development (Elkonin, 2005). This kind of play has the following characteristics:

1. Symbolic representations and symbolic actions
2. Language is used to create a pretend scenario
3. Complex interwoven themes
4. Rich multifaceted roles
5. Extended time frame (over several days)

While some of these characteristics are just emerging in the play of 3-year-olds, all of them should be present by the time children leave kindergarten.

1. *Symbolic representations and symbolic actions.* In advanced play, children use objects and actions symbolically to represent other objects and actions. Children who play at this level do not discontinue their play if they do not have the exact toy or prop. They merely invent or substitute something else. They may even agree to pretend to have the object and not require a physical substitute. Children at this level treat actions symbolically as well. They may agree that the building has fallen down and do not need to make the structure fall. They only need to say, "Let's pretend it fell down."

2. *Language is used to create a pretend scenario.* Children use language to create the scenarios they play out. Language is used to communicate what props stand for and how they will be used.

"Let's make this the telephone," says Jonah as he picks up a block. The play scenario is planned and discussed as it is played. "Let's pretend that we are going to Mexico and we have to get on a plane. First we have to pack our bags, then we get our tickets," says Estefan to Rosa and Katie. "OK, then we have to get our babies, too. We must take our babies, too," adds Rosa. After they get their "bags" packed—actually a purse and a shopping bag—they pretend to go to the ticket counter. Estefan says, "Now, I'm going to give you a ticket," as he rips a piece of paper he finds on a shelf and scribbles on it. "We need 3 for me," says Rosa. "I need 2, no 3, too," says Katie. Each scenario is verbally planned and then acted out. Language enables the players to communicate who is who and what will happen next.

3. *Complex interwoven themes.* Advanced play has multiple themes that are interwoven to make a whole. Children easily incorporate new people, toys, and ideas without disrupting the flow of play. Children also integrate seemingly unrelated themes into an imaginary situation. For example, they might pretend that the mechanic gets sick fixing an ambulance and has to call the doctor, thus merging a hospital theme and a garage theme.

4. *Rich, multifaceted roles.* In advanced play, children simultaneously assume, coordinate, and integrate many roles. In less-advanced play, children enact stereotypical roles tied to one theme, such as being the mommy who feeds the baby and does dishes. Once play becomes more advanced, "Mommy" can go off to work and later to the hospital with a sick child. There she can turn into the doctor who heals the child, then play out the role of the child patient, and finally return to the original mommy role. Each role is planned as part of the play scenario and is often signaled by a change in voice, gesture, or prop.

5. *Extended time frame.* The extended time frame of advanced play refers to two different aspects of play. First, it refers to how long the child can sustain the play. The longer a child is able to move the scenario along by flexibly creating needed roles or plot lines, the more advanced the play. Second, it refers to whether or not the play lasts longer than one day. Older children typically continue the same "battle" or "hospital" for several consecutive days. With assistance, even 4-year-olds can sustain play for several days. Most early childhood teachers do not consider extending play for several days because they usually think in terms of a single day's play session. According to Vygotsky and Elkonin, continuing play over several days pushes children to the highest level of their ZPD by requiring more self-regulation, planning, and memory.

Levels of Play Found in the Preschool/Kindergarten Classroom

Play used to be something that children learned at home; they then brought these play skills to the classroom. Children used to play in neighborhoods in mixed-age groups that included children from 3 to 10 years of age and even older. It is a very sad fact that children do not play the way they used to. Children today almost always play with same-age peers whose play skills are as immature as their own. Today's children also participate in many more adult-directed activities, such as soccer practice or dance lessons, at a younger age than in the past. While there are other children at these activities, they are designed to teach specific skills and seldom involve dramatic play. Additionally, children now watch more television and play on computers at earlier ages. While entertaining, these activities do not offer the same benefits as make-believe play.

These changes in the activities of childhood result in most children entering preschool with immature play skills. Children can leave kindergarten not knowing how to play if they do not get support for it in the early childhood classroom. A recent research study in Russia replicated a study done in the 1940s that compared preschoolers' and kindergartners' ability to follow directions in play and nonplay settings (Elkonin, 1978). The preschoolers of 60 years ago followed directions better in play situations than in nonplay settings but now that difference does not show up until the children are much older. It had been a characteristic of preschool children but this no longer is the case (Smirnova & Gudareva, 2004). Also, the ability to follow directions at all ages and in all conditions had generally declined compared with that found in the 1940s study. They found that the 7-year-olds of today have self-regulation levels more like those of the preschool child of the 1940s. The authors attributed this phenomenon to the decline in both quantity and quality of play in preschool and kindergarten.

Table 11.1 compares the play of children who are immature and have had little experience in play with that of children who are mature players, engaging in the kind of play that Elkonin was thinking of when he described it as the leading activity for this age group. We use the terms *immature* and *mature* to distinguish the kind of play that is common in younger preschoolers and the kind of mature, developed play skills that should emerge at the end of kindergarten.

Early childhood teachers must find ways to help children who are playing in an immature way to engage in play at a higher level. Without scaffolding from the teacher, these children will not be able to engage in the play that will become their leading activity.

Enriching Play

Our observations in a variety of kindergarten, preschool, and Head Start classrooms reveal a generally low level of make-believe play, with 4- and 5-year-old children playing in a way one generally expects in toddlers. These children rarely attempt new themes, preferring instead to act out the same familiar scenarios of family, school, and doctor. Even worse, some act out scenes from violent movies and television shows. In their play, children in these classrooms often depend on realistic toys and props, seemingly incapable of using their imaginations to create a substitute for a prop they do not have. The immature levels of play we have observed in most classrooms are not sufficient to provide children with all the potential benefits of this important activity. Given the benefits mature play affords

Table 11.1   Immature and mature play

Immature Play	Mature Play
Children repeat the same actions over and over again, such as chopping vegetables or washing dishes.	Children create a pretend scenario and act out a scene that is developed in that scenario.
Children use objects realistically and cannot invent props.	Children invent props to fit their roles.
Play does not have roles or may have a primitive role based on one action or on the prop.	Children play roles that have specific characteristics or rules for action. Children may play several roles at once, changing their language and actions to indicate a new role. Children can assign a role to an object and then talk and act for that object.
Children use very little language to create the play scenario or their role. Language tends to be limited to labeling the person or action: "I'm the mom" or "wooosh."	Children engage in long dialogues about what the play scenario will be, what the role will be, and how the scenario will unfold. Children use language intensively when playing to label the props, explain their actions, direct the behavior of other players, and to imitate the speech of the characters they are playing.
Children do not coordinate interactions but engage in parallel play.	Play is coordinated with multiple roles and themes. All of the roles play a part in the play scenario. Children may play more than one role (the cook and the customer in a restaurant). New ideas are added to the mix.
Children cannot describe what they will play in advance of beginning the action.	Children can engage in extended discussions about their roles, actions, and the use of props prior to starting their play as well as when the play scenario is about to be changed.
Children argue and fight over props and roles.	Children solve disputes and disagreements and invent props instead of fighting over them.
Children are unable to sustain play for longer than 5 to 10 minutes before moving on to another activity.	Children become immersed in play and can continue the next day or for several days to explore and expand a pretend scenario.

children for the development of literacy and other cognitive skills, it is imperative that teachers intervene in their play to improve its quality (Bodrova & Leong, 2001).

When we recommend that teachers intervene in play, we do not mean that teachers should play with children or direct play as a member of the group. Interaction with an adult places the child in a very specific, subordinate role, and no matter what the teacher does, the child is still the "child." If a teacher takes too much of the lead in play, children never get a chance to see what it is like to pretend on their own. Even when the teacher is asking the children to tell her what to do, she is still directing the play, although subtly, and thus play is now a teacher-directed activity.

Another disadvantage of too much adult direction is that the teacher will not be able to observe what lies within each child's ZPD. Only by stepping back and watching the child interact with peers can the teacher see the child's potential in a different social context. This other social context may show a side of the child the teacher would never otherwise know.

Teachers, nonetheless, have an important role in assisting the play process. Sensitive teachers who provide appropriate scaffolding have a positive impact on the level of play in their classrooms (Berk, 1994; Bodrova & Leong, 2003a; Smilansky & Shefatya, 1990). In on our work in preschool and kindergarten classrooms, we found the following interventions to foster higher levels of play:

1. Make sure children have sufficient time for play.

2. Provide ideas for themes that extend children's experiences and enrich the play.

3. Choose appropriate props and toys.

4. Help children plan their play.

5. Monitor the progress of play.

6. Coach individuals who may need help.

7. Suggest or model how themes can be woven together.

8. Model appropriate ways to solve disputes.

9. Encourage children to mentor each other in play.

1. *Make sure children have sufficient time for play.* Preschool children need a substantial block of time, between 40 and 60 minutes of uninterrupted time each day, to develop the themes and roles characteristic of rich, mature play. At the beginning of the year, teachers should start with 20 minutes and slowly increase the time allotted until they reach the full 40 to 60 minutes. By uninterrupted time, we mean that teachers should not pull children out for other activities or change the direction of ongoing play. It takes time for themes and roles to develop. When children are pulled away for other activities, it disrupts the development of roles and themes. At this age, children cannot stop and restart play unless they have attained the most mature level of play.

However tempting, teachers should not interrupt the flow of play to insert academic concepts. For example, we would consider it an interruption if the teacher would ask children who are playing car mechanic in the block area to find all of the square blocks and put them in a pile and file all of the rectangular blocks and put them in another pile. Also inappropriate would be a comment such as, "Did you notice that the wheels on the cars are round? How many wheels do your cars have all together?" These comments take the play in another direction and actually turn play into a teacher directed mini-lesson. Teachers can convey information in helpful ways such as, "Tell John what shaped block you need next so he can hand you the right one." (The child points to a rectangular block.) "Oh, you need the rectangular one. Ask him to give you the rectangular one." The teacher gives the child the information about shape that will help the child play with his friend. Knowing to ask for a rectangular block helps John to build the tower the way he wants to.

It is not just in preschool classrooms that play needs to be supported: it should be part of the kindergarten schedule, as many kindergartners have not yet achieved the level of mature play. With the emphasis on academics, particularly for at-risk children, many elementary schools have cut back on play, delegating it to recess time. We suggest that all kindergarten teachers allow time for play within the classroom's daily schedule. Kindergartners should be mature enough to begin their play using a story as the theme. For five-year-olds, the themes can come from books and stories rather than from experiences that the child has had directly. Fairy tales are a perfect example of stories that can serve as themes for play. Teachers can read several versions of a tale and the children can use the story as the starting point for their play. Children should be encouraged to embellish and add on to the story as the play evolves. Nonfiction books about space, oceans, sailing ships, or even historical periods can also be the source of great play themes.

2. *Provide ideas for themes that extend children's experiences and enrich the play.* Mr. Eversol took his preschool class to visit the local pediatrician's office. The nurse showed the children around the office and talked to them about good nutrition. When the children came back to class, the teacher tried to set up a doctor's office in the play area. He was disappointed because the children tended to fight over who would be doctor and who would have the stethoscope and the prescription pad. The inability of children to create new roles for their play is a common problem when preschool teachers try to expand the children's play beyond playing house or superheroes.

The problem seems to be that children do not have a repertoire of roles other than a few restricted ones and consequently, are unable to generate the necessary new ones to make their play rich and varied. When introducing new play themes, we suggest that teachers identify the roles and actions that go along with them. This gives children an opportunity to try out fresh roles. Just because a child has experience with a specific situation does not mean that he is paying attention to the roles being enacted before him. He may be focusing on the interesting objects rather than what people do and say. Therefore, the only thing he can do is to play with the objects rather than develop the rich play scenario.

For example, during the field trip to the actual doctor's office, Mr. Eversol could identify four different roles that children could act out in their pretend hospital back at school. For example, he could ask the doctor, the nurse, and the receptionist to individually demonstrate what they might do and say, while he plays the role of a patient or a parent of a sick baby. Each role is acted out in front of the child. The person playing the role tells the children who he interacts with, what he says, and what he does. This preparation for play would go something like this:

When the children are standing in the reception room of the doctor's office, Mr. Eversol points out that this is where the parents wait with their children to see the doctor. He explains that the parents have to talk with the receptionist first. He says, "This is Mrs. Johnson, and she is the receptionist. Mrs. Johnson, please tell the children what you do, and show us what you do and say if a sick child comes into the office." Mrs. Johnson says, "I'm the receptionist. I say hello to the parents as they come in. I make sure they sign in and then I get the chart–the nurse's and doctor's report of what happened the last time the child was sick. So let's pretend Mr. Eversol is the parent." Mr. Eversol walks up to the counter. Mrs. Johnson says "Hello, could you please sign in here," as she hands Mr. Eversol the sign-in chart. Mr. Eversol signs in and then he shows the children what he did. Mrs. Johnson says "Do you have an appointment?" Mr. Eversol says, "Yes, I have an appointment." Mrs. Johnson says, "Who is the patient today?" Mr. Eversol says, "Jody, my baby Jody is sick." Mrs. Johnson says, "Have a seat, the nurse will see you in a moment. I am going to get Jody's chart." Mrs. Johnson says, "I then get the chart and put it over here and then I tell the nurse that Jody is waiting for her." Mr. Eversol says, "Now I sit down with my baby and I read a magazine or I play with my baby while I wait for the nurse."

Each role is acted out in the same way with the person explaining what they say and do. Then they pick books that have pictures and demonstrate who they interact with. During the field trip, Mr. Eversol takes a picture of each of the people in the office doing a typical task. These photos will be used as reminders later when the children are back at school.

This technique of alerting children's attention to the actions, words, and social interactions among the people involved in various situations can be done with books or classroom visitors as well. For these demonstrations, books are used that have text describing what the people in those settings do and say. If the book has only a general description, the dialogue is made up by the teachers. Tell classroom visitors to plan on discussing at least four different roles within their setting. Give them a simple prop that you might use in the center or ask them to bring something that will characterize each role. Ask them to act out the procedures used in their workplace.

Instead of visiting the doctor's office, Mr. Eversol could invite Mrs. Lupina, who is the parent of one of his students and also a nurse in a doctor's office, to act out several different roles in front of the children. Ahead of time, he explains to Mrs. Lupina exactly what he wants her to do. When there is something he particularly wants to emphasize, he tells her that he might ask her to repeat that portion of the episode. He asks her to show the class what would happen if a dad came in with a baby who had a fever. Each time Mrs. Lupina demonstrates a role, she uses a distinct prop, shows what that person does and says and explains with whom the person interacts. This would go something like this:

Parent Role: Mrs. Lupina puts on a tie and picks up the baby doll. She says to the children, "Now I'm the dad and this is my baby. I could be the mom, but today, I am the dad who brings his sick baby to the doctor's office. I bring my baby in if my baby is sick and has a fever or has broken her arm. Today, my baby has a fever, so I say to the doctor or nurse, 'I think my baby has a fever, I'm worried about her.' I give my baby to the doctor or nurse."

Nurse Role: Mrs. Lupina puts down the baby and the tie and puts on the nametag that says "nurse." She picks up a chart and a rectangular block. She says, "Now

I'm the nurse and I talk to the dad and take the baby's temperature to make sure the baby has a temperature before the doctor comes in. I say, "When did your baby get sick? Was it in the morning? Was it after she ate breakfast?" I write down what the dad tells me. (She shows the children what she has written on the chart.) I take the baby's temperature (she demonstrates by holding the block near the baby's ear and looking at it), and say "Oh dear. Your baby has a temperature. We will have to tell the doctor." I write the temperature on the chart. (She shows the children that she has written a number on the chart.)

Pointing out the roles and what people do and say when they are interacting with each other provides a set of roles and actions that children can use to create their own play scenario. The children should use, as much as possible, the actual words that the adults whose lives they are acting out would use. Teachers can explain new vocabulary words to children and show them how they are used. For example, the teacher can encourage the word *injury* rather than *owie*. Encouraging the use of specific grown-up language that is associated with various situations provides an opportunity to expand vocabulary as children play.

By kindergarten, children should be able to create pretend scenarios and roles with much less physical support and with less involvement on the part of the teacher. Once they have the idea that they can use stories as play themes, kindergartners are adept at bringing different stories together, even using pictures in books to spark play. Teachers need to make sure that the stories they are reading are rich enough to sustain play at this age. Chapter books in which characters encounter more than one episode provide wonderful ways both to enhance literacy skills and to provide sufficient play material. Also, nonfiction and fiction books can be woven together to create ideas for play.

3. *Choose appropriate props and toys.* Play props serve several functions. First, they are an important part of making play a context in which children can operate on a "mental plane." In play, they are not just dealing with physical objects but are manipulating them mentally, as when they pretend that a block is a cell phone. The child has to mentally separate the usual meaning of an object, a construction block for instance, from what he is pretending it is. A child deciding to use a block as a telephone makes a greater cognitive leap than when he uses a toy telephone as a telephone. When the block becomes a phone, the child acts according to internal ideas and not external reality, thus separating thought from action. The prop acts as a generalized model because the block represents all actions that one does with telephones, including answering them, punching in numbers to call out, and hanging up.

According to Vygotskians, the teacher should stock the play area with toys and props that have multiple functions. For example, several large pieces of colorful cloth are better props than a specific princess dress. Use toys from different cultures; for instance, demonstrate how the child playing mom can carry her baby in a Snugli™, tied to her back, or in a sling. Encourage children to make their own props. When children cannot find the exact prop they want, encourage them to make one up. They might use another object, like a block, or they can just pretend they have the object. They can make the menus for the restaurant, the tickets for the airport, and the toppings for the pizzas.

Second, props can also serve as external mediators to help children remember and self-regulate their actions. In Mrs. Ang's classroom, a group of children are playing restaurant. Tony is supposed to be the chef, so he goes to the kitchen. He picks up the menu that the children made the previous day and, forgetting that he is the chef, he takes up a pad and pencil. He starts acting like the waiter, which makes Michelle angry as she is the waiter. Mrs. Ang comes over and sorts out who is who. She gives Tony a "chef" jacket and she gives Michelle the "waiter" apron. Michelle and Tony now play together without arguing. Tony says "I want to be the waiter next, OK?"

Props, in helping children to remember their roles, can sustain the length of the play scenario. These props should be simple and iconic. Although it is fun to dress up to play a role, remember that the important function of play is about learning to function mentally. Elaborate costumes are not necessary to remind children of their roles and it is the role-playing that is the important aspect of play and not the costume.

Prop use in kindergarten becomes even more abstract and iconic. Kindergarten children should be able to play with very few physical props at all. They should be able to create mental images through language alone. Children should no longer need a prop in order to stay in a role, and they may play several roles at the same time. Children in kindergarten also use objects as actors rather than playing the roles themselves. For instance, they can make the doll walk and talk by moving her around the table and using a specific voice as they talk for that doll. They will create imaginary props for those objects as well.

4. *Help children plan their play.* Immediately before play time begins, ask children what they plan to do. Although the children do not have to follow that specific plan, verbalizing ideas promotes better mutual understanding and establishes a state of shared activity. Since mature play involves planning multiple scenarios and then acting them out, children may have to be supported as play progresses to talk to each other and plan what they will do together. Help them identify new props or roles.

The best time to help children plan their play is right before the children begin playing. In some programs, a planning time at the beginning of the day is used to describe what will be done. Because most children in preschool do not have deliberate memory, they may find it difficult to remember what they decided to do several hours earlier. If they do not have a reminder of the plan just before they begin playing, they will not make the connection between their planning and their actual play. Many programs have children review their plans only at the end of the day; this is not sufficient to enable young children to make the appropriate connection between their planning and their actual activities. When they are reminded of their plan at the end of the day, they may not remember their original plan and whether or not they did it. Instead they will remember the last thing they did, which may have evolved to be something very different from their original plan.

A better idea is to have children review their plans immediately after their play is over. As playtime ends, ask the children if they want to continue this scenario tomorrow, and encourage them to figure out what props they need to put aside for tomorrow. This strategy extends the play for more than one day. Begin the play the next day by going over the previous day's plans and activities. Remember that sticking to the plan is not a goal in itself. It is just a means of helping children see continuity in their actions.

Play planning in kindergarten is even more detailed. Children may play more than one role and consequently plan more than one role. Children can plan in groups, discussing the scenarios that might happen. Children may spend more time planning than actually acting out the play.

We encourage the creation of written plans prior to starting play in centers. The children should draw a picture of themselves and where they are going to go or the objects they are going to play with (see Figure 11.1). If teachers wish, they can take dictation from the child as to what they are going to do and who they are going to be. These written plans help children remember what they are going to do better than a verbal plan, which is easily forgotten. It is important that the child say something about the role she is going to play when she goes to the center. If the teacher knows that there are several children who want to play the same role, this conflict should be discussed prior to the children going to the center. Having these ideas in mind will promote much better social interaction as it can happen with the teacher's support and suggestions. Ms. Abogada knows that there is only one ballerina costume in the dramatic play area and that both Tomita and Veronica want to be ballerinas. Ms. Abogada supports their play planning by saying "There is only one ballerina costume. How will you work this out?"

5. *Monitor the progress of play.* Watch what the children do as they play. Think about the characteristics of mature play and what you might suggest to further their skills during the play period. It is important not to be too intrusive or to make too many suggestions.

Here are some suggestions geared to children at different levels of play:

Children who do not seem to be playing a distinct role. These children may be taking things in and out of cupboards or may be mindlessly handling props. Describe what children are doing in terms of the role they might be playing. "Are you the vet or are you the patient?" or "I see Marty is going to work."

Children who cannot stay in a role. Help children recall their roles and the actions that go along with the role. "Who are you? Are you the doctor? What are you going to do and say?" Make sure the child has a small prop to remind him/her of the role.

Children who are not talking to each other as they play. Help children to develop a play scenario. "What are you playing? Who are you (to each child)? What is going to happen next?" Suggest roles or new actions that might occur. Suggest twists in the scenario.

Children who were playing well but seem to be losing the thread of the play. Ask children what will happen next. Intervene temporarily by entering the play long enough to get the children to interact with each other. For instance, when the children are playing restaurant, pretend to call them and order something for take-out. Help them plan the next scenario and act it out and then help them plan another scenario without as much input from you.

Figure 11.1 An example of children's play plans

6. *Coach individuals who may need help.* Watch for children who avoid the play area. These children may need support in joining the group, accepting new ideas, or including new partners.

Look at the child's level of play. If he is primarily playing with objects, then providing support at the next developmental level will be beneficial. The teacher can help this child by adding the imaginary context that the child is not yet verbalizing. A teacher can ask a child who is making mudpies, "Are you making mudpies for a party or are you going to sell them in the store?" Sometimes this is enough to trigger imaginary play.

7. *Suggest or model how themes can be woven together.* Read and act out stories with different variations of a single theme. For example, read stories about bears in the zoo and bears in the wild to show how the same bear theme can be used in different ways. You can interject "what if" comments to combine themes that seem different but can be merged. For example, if Mara wants to play school and Tony wants to play cars, the teacher can suggest, "What if Mara's class wants to go on a field trip? How could Tony help her?"

8. *Model appropriate ways to solve disputes.* In play, children learn how to solve social disputes. Teachers cannot expect them to always be able to work out these problems alone. Children with poor social skills need additional assistance. Teachers can model ways of talking that will help children work through disagreements, such as "I feel _____." "I don't like it when _____," or "What if we _____ instead of _____?" The use of external mediators, as discussed in Chapter 5, is also helpful. One teacher keeps a "dispute bag" containing a coin, dice, straws of different lengths, a dreidel, a spinner, and cards with rhymes on them (such as "One potato, two potato") to help children solve disagreements.

9. *Encourage children to mentor each other in play.* If you are lucky enough to have a mixed-aged classroom or if you have children from higher grades come and visit, you will have a ready-made source for play mentors. Siblings who visit for the day can be encouraged to help younger children play. Older children who have developed more mature play skills can elevate the level of play for all of the other children by taking more responsibility for identifying props, describing scenarios, and defining roles for the less accomplished players. We have found that as the less mature player becomes more mature he/she will assert and interject more ideas into the scenario. At this point, the play mentor usually facilitates the interweaving of themes, taking into consideration the role the younger child wants to play. Other children are much more effective mentors for play than the teacher, because the child is a "child," which means that they can engage in play without making it a teacher-directed activity.

Scaffolding Other Activities in the Preschool/Kindergarten Classroom

Although play is the leading activity and most of the teachers' efforts should be directed toward play, other activities that have been extensively studied from the Vygotskian perspective are valuable as well. To review, these activities are:

- Games with rules
- Productive activities (drama and storytelling, block building, art and drawing)
- Preacademic activities (early literacy and mathematics)
- Motor activities (large-muscle activities)

Games with Rules

Like Piagetians, Vygotskians think that children are able to engage in games at around 5 years of age. Vygotskians, however, consider games to be a direct outgrowth of play, in that they also have imaginary situations and rules. Games are distinguished from imaginary play by the fact that the imaginary situation is now hidden (and not explicit as it is in pretend play), and the rules become explicit and detailed instead of being hidden or implicit:

> For example, playing chess creates an imaginary situation. Why? Because the knight, king, queen, and so forth can only move in a specified way; because covering and taking pieces are purely chess concepts. Although in the chess game there is no direct substitute for real-life relationships, it is a kind of imaginary situation nevertheless. (Vygotsky, 1978, p. 95)

Another example is playing motor games in which children agree to follow rules that make them pretend that they cannot perform some action(s) even if, in fact, they can. For example, a child agrees to "freeze" and not move when tagged or to jump only on a certain square playing hopscotch. In both these games, there is a rudimentary imaginary situation, though not as prominent as in pretend play.

Compared with play where rules are implicit, rules of the game become the most salient characteristic of the interaction. Instead of rules staying hidden in the role until they are violated, in games, rules are the way the players interact with each other and changes to the rules are mutually agreed upon. In many instances, the rules are written down, thus presenting a standard with which children can compare their actions. For this reason, when children play a new board game, adults may need to assist them with learning the rules until they internalize them and are able to follow them independently or with the help of their peers. This learning to compare one's own actions with a clearly set standard shared by others is very beneficial in preparing kindergarten students to engage in *learning activity* (see Chapters 12 and 13) in the following years.

Games with rules offer children experience with emotional issues that they will encounter in the formal learning activities of elementary school (Michailenko & Korotkova, 2002). Losing, an inevitable part of playing games, prepares the child to accept the frustration and the unavoidable temporary failures that are part of learning. In the process of learning something difficult, one usually makes mistakes along the way. Learners face times when they are not able to solve a problem. Games help children to practice dealing with temporary failure or losing because they offer opportunities to play again and perhaps win the next time.

Unlike pretend play that is innately motivating, games with rules motivate children by offering them an opportunity to win. Winning, however, is often associated with mastering the game, which comes with practice. The initial steps in mastering the game are not as much fun for children as when they can play it well. This difference between play, which offers immediate gratification, and games, which initially require time and effort to learn, is very important in preparing children for the transition to learning activity. Game playing offers a bridge to the necessary ability to pursue delayed goals as required by formal learning.

Because they are a cooperative, shared activity, games can also support academic learning by giving children more opportunities to work together. Didactic games, games that are actually designed to teach content, can support the learning of particular concepts or skills. Kindergarten teachers have all sorts of didactic games, from pancake math to word bingo, that use a game format for academic instruction.

Productive Activities

Under the umbrella term *productive activities*, Vygotskians place storytelling, block building, art, and drawing (see Chapter 10). All these activities were described by Zaporozhets (1978) as amplifying development of preschool- and kindergarten-aged children.

Storytelling.   Storytelling is beneficial for language development and creativity. In the Vygotskian framework it is also used to promote the development of deliberate memory, logical thinking, and self-regulation. When children retell stories or create new ones, they are not absolutely free in their choice of episodes; the story must make sense to other people. In this way, storytelling is similar to play; both lead children from spontaneous to deliberate behaviors.

By retelling familiar stories and creating their own, children learn about the general patterns common to all stories. The use of these patterns, called "story grammar," involves putting events in a logical sequence and recognizing why a specific sequence is appropriate. *Story grammar* imposes limits on the content of a story. For example, children learn that if a main character disappears, he will not be able to do anything until something magical takes place to reintroduce him. Familiarity with the idea of story grammar helps children master basic logical concepts such as cause and effect, mutually exclusive events, and so on.

Children cannot learn about the logic of a story merely by listening to the teacher read. Listening allows children to understand fairly simple texts. More complex stories require much more contextual support, such as external mediators and the children's use of language. In the beginning of the school year, 3- and 4-year-old children will need assistance in retelling simple stories. Simple external mediators will help them remember the sequence of events. These mediators can be teacher-generated at first and later, child-generated. It is very important that a child learns to use her own symbols to keep a story line straight. The pictures or scribbles need to make sense only to the child, and can be different from the ones in the book. Make the purpose of the mediator explicit to the child by saying, for example, "These pictures will help you remember the story."

After retelling the story enough times so that the story line is very familiar, children can be encouraged to see how alterations in the sequence of pictures might change the story. For example, the teacher can rearrange the pictures for *Goldilocks and the Three Bears* so that Goldilocks is eating the bears' porridge before she goes to the bears' house. Ask the children if the pictures still make sense in this sequence.

Older children can mentally experiment with the elements of a story without much external support. They can be given different versions of the same story to compare, such as the traditional version of *The Three Little Pigs* and *The Real Story of the Three Little Pigs* by Jon Scieszka. Older children can also practice creating new episodes when given the beginning of a story line, or they can choose various different endings to a story, as in the *Choose Your Own Adventure* series. To help children make the transition from retelling familiar stories to creating stories of their own, we recommend using the techniques developed by Gianni Rodari (Rodari, 1996). Rodari suggests a number of ways to generate new stories, including combining two episodes or characters from different stories (the less compatible they seem, the better) and using this combination as a starting point for a new story. For example, with *Sleeping Beauty,* the teacher could ask children to imagine what might happen if, instead of a prince, the Big Bad Wolf woke her up.

To assess how a child's mental abilities have grown from storytelling activities, one can ask:

- Is there growth in the child's ability to retell a familiar story? Can the child use the major elements of the story? Do the episodes follow each other logically?

- Is there growth in the child's ability to remember a story? When the child retells a familiar story, are there missing episodes or episodes that are different from the original? What kind of assistance or external support does the child need to retell a story (e.g., external mediators, prompts from peers, or hints from the teacher)?

- Is there growth in the child's ability to comprehend stories? What are the elements of the story that the child focuses on when comparing different stories? Are these elements essential for comprehension or just superficial?

- Can the child change elements of the story and still generate a story line that makes sense?

Block Building.   For younger preschool children, block building fosters self-regulation, planning, and the coordination of roles. Further, block building for kindergartners facilitates the ability to move back and forth between symbolic representation (drawing) and physical manipulation. To promote children's mental development, block play must be a shared activity (see, e.g., Brofman, 1993). It must involve more than one child in order to evoke the use of language as the children discuss their construction activities. For Vygotskians, the objective of block building is like play, to create a shared experience. The building of the structure is a by-product of this experience. When children are building next to each other but are not talking or jointly constructing, then the block building is not considered to be an effective activity for promoting mental development.

To help children engage in block building, the teacher should help children articulate a plan for what they are going to do together. For example, the children might say they are going to build a road or a house for the farm animals. All children should be encouraged to describe what they plan to build before they begin using blocks, even though younger children will not be able to carry out a specific plan all the way through. The plan can be changed or abandoned as the building progresses and as the children negotiate what they want to construct. Children who are building alone are encouraged to join others.

This will necessitate amending the original plan to include the new child's contribution. Maggie is building a house for her dolls next to a group of boys who are building an airport. The teacher suggests that Maggie's building might be the pilot's house or a passenger's house. She suggests that the road the children are building might need to extend to Maggie's. Before long, the boys have begun to ask Maggie questions. They give her a car so she can get to the airport.

In kindergarten, block building can be set up as a shared activity with specific roles assigned by the children or suggested by the teacher. Encourage children to work on the structure together. Through this shared building, children learn to regulate each other, to be regulated themselves, and to talk about their ideas. Once the cooperative nature of block building has been established, teachers foster further development of cognitive skills by having children build a structure that will meet certain external criteria, such as "big enough for a toy elephant" or "large enough to be a home for six animals." This type of building requires an even higher level of planning and sharing/other-regulation.

In addition, block building activities can be designed to alternate between representational drawing and physical manipulation of the blocks. By moving back and forth between these two types of activity, children strengthen the connections between them and move to higher levels of abstraction and planning. Children as young as 3 years of age can plan their structures on paper with the use of colored pieces of paper in the shape of the blocks (see Figure 11.2). Once they have made a plan, they build it themselves or, even better, have another classmate build it. Then they can compare the real structure to the plan. Children 5 to 8 years of age can use templates, their own drawings, or a computer program to generate plans. With older children, the buildings will become more complicated, and sophisticated roles can be assigned, such as architect, builder, and building inspector.

If block building is structured appropriately, teachers should see growth in:

- The ability to articulate a plan for what is going to be built. How detailed is it?
- The ability to cooperate with others to plan the structure's characteristics and to negotiate roles. How much teacher support is necessary to sustain a 5-minute interaction?
- The complexity of the structures the child plans on paper.
- The ability to take on different roles in planning, carrying out the plan, and checking the plan.

Art and Drawing. Leont'ev (1931, 1981), Luria (1979), and a group of more contemporary post-Vygotskians (e.g., Venger, 1996) have argued that drawing plays a particularly important role in the development of memory and written language in addition to the development of aesthetics (see Stetsenko, 1995 for a review of the Vygotskian approach to children's drawing). Leont'ev (1931) studied the effects drawing had as an aid to children's ability to remember and found that even primitive marks boosted memory.

Figure 11.2   A child tracing the blocks

Venger suggested that this occurred because the drawing was an abstraction, the creation of a mental model (see Chapter 10).

Luria showed that children at first do not distinguish between writing and drawing (Luria, 1983). They actually write-draw. Drawing is an integral part of early spontaneous attempts to write words. Thus, drawing is a support to writing and conceptualizing, and is particularly important when children do not yet have sufficient sound-to-symbol correspondence skills to actually be able to write with words. Drawing not only communicates to others, but, like writing, helps children remember.

There are many missed opportunities in most preschool classrooms to make drawing into the rich intellectual activity that Vygotskians suggest it can be. Drawing is often relegated to the art center or an art activity rather than being integrated in an experience where remembering is important. Teachers seldom have children draw to record the experiences of a field trip or to recount a story they have just heard. Teachers are much more likely to write out accounts of activities on a chart, such as when they have children dictate a recipe for the cooking experience they have just had. A more effective way of helping children to remember the experience and to make the link to literacy would be to ask children to draw the recipe for themselves and to "write" something about the recipe.

Preacademic Skills

As they did with productive activities, Vygotskians conducted extensive research on the way to introduce content skills in literacy, math, and science (see, e.g., Venger, 1986, 1996). There are several distinctive features in the Vygotskian approach to supporting the development of preacademic skills. First, the preacademic content is used to help children develop underlying cognitive skills such as focused attention, deliberate memory, and self-regulation. Second, when appropriate, preacademic content is used to prepare children for the leading activity of the next stage: *learning activity* (see Chapter 12). Children will need to learn that certain activities have standards for their performance. In mathematics, for example, $5 + 5$ must equal 10; if you do not get "10" when you add these numbers together then you must revisit what you did because "10" is the answer. In preschool and kindergarten, children are engaged in many activities for which are "standard" does not exist. When the teacher asks you what you like about a story, there is no one correct answer. In play, there is not one right way to be the mommy. There is considerable leeway in what a child can do without violating the implicit rules of "mommy-ness." Therefore, pre-academic activities, like learning to recognize and write your name or learning to count out 10 objects, are well suited to helping children understand the existence of standards in academic areas.

By engaging in carefully planned preacademic activities, children can begin to internalize this idea of working toward a standard. In Vygotskian-based preacademic activities, scaffolding is planned into the activity and provided in different ways depending on where children are in their development. Much support is given in the form of shared activity, where children help each other or work in pairs and groups to solve problems. In other cases, special manipulatives and mediators are used as scaffolds. This support is designed to help a particular child learn a certain concept or skill and then as the child can perform it independently, the support is removed.

Finally, the context in which children learn the content is important. The activity has to be meaningful so that children see the reason for doing something as they learn how to do it. For example, writing their names on a list so that they can use the computer next is more valid than writing their names several times on a piece of paper in a name-writing activity. Instruction conducted in small groups where children are all participating and interacting together will ensure more mental engagement and language use than the same activity done in a large group. Especially when the teacher calls on individual children to answer questions, large group instruction often leaves children behind as they are not that interested in what other children have to say and they only act when they are called upon to answer. While older children may mentally answer a question when it is asked of another child, most preschool children just stop paying attention. Consequently teachers should plan one-to-one interactions, pairs of children working together, or small groups with eight children or less as the context to teach preacademic skills.

We have adapted these ideas and used them in classrooms in the United States (see, e.g., Bodrova & Leong, 2001, 2005; Bodrova et. al., 2001). Because of the differences between Russian and English, we have made substantial changes and have invented new ways of teaching, applying Vygotskian approaches to new situations. In this section, we give examples of early literacy and math activities we developed to support the preschool and kindergarten child's cognitive development.

Learning to Recognize and Write Your Name.   Learning to write your name is a typical expectation in preschool and kindergarten, and children arrive at school with different capacities to do this. In the course of learning to recognize and write one's name, children learn to focus attention on specific aspects of print, and they get practice in remembering deliberately. The activity has relevance and meaning because the activity is done in a context, where writing one's name is important; for instance, when it helps a child find his own finger painting. Children learn to write their letters to a specific standard, because if they are not legible, no one else will be able to read it.

The teachers we work with usually create an external mediator, which both helps children remember and serves as the standard. We use a small laminated card with the first name on one side and the child's last name on the other.

Teachers create activities in which recognizing and writing your name is valid and important. For example, to improve the social interaction in the classroom, you might put nametags out at snack so that children sit next to different children each time. Finding one's name is meaningful, especially when snack is pizza! Writing their names is a valid way to label their possessions, their artwork, or their play plan (see Figure 11.1). Writing their names to sign up for something, like a turn on the computer, or to voice their opinions ("I love broccoli") are other examples of creating contexts where name writing has meaning. In addition, writing legibly to the standard in these situations also makes sense, because if one writes the letters any old way, other people may not be able to read them.

Following are examples of how teachers can provide specific support to children at different levels of development within the meaningful activities described previously. More examples of how to scaffold children's writing of their names are provided in Chapter 14.

Children who cannot recognize their names without help. When Jeremy is trying to find his name so he can sit down, other children will often help him out by telling him when he is in the wrong seat. The teacher can help the child notice specific details about his name that would help the child to find it easier. For example, you might say to the child "Your name starts with a *J.* See a *J* has a hook at the bottom." If there are other children's names that start with the same letter, you might say, "Both you and Jason start with the same letter, but Jason is spelled 'Ja' and Jeremy is 'Je.'" So that the child might check himself, she can add the child's picture, taped to the back of his nametag so he can turn it over to check. Once the child recognizes his name, she removes the picture.

Children who cannot write any of the letters of their names. The teacher can provide language to help the child learn to write the first letter of his name. Placing a colored line under that first letter also helps the child pay attention to that specific letter. For example, for Jeremy, the teacher would make the sound of the letter *J, juh.* "You write the letter *J* down with a hook." She would demonstrate that and then talk the child through writing the letter, using the same words as he attempts the letter. If he does not write it correctly, she points out the differences, "Your hook went that way, this hook goes this way." If he still cannot write the letter, she provides support by putting her hand over his.

Children who write their names from right to left. The teacher should place a green dot under the first letter of the name and a green arrow pointing to the left under the rest of the name on the nametag. If the child still cannot write it with this support, the teacher could add a similar dot and arrow on the child's paper where the child is to write her name. When the child remembers where to start on her own paper, the teacher stops putting the dot and arrow on the child's papers. When the child is able to consistently write her name from left to right, the teacher removes the mediatoz from the name tag.

Children who write their first names correctly. The teacher turns the nametag over and begins to help children write their last names.

Children who write their first and last names. The teacher doesn't give them their nametags for writing activities in which the children write their names, because they can write their names independently.

Patterns.   Patterns are an example of a common preschool and kindergarten math activity that can be adapted to Vygotskian purposes. Understanding patterns is one of the national math standards for young children (National Council of Teachers of Mathematics, 2000). These include simple repeating patterns (AB AB AB) for younger children and patterns with more items (ABC ABC ABC), repetitions within items (AABC AABC or ABBBC ABBBC), or growing patterns (ABC AABBCC AAABBBCCC). Pattern-making is used as a context to teach underlying cognitive skills of remembering on purpose, focused attention, and even self-regulation. By engaging in patterning activities, children also learn about symbolic substitution and about the idea of standard as they play games in which they try to make the same pattern (standard) in different ways. The following are only some examples of how pattern activities can be used:

Children translate a pattern into motor movements. These movements are changed every two or three repetitions. Children "read" the pattern, moving only the same number of movements as elements in the pattern. For example, using a certain pattern card that displays a circle and a square, children are initially told to touch their noses when the teacher points to the circle and to touch their shoulders when she points to a square. After a few times doing this, the children and teacher decide to change the movements so that now pointing to a circle means the children clap their hands and the square means that they snap their fingers. They change the pattern again to stomp and hop.

Children translate a pattern into other objects. Children play a game with individual pattern cards. The teacher gives them a manipulative for each item in the pattern. Children make the same pattern as is on the pattern card, but have a blue bear for the circle and a red bear for the square. Again, the objects used to represent the pattern are replaced with different manipulatives, such as dinosaurs or sea shells.

Children record patterns on paper. Children are asked to draw a representation of a pattern they see. This can be the translation of a motor pattern into a written one. The teacher plays a pattern using two musical instruments behind a screen, for example, tapping a drum three times and clanging the cymbals once. The children draw the pattern or, more simply, pick out one pattern from the two cards she shows them. Children can also be asked to translate patterns they see in the environment into a pattern that they draw on paper. For instance, they might notice that the gardener has planted a big tree and then a small tree, a big tree and a small tree along the path to their school. They can be asked to draw a representation of this pattern and then also draw a translation of the pattern into squares and triangles.

Motor Activities

As discussed in Chapter 10, motor activities are important in helping children to develop self-regulation. The most beneficial games are those in which children stop and start on cue several times during the game. Games such as Simon Says, Freeze, Follow the Leader, and Duck, Duck, Goose all require that the child wait until there is a verbal command before moving. The commands can be given by other children or by the teacher.

Songs in which children must make a specific movement along with the words, finger plays, and acting out stories also require the inhibition of motor behavior. Activities such as hopscotch, jump rope, clapping to a beat, and hopping to a beat all require specific motor responses. These are more difficult than games like Simon Says because the child must hop only at a certain place or clap in a specific way.

Games with specific rules are also excellent for promoting motor control in older children. These games can be simple, such as Red Rover, or they can be complex, as in soccer or baseball.

Modify games in which children take turns by passing around an external mediator such as a ball or stick as a signal for "my turn." Teachers have used this technique during circle time to help children take turns talking. One teacher has a welcome song in which all of the children chant their names. She uses a beanbag that is passed from child to child as each says his or her name.

Scaffolding School Readiness

Kindergarten teachers today face pressure to make their classrooms into scaled-down first grades with worksheets and drills. This is thought by some authorities as a way to make sure that children are prepared for first grade. As we noted in Chapter 10, this type of kindergarten classroom is not in the best interests of children because it does not provide the underlying skills that make learning more efficient and effective in the long run. It may seem that children are behaving appropriately during large group instruction when they correctly respond to the teacher's questions, for example, but this kind of learning situation does not teach true skills of self-regulation. Instead they are learning what we call "teacher regulation" which means they can control themselves when the teacher is present but cannot without her. As soon as the teacher leaves, the children can no longer sustain their focus. Furthermore, many children in large group instruction look like they are paying attention, when in fact their minds are somewhere else. Self-regulation means that the child can voluntarily perform with or without an adult present. When kindergarten teachers help children to develop self-regulation skills, Vygotskians believe children will be able to learn cognitive skills and concepts effectively and be prepared for the *learning activity* that is the leading activity for the next stage of their development.

For Further Reading

Berk, L. E. (1994). Vygotsky's theory: The importance of make-believe play. *Young Children,* *50*(1), 30–39.

Berk, L. E., & Winsler, A. (1995). Scaffolding children's learning: Vygotsky and early childhood education. *NAEYC Research and Practice Series, 7.* Washington, DC: National Association for the Education of Young Children.

Elkonin, D. (1977). Toward the problem of stages in the mental development of the child. In M. Cole (Ed.), *Soviet developmental psychology.* White Plains, NY: M. E. Sharpe. (Original work published in 1971)

Elkonin, D. B. (2005). Chapter 1. The subject of our research: The developed form of play. *Journal of Russian & East European Psychology, 43*(1), 22–48.

Vygotsky, L. S. (1977). Play and its role in the mental development of the child. In J.S. Bruner, A. Jolly, & K. Sylva (Eds.), *Play: Its role in development and evolution* (pp. 537–554). New York: Basic Books. (Original work published in 1966)

CHAPTER 12

Developmental Accomplishments and Leading Activity: Primary Grades

Vygotskians argue that many cultures change their expectations for 6- to-7-year-old children; they are considered ready to start formal instruction in the skills and understandings important to their culture. This emphasis on the importance of schooling as the principle context for development for children of 6 and 7 years old is hardly new. Many psychologists and sociologists have acknowledged this fact (see Cole, 2005, for a discussion on this topic). Children enter the primary grades expecting things to be different, harder, and more serious than in preschool and kindergarten. All schools—regardless of whether they are public or private, religious or secular—have a special kind of social organization and special forms of interaction.

Vygotskians make a distinction between formal instruction and informal instruction, such as an apprenticeship, where one child works alongside an adult, such as when a mother teaches her child to sew. They do not devalue the learning in apprenticeships but argue that the way learning occurs in this context is different. The parent provides different interactions than the teachers do because she has only one child to teach and because she is in the midst of doing the task herself. Because Vygotskians are concerned primarily with formal instruction, the developmental accomplishments and the leading activity for the child beginning at 6 years of age are school-related, dominated and fueled by the child's quest to learn.

The primary grades encompass only the first part of the age period during which these developmental accomplishments come to fruition and during which learning activity is the leading activity for development. Consequently, to understand how these concepts apply to primary-aged children, we will first describe the Vygotskian view of formal schooling, then the developmental accomplishments that appear by sixth grade, and finally the *learning activity* as implemented throughout the elementary years. The chapter ends with a discussion of how these apply to the primary grades.

Formal Schooling and Development in the Primary Grades

Vygotskians argue that the function of schools in Western society has changed over time. In past centuries, the emphasis was on equipping children with specific skills and knowledge that would be immediately applicable in the real world. Vygotskians have come to think that schools should "arm children with cultural tools" that allow them to adjust to the ever-changing demands of evolving workplaces. Many postindustrial societies now share the expectations of what a school graduate should know and be able to do; the ability to plan, monitor, and control one's own cognitive processes being a part of these expectations (Gellatly, 1987; Ivic, 1994; Scribner, 1977).

Schools across the globe share similar characteristics that set them apart from other social contexts such as families, peer groups, and individual apprenticeships where children's learning also takes place. For example, in a school setting, the teacher works with a number of children at the same time. The teacher uses books to teach, and children use books to learn. The content that is being taught is sequenced in a specific way. Children learn abstract, scientific concepts and in doing so, learn to think in an abstract, logical, and systematic way and to apply this logical thinking to a variety of problems across subjects. This entire process can take up to 12 years, and the primary grades are the time that children take their first steps in this direction.

Some children arrive in elementary school equipped with the developmental accomplishments of preschool and kindergarten (see Chapter 10), so that the transition is easy for them. Other children arrive lacking the prerequisite skills that would provide a smooth transition, so they can have trouble adjusting. To succeed in school, children need to have cognitive, linguistic, social, and emotional competencies along with an understanding of what is expected of a student and the will to take on this role (Carlton & Winsler, 1999). All of these competencies and attitudes continue to develop during the first years of school. Thus, properly designed instructional processes can help children who have not yet attained the developmental accomplishments of preschool and kindergarten years.

The principle role of the elementary school teacher in the primary grades 1 to 3 is to help children learn how to become students. In upper grades 4 and 5 the teacher's role is helping children act as students and then the sixth-grade teacher prepares children to learn formal disciplines taught in junior high, high school, and beyond. At each grade level, the child must learn to adjust to a different kind of relationship with the teacher, additional and different cognitive and social demands, and a different way of learning. Therefore, the teacher's role is more than just teaching content. It is also helping children learn how to learn in a way that will make them more effective students, capable of tackling the difficult and diverse knowledge base that they must acquire to become productive adults in a technological society.

The Developmental Accomplishments of the Elementary School Child

As they successfully engage in the learning of literacy, math, science, art, and other subjects by the end of elementary school, children attain the developmental accomplishments of this period: the beginnings of theoretical reasoning, the emergence of the higher mental functions, and the motivation to learn (Davydov, 1988; Elkonin, 1972; Kozulin & Presseisen, 1995). These are built on the developmental accomplishments of the preschool/kindergarten period and emerge only if the learning environment in elementary grades is organized in specific ways.

As is the case of other developmental periods described in earlier chapters, children must engage in the leading activity of this period—learning activity. If they do not, the developmental accomplishments of this stage will only be partially attained, and will not be sufficient for success in the next stage. In the following discussion, we will describe the developmental accomplishments that emerge by the end of elementary school. We will focus on the developmental accomplishments that happen in grades 1 to 3 in a separate section.

Beginnings of Theoretical Reasoning

Theoretical Reasoning in Elementary School.   The term *theoretical reasoning* describes the way children will come to think about the content of math, science, history, and other academic disciplines. Theoretical reasoning, however, is not limited to the subjects taught in school, but is also used to solve real-life problems more efficiently than through trial and error. When reasoning theoretically, children deal with the essential properties of objects or ideas, which may or may not be perceptually visible or intuitively obvious, such as the concept of density in relation to sinking and floating objects.

Theoretical reasoning allows the child to have a deeper understanding of *scientific concepts*. At the same time, in the course of learning scientific concepts, theoretical reasoning develops further (see the next section of the current chapter for a discussion of Vygotsky's theory of everyday and scientific concepts). It is important to note that the word *scientific* does not mean that the concept pertains to biology or chemistry only. The word *scientific* means that a discipline, including art, history, and economics, has a core of theoretical principles that organize it. Thus, there are scientific concepts in art, history, economics, and so forth. For instance, learning to analyze metaphors and similes as a part of literature analysis in the language arts curriculum, and learning the concept of colony in history are examples of scientific concepts in areas other than science.

Theoretical Reasoning in the Primary Grades.   Between 6 and 10 years of age, children are just beginning to acquire theoretical reasoning. The process of its development is not completed until age 18 or even later. However, the primary grades are formative years for the development of basic literacies, the most basic units or concepts of the content area that will facilitate the development of theoretical reasoning. For example, number as the organized way of accounting for quantity is one of the basic concepts of mathematics, and the content of mathematics instruction should be centered on it. To understand how these literacies develop, we must address the difference between everyday and scientific concepts.

In everyday concepts, meanings are constructed in context through the child's own direct experiences (Vygotsky, 1987). From these, children generalize ideas about the phenomena they see. These ideas are usually unsystematic, empirical, and unconscious (Karpov & Bransford, 1995). Children form these generalizations in a haphazard way, depending on how the experiences happen and without planning or monitoring the conditions of the experience. Empirical learning is based on comparing objects, figuring out the common characteristics observed, and creating a general concept about the kind of object. For example, as children observe many things that sink and float, they can generalize rules or concepts from what they notice about what will sink and float and why certain things sink and float. Being limited to only properties they can observe directly, children will come to some conclusions that are consistent with the scientific concepts of density and displacement (e.g., that light objects float) and some that are not consistent with them (e.g., believing that metal objects always sink). However useful in daily living and however important for the later development of scientific concepts, everyday concepts are not the same as scientific concepts.

The essential properties of scientific concepts have been identified by a specific scientific discipline and are not necessarily a product of everyday experience. Scientific concepts are taught and presented within a conceptual system that enables children to use ideas that they cannot see or that are not intuitively apparent. Every scientific field has its own basic assumptions and language. These are introduced as definitions that must be learned in order to understand the concepts of that science. The concepts only make sense when the child knows the basic assumptions and definitions: for example, the concept of mammal has meaning because it is part of the taxonomy of kingdom, phylum, class, order, family, genus, and species.

Unlike everyday concepts, most scientific concepts have been developed through the history of that particular discipline, leading to an agreed-upon procedure for determining whether a specific example fits the criteria for that concept. These procedures can be a set of specifically designed experiments with carefully controlled conditions or a set of prescribed logical steps. Unlike everyday concepts, they are based on the essential properties of objects or events of a certain type that may or may not be observable. Scientific concepts are presented with symbolic and graphic models or through a set of specific procedures. In learning them, students learn a specific method of analysis particular to a given discipline. Unlike everyday concepts, scientific concepts further problem solving, because they have distilled within them the general and optimal methods for dealing with certain classes of problems. So instead of only having his own experience to depend upon, the student can apply the knowledge and experience of those who preceded him. For example, street children in Brazil learn to add multiple numbers without any formal schooling (Saxe, 1991). This knowledge serves them every day as they earn their living through buying and selling. However this facility with addition and subtraction is not the same as the formalized instruction in mathematics that would lead them to be able to comprehend algebra and calculus. To enable children to understand mathematics principles and solve these more advanced abstract problems, they must go through the process of learning math through formal instruction. They will not discover algebra and calculus on their own.

To learn scientific concepts, children must learn more than a set of definitions. They must learn the rules and the set of procedures associated with it. Knowing the definition of an angle is not sufficient; the child must be able to identify and use the concept of angle to create angles, to analyze geometric figures, and to solve problems. The definition and the procedure/process for their use are married together so that the child's understanding is more than knowledge at a superficial level, but understanding in a generative and deeper sense.

Scientific concepts, Vygotsky says, "grow down" into existing everyday concepts, and everyday concepts "grow up" into scientific concepts (Karpov & Bransford, 1995). Once children learn scientific concepts, their everyday concepts take on a new meaning and their use becomes more accurate and systematic. For example, learning about the rotation of the earth leads to a different understanding of the concept of night and day that was previously an everyday concept based on a child's own experience. Similarly, learning that there is a difference between stars, planets, and moons, gives stargazing a different meaning. Being able to construct a sentence when talking is different from being able to diagram that sentence showing the parts of speech. If, however, a child lacks background knowledge or if his everyday concepts do not match conventional meanings, the child will have trouble acquiring scientific concepts. For example, a child who does not have the everyday concepts of "more" and "less" cannot understand the idea of "greater than" (>) and "less than" (<) when applied to numbers.

An example of the difference between everyday and scientific concepts is shown in Mr. Johnston's second-grade class. In class, he asks children to generate a list of what they know about the rain forest. This list ends up being a catalogue of the children's everyday concepts about the rain forest. The children write things like, "It has trees," "We cut the logs and then ruin the land," "The birds die because they don't have a place to live," and "I like the rain forest." Mr. Johnston then presents information about the rain forest in the form of related scientific concepts. He discusses the rain forest as an ecosystem with specific characteristics that make it different from other ecosystems, and he explains the effects of destruction of habitat on the survival of animal and plant species. After studying the rain forest in a project, the children are asked to write down what they now know. Mr. Johnston can see that the scientific concepts are growing into the everyday ones because children are beginning to use scientific language in their writing. Now they write things like, "It is a habitat with dense trees and lots of raining," "It is not a desert," and "There are many kinds of plants and animals living there that need rain water to survive." The scientific concepts have altered the way the children think about the idea of rain forest. At the same time, the children's intuitive concepts were used as a starting point for the scientific ones.

Scientific concepts form the basis of *theoretical reasoning* and instruction in scientific concepts drives its development. Unless children engage in the kind of activities that promote scientific concepts, this developmental accomplishment will not emerge.

Emergence of Higher Mental Functions

Higher Mental Functions in the Elementary School. The second developmental accomplishment is the *emergence of higher mental functions* (HMF) that were described in Chapter 2. Like some other psychologists, Vygotsky believed that HMF are tied to abstract, reflective, logical thought. HMF are purposeful, deliberate, and mediated. They are linked to the internalization of mental tools, occur in a system of interrelated HMFs, and emerge through the transition from shared to individualized functioning.

Children in elementary school are just beginning to develop HMF, which are not fully developed until about age 18. However, to succeed in elementary school, children have to operate at some levels of HMF. For example, children must be able to learn on demand and to learn according to the teacher's plan for success in the primary grades. They have to be able to focus attention and to remember on purpose. They must have the beginnings of self-regulation of their own mental processes so that they can compare their own learning with what the teacher expects them to know. Without the partial acquisition of HMF, children will not succeed in school even in the primary grades.

Take, for example, the type of focused attention required in the primary grades. In preschool, teachers use the words "pay attention" to signal that the child must ignore distractions and pay attention to what the teacher is doing or saying. It involves sitting still, not talking to others, and looking at the teacher. The meaning of these words changes in elementary school. The children must now "look through" the teacher to the skill, concept, and process that the teacher is demonstrating instead of concentrating on just the teacher's actions. The children must look through the surface of his words and actions to understand the specific thing the teacher is teaching. The children must infer from what the teacher presents what is to be learned.

It is interesting that we say to children who are not doing well or who are making mistakes that they should "pay attention," as if this were some kind of mystical ability that by sheer willpower they can bring to bear on the situation and thus "learn." Actually, it is often not that children are not paying attention, but that they are attending to the wrong thing. It would be closer to the truth to say "pay attention to this characteristic and not that characteristic." Delia must find the grammatical errors in the sentence that is posted on the board. The sentence reads "We wents to the store to buys a apple." She reads the sentence and decides that there are no errors because yesterday the class did go to the store to buy apples for apple pie. It isn't that she is not concentrating, or that she did not read the sentence or did not participate in the activity—it is that she focuses on the wrong thing. Instead of paying attention to the grammar, she attends to the meaning of the sentence.

Higher Mental Functions in the Primary Grades.   In the early primary grades, higher mental functions are just emerging, so children are able to perform some strategies but need contextual support or assistance to use them effectively. These can be shared activities with peers or with the teacher. Because they are just beginning to plan, monitor, and evaluate their own thinking, children may not be fully aware of their own thought processes, and will require shared activities to perform at a higher level of their ZPD (Zuckerman, 2003). Studies done by Vygotsky's colleagues found that it was during the primary grades that children got the maximum benefit from visual aids and manipulatives, and from other learning supports described in Chapter 5. Primary children make greater gains in memory, attention, and problem solving when they are given these mediators. In addition, participation in cooperative/shared activity can boost the use of HMF in thinking. Verbal reminders and prompts made by the teacher or a peer are also useful. Writing and drawing provide additional support for reflective thought. As they progress through the elementary grades, children depend more and more on writing as a primary support for learning. Consequently, written language becomes a primary mental tool that aids in the development of HMF. The increasing degree to which learning depends on books and the written word as opposed to oral communication continues through high school and beyond. Continued experience with learning activity will strengthen and nurture further development of higher mental functions throughout the child's school years.

Motivation to Learn

Motivation to Learn in the Elementary School.   The final developmental accomplishment of this period is the *motivation to learn*. The motivation to learn includes accepting the student role, internalization of standards of performance, and *pozenavatel'naya* or enquiry motivation (intellectual curiosity). As we discussed previously, children realize that the learning in elementary school is much more serious than in preschool and kindergarten. Studies of children's attitudes about school (see, e.g., Elkonin & Venger, 1988) show that they give much more status to the learning in elementary schools, and consider preschool and kindergarten to be play, which they view as less serious and worthwhile. This attitude about the seriousness of "real school" prepares children to put in the mental effort, to put up with the frustrations, and to take achievement seriously—qualities necessary for school success. Children who do not buy into this attitude about the importance of school have difficulty staying motivated. Teachers have always mourned the fact that some children are so difficult to motivate. Vygotskians would argue that these children can develop the motivation to learn depending on how their school experience unfolds. By succeeding in learning, children can develop more motivation to learn. Motivation is not viewed as a personality trait set in stone, but as something malleable. Many other psychologists agree with this perspective (see Stipek, 2002, for a discussion of different approaches to motivation).

Vygotskians add another facet to the idea of motivation to learn, defining it as more than just the desire to learn. It also includes the gradual internalization of standards of performance. These entail understanding the goal of an activity and the level of mastery that must be achieved. At first this knowledge lies outside the child, as the teacher tells children in a general way what she is teaching and whether children's responses are correct or not. Eventually, children internalize this standard and become capable of predicting, prior to the teacher's grading or feedback, how well they are doing. This internalization of standards is not seen as something negative that deflates the student's desire to learn but rather as a means of developing an internal compass that helps children avoid potential failure and frustration.

If we think of standards as signposts telling children how close they are getting to mastery, it becomes clear that setting vague or inaccurate standards is a sure way to have children lose motivation to learn. For example, which of these two children will become more frustrated: a child who knows that there are five elements to a paragraph, that she has achieved three and is missing two or the child who only knows that he has not "written enough"? Obviously, the child who knows exactly what is missing and how to fix it will be more motivated to do better on her next writing assignment. The child who has not "written enough" will become discouraged because he does not know what "enough" mean. Is he supposed to write two more pages or elaborate on a specific subject? And what does he need to do to get a better grade next time?

Children learn for all kinds of reasons. Some learn to please their parents, others learn to impress their friends, and still others learn to please their teachers. Children with *enquiry motivation* or intellectual curiosity have a pervasive curiosity and intensity of purpose, which they apply to many areas of learning, not just those introduced by adults (Davydov, Slobodchikov, & Tsukerman, 2003). The goal of this developmental period is to establish enquiry motivation in children so that they become interested in and begin to pursue study without being asked to do so. When asked to study something, they will find something that interests them. These children have what is called nonpragmatic curiosity (Bogoyavlenskaya, 1983; Poddyakov, 1977), interest that exists even though there may be no tangible payoff. Kevin is writing a two-paragraph summary of a chapter in his reading book on Benjamin Franklin's experiments with electricity. He wonders if Franklin has any other inventions, so he goes to the library to find other books about Franklin's inventions. This leads him into wondering about electricity, and soon he is off looking at books about electricity. Kevin's curiosity leads him in many different directions, and through this he shows enquiry motivation. Children without enquiry motivation, Davydov notes, are primarily motivated by grades or by praise from the teacher. The word enquiry is the translation of the Russian word *poznavatel'naya* and although it is similar to the Western idea of intrinsic motivation, it is also different in the emphasis on learning and intellectual curiosity.

For Vygotskians, the lack of enquiry motivation (intellectual curiosity) is caused by failures in the interaction between the child and his social context (Elkonin, 2001a; Leont'ev, 1978). Either the social context does not support or value learning or the child cannot yet differentiate between learning and nonlearning endeavors such as play or social interaction. The social context must convey a set of expectations relevant to the essence of the learning, thus fostering the internalization of standards. If every morning before school, Jessica's parents tell her, "Be sure you do what the teacher tells you to do. Don't get into trouble," she is much less likely to develop enquiry motivation than if they tell her, "Be sure to learn something today." The classroom can convey messages about expectations about learning, too. If most of the classroom activities consist of drills on specific facts with little time to brainstorm and talk about ideas, this conveys to children that memorization is more important than curiosity. Some children come to school without understanding the difference between learning and social interaction. Instead of paying attention to the teacher, they talk and chat with other children. The way the teacher handles this confusion can lead to a positive outcome if the teacher stresses that you have to pay attention to learn.

Motivation to Learn in the Primary Grades.   The motivation to learn in formal ways is just developing in the primary grades. Many children will not have achieved it, especially if they have not had a preschool/kindergarten experience that gave them the self-regulation skills necessary to be successful in the new on-demand learning context of the elementary school classroom. Teachers will need to provide a great deal of support for each aspect of motivation. For example, the learning standards the child needs to internalize have to be made explicit by the teacher. Peers may also provide support for the use of standards and help children to maintain motivation. Successful achievement is critical for the development of motivation.

Leading Activity: Learning Activity

Elkonin (1972) and later Davydov (1988) defined the leading activity of the primary grades as learning activity. *Learning activity* is defined as child-initiated activity driven by enquiry motivation (intellectual curiosity). It starts as a process modeled and guided by adults around specific content that is formalized, structured, and culturally determined such as learning parts of speech, operations on numbers, or how to read music. In its early stages, learning activity is not carried out by any individual child but rather unfolds as a group activity with several children participating. At its mature state, learning activity is something a child can engage in various contexts and situations. It is not limited to a classroom setting.

The goal of learning activity is not just learning facts and skills, but transforming the learner's mind by the mastery of *sposoby deyatel'nosty,* which is Russian for the "methods and the means" or the "ways and means" of his actions (Elkonin, 2001b). It is not enough for the child to create the same product as the teacher or the correct answer. The answer must be the result of the appropriation of the right mental process.

In contrast, much of the teaching that goes on today takes for granted that if the child produces something that looks like the teacher's model, the child has in fact gone through the same process to get it. Take something as simple as writing a sentence using a model sentence that is put on the board. Some children will just copy the model sentence, looking at each letter as an isolated "picture" that they copy on their paper. Other children will read the model sentence and try to remember it and write it on their own, using the model as a check to see if they have spelled words correctly. Although all of these children will produce something that looks like the teacher's, the process the children went through to write the sentence is very different. In learning activity, the learning process is planned so that the teacher can tell if the children are using the process that she wants them to learn. The fact that the product looks like the teacher's is a by-product of the children's learning the right process and not merely copying.

From the children's perspective, engaging in learning activity feels very much like discovering processes and ideas. Learning activity has the same "aha" moments as discovery learning except that the process is guided by the teacher. For example, in a transcript of a Russian teaching session using learning activity, the teacher asks children how they think they could represent "a + 4a" graphically. The children come up with two solutions, one of which is not correct because the size of the "a" segment is as big as the size of the "4a" segment. The teacher then asks children to show her how one is right and one is not. The children propose ideas pro and con. The teacher continues to ask questions to reveal the process she is trying to teach. From the children's perspective, this is a journey of discovery. The first part of the lesson ends with the correct graphical representation on the board. The lesson continues with the teacher presenting more examples to have children test out the graphical model using different number combinations (Berlyand & Kurganov, 1993). The teacher guides by asking questions, leading to the correct answer. The teacher does not tell the children the correct answer.

Definition of Learning Activity

Just as in the case of play, Vygotskians have a strict definition of what comprises a learning activity (Davydov & Markova, 1983; Elkonin, 2001a). To qualify, an activity must have the following:

1. *A learning task* as the generalized way of acting that is to be acquired by the student
2. *Learning actions* that will result in the formation of a preliminary image of the action that is being learned
3. *Control actions or feedback* where the action is compared with a standard
4. *Assessment or self-reflection action* showing the learner's awareness of what he or she has learned
5. *Motivation* or the desire to learn and participate in the learning task; intellectual curiosity built into the activity so the child sees the task as something worthy of learning, interesting, and useful

Learning Task

In learning activity, the goal is not the acquisition of facts, but of the generalized action the child is expected to learn. The facts are the specific cases or exemplars used to practice this generalized action. Vygotskians make a distinction between a specific task at hand and the learning task. The solution to the specific task at hand is useful only if it causes the child to use the generalized action. Thus, learning moves away from the goal of getting the answer correct to getting the answer correct because a specific process was used to get that answer. Memorizing words for a spelling test would be considered a task at hand; learning rules for constructing a specific type of word would be the general principle. Vygotskians argue that emphasis should be placed on the latter.

Elkonin gives an example of teaching children how to break numbers down so that they can add numbers in their heads (Elkonin, 2001a). The teacher leads children to the discovery of a general pattern that exists in the sums of numbers such as 7 + 8 and 6 + 7. The learning task is to discover how to break down numbers that are less than 10 to facilitate adding using the number 10 as a strategy. In this example, the emphasis is on teaching the generalized principle rather than the specific cases. Children are not simply memorizing math facts from 11 to 20 but learn these as examples of the generalized rule.

Learning Actions

To solve a learning task, the child must perform certain learning actions. Following are examples of learning actions:

- transforming the learning task to discover a general principle
- modeling the identified general principle using pictures, schemas, symbols, etc.
- manipulating a model or models to crystallize and refine the general principle
- applying the general principle to a variety of specific problems

Each learning action that is being internalized must first exist in a sequential, explicit form. As the child first learns the process, she must proceed in a step-by-step way using mediators and manipulatives that make these steps concrete and discernable. These learning actions help the child form a visual, generalized image of the concept-process being learned. As the child internalizes the learning action, the need for tangible manifestations of each step become unnecessary, and she begins to use symbolic representations of the actions. Eventually the steps become automatized and folded, meaning that the learner will no longer be aware of each separate step but will see the process as an undifferentiated whole.

In the previous example of adding numbers using 10 as a facilitator, the learning actions involve presenting one number in each sum in a very specific way. It has to be broken down into two numbers, one of which, when added to another member of the sum, will equal 10. For example, 8 + 7 would be presented as (5 + 3) + 7 which is the same as 5 + (3 + 7) which is the same as 5 + (10). Similarly, 6 + 7 would be presented as 6 + 4 + 3. Breaking numbers down may involve the use of counters, Unifix cubes, or graph paper. Other learning actions involve applying the general pattern of addition to new examples, such as 4 + 8.

Another example would be the use of Elkonin boxes, which are used by children just learning phonemic awareness (see Figure 12.1). The original use of Elkonin boxes has been adapted by a number of literacy programs in the West to serve other purposes, for example helping children learn the sound-to-symbol correspondence (Clay, 1993). In its original version, it is a good illustration of the concept of a learning action. Elkonin boxes are designed to teach children the idea of "phoneme." Children are shown a card with a picture and a set of connected boxes underneath it representing the phonemes. Children push tokens into the boxes as they separate the phonemes of that word (see Figure 12.1). For example, the word *fish* is represented by three boxes. Children say "f" "i" "sh" as they push three tokens into the corresponding boxes one by one. The action of pushing each token into the box as they say the sound helps them

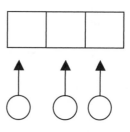

Figure 12.1   Elkonin boxes

create a mental image of the phonemes in that word. This image has kinesthetic, auditory, and articulatory properties tied to it. This learning action is very effective in establishing the idea that words are made up of phonemes. Within a few weeks, when children are asked to generate their own three- and four-phoneme words, they have no difficulty doing that, nor do they have trouble with words the teacher gives them, whether or not the word can be represented by a picture. So the learning action results in children developing phonemic awareness through the process of isolating and then blending the phonemes in a word.

Learning actions involve the exploration of the model and its characteristics as well as testing the model on concrete problems. For instance, in the previous example, children are given many pictures with Elkonin boxes so that they can explore the model. They try identifying the phonemes of many different words. They come to comprehend the idea that a word is made up of these components. Then, once they seem to understand the model, the teacher presents different words and asks the children to try to identify the number of phonemes. Children may still use manipulatives or a picture of three boxes and four boxes to remind them of what they are supposed to do. Children are asked to generate words with different numbers of phonemes. The learning action involves both exploring the phonemes in a particular word and eventually testing this newfound knowledge on new words. The transfer of this new knowledge to new situations is planned as part of the learning action.

Once the children have learned the general principle, part of the learning action is to use it as the basis for analyzing other problems that require an ever-deeper understanding. Children are given examples that vary more from the ones given at the initial stages of learning. These planned variations are designed to force children to decide how to apply the original principle. When errors occur in these more complicated cases, children are encouraged to revisit the original model.

Control Action or Feedback

The third characteristic of learning activity is the built-in control action or feedback. A particular learning activity should have feedback built into it so children know if they are right or wrong. Sometimes that feedback is simple, in that it tells children immediately if they are right or wrong. Returning to the example of the Elkonin boxes, children know if they have produced the right number of sounds because there are only the right number of chips and boxes. If they say "fi" "sh" or "f" "ish," they know this is wrong because there is one chip and one box left. They know that they did not produce enough sounds when they pulled the word apart. It leads them to look for their errors. They can then self-correct without having to wait for the teacher's feedback.

Another aspect of feedback allows the child to compare her performance with a standard or benchmark, which shows her how far she is from mastery. This is very important because, through this action, children begin to internalize the standard for a particular task. Research in learning indicates that one of the differences between good and poor students is this ability to know when you know something (Zimmerman & Risenberg, 1997). Good students are able to estimate how close their performance is to mastery. Poor students often have no idea if their answers are correct or incorrect. In correctly designed learning experiences, the act of internalization of the standard is built into the activity. Children begin to learn how to judge the distance between their current performance and mastery. This helps with motivation as it makes clear the necessary next steps. Children can then think ahead so self-corrections are meaningful to future performance. Instead of just continuing to guess, children revisit their own work and make changes that will have a greater chance of furthering the learning process.

Learning activity involves several cycles of exploration of the model that require children to apply the concept/process to increasingly diverse examples of that concept. Thus, children have to continue to evaluate their mastery. Built into the process is the revisiting of one's understanding of the original concept/process to build confidence and a deeper understanding. When there are errors, ways of analyzing the reasons for those errors are part of the learning process, revealing misunderstandings and aspects of the concept that are unclear. The errors are helpful in deepening learning and understanding.

Vygotskians argue that often learning and the practice that follows it are not constructed carefully enough. Consequently, errors do not yield much information for the learning process except that the child is wrong. The learner is left to figure out on his own why he got the answer incorrect. Rather than the error showing the child what he does not understand, it often makes the child more confused.

Davydov and his colleagues emphasize that there is a huge difference between grading and feedback in learning activity. Grades tend to summarize performance, but do not indicate to children the steps necessary to attain proficiency. They tend to take the child's focus off of process and onto the product. Also, grades are given by the teacher so they place the teacher in the role of controlling the learning process, rather than sharing that responsibility with the child. To succeed in school, children need to be able to evaluate themselves.

This capacity to control action or feedback is something that most young children cannot do without help. For this reason, Vygotskians advocate careful teacher guidance along with using the peer group to help children practice this action on each other. An example of such other-regulation is an activity in which children are paired to do sound analysis with Elkonin boxes. One child does the action (e.g., says a word sound-by-sound) and the partner checks it against a set standard (e.g., by physically pushing the tokens into the boxes). When children work together, they can sound out the words more accurately than when they work alone. Therefore, during the primary grades, control action involves not only self-correcting materials or a mechanism to figure out if you are correct, but also the support of a peer (Zuckerman, 2003).

Self-Reflection

In learning activity, children are asked to reflect and make a self-assessment of what they have learned. According to Davydov, children must be able to step back and become aware of what they can do as a result of having participated in the activity that they did not know or were not able to do before. Being able to independently comprehend and express the result of learning is a developmental goal for older children. Such self-reflection does not appear in children until the end of elementary school or even into junior high and high school.

Learning Activity in the Primary Grades

Davydov, Elkonin, and others have implemented this learning activity approach in many subject areas as early as first grade in Russia (Davydov, 1988; Davydov, Slobodchikov, & Tsukerman, 2003; Elkonin, 2001a, 2001b). One of the primary lessons from these applications is that primary-aged children are not ready to engage in the control action/feedback and self-regulatory aspects of learning activity without substantial support. Therefore, Vygotskians advocate using the peer group to help children incorporate this important aspect of learning. They argue that other-regulation is similar to what the child will eventually do for himself as he matures. He will be able to perform the learning action and simultaneously engage in self-feedback. Other-regulation is control of action in a shared state where the child engages in control action/feedback for another child. Eventually, after much practice, the child will be able to self-critique. An example is an activity in which children are paired to do editing of their writing. One child writes his story. The other child looks for mistakes using a list of sight words. The editor underlines the incorrectly spelled words and gives the writer feedback about which words were not spelled correctly. One child does the activity and the other child gives feedback. Activities in which other-regulation is actually built into the learning process give children much needed feedback skill (Zuckerman, 2003).

Another example is to present information in class in such a way that the peer group continues to interact with each other to find solutions to problems or questions. This is very different from the current practice of asking each child to give his/her own individual answer. The teacher can present the problem in a small or large group, but encourages the children to dialogue with each other in proposing solutions. In this way, the teacher acts more as a moderator of ideas, helping children sort out the ones that overlap or are erroneous. Children are encouraged to exchange ideas. It can be a sort of guided brainstorming session, where children propose lots of ideas and then use the principles/concepts/processes being taught to evaluate the ideas proposed in the group.

Self-reflection is, at this point, just developing in children. The learning goal must be restated at the end of the learning activity to remind children of what they were trying to do in the activity. Teachers must provide opportunities for self-reflection on the learning process. Ideas for supporting self-reflection are given in Chapter 13.

For Further Reading

Davydov, V. V. (1988). Problems of developmental teaching: The experience of theoretical and experimental psychological research. *Soviet Education, 30,* 66–79.

Elkonin, D. (1972). Toward the problem of stages in the mental development of the child. *Soviet Psychology, 10,* 225–251.

Karpov, Y. V., & Bradsford, J. D. (1995). L. S. Vygotsky and the doctrine of empirical and theoretical reasoning. *Educational Psychologist, 30*(2), 61–66.

Zuckerman, G. (2003). The learning activity in the first years of schooling: The developmental path toward reflection. In A. Kozulin, B. Gindis, V. S. Ageev, & S. M. Miller (Eds.), *Vygotsky's educational theory in cultural context* (pp. 177–199). Cambridge: Cambridge University Press.

CHAPTER **13**

Supporting the Developmental Accomplishments in the Primary Grades

As described in Chapter 12, children in the primary grades are developing elements of the intellectual capacities that will emerge in later grades. These early elementary years are the formative years for learning the basic literacies that are the building blocks of theoretical reasoning. Children are introduced to the basic units of mathematics and understandings about literacy, such as the concept of "word" and metalinguistic awareness. Children acquire written language, a critically important cultural tool, which will transform their ability to learn by increasing its efficacy.

Higher mental functions (HMF) are also emerging at this age. Most children can now remember on purpose, focus attention, and self-regulate some aspects of their mental behavior, but memory, attention, and self-regulation still have a ways to go before reaching the levels needed for success in later grades. The motivation to learn in formal ways is just developing, as children move from having play as their leading activity toward taking on the student role and developing enquiry motivation (intellectual curiosity).

It is hoped that children enter the primary grades with the developmental accomplishments of the preschool and kindergarten years well established. Unfortunately, this is sometimes not the case, as many teachers in primary grades find that their students are actually still "preschoolers." Teachers are often faced with the problem of building the underlying competencies that make learning effective along with teaching the skills of the primary grades.

In this chapter, we will address the two major challenges related to scaffolding that confront teachers in the primary, (first to third) grades. The first is providing a classroom environment that has learning activity geared to the growing skills of children at this age. Children are not yet ready to engage in full-blown learning activity on their own. They need support for its development built into all classroom experiences. Teaching strategies have to be modified to create conditions in which the developmental accomplishments needed by sixth grade will emerge. However, they must also be geared to the skills and learning levels of first and second graders. The focus in the primary grades is on helping children learn how to be learners—how to engage in learning activity as well as the other activities that occur in the classroom in the most productive way.

The second challenge for primary teachers is to help the children who have not attained the accomplishments of preschool/kindergarten and who, consequently, have difficulty coping with the demands of formal schooling. How can teachers support these children so that they do not fall farther behind their more prepared classmates? By the end of the primary grades, children should be maturing into competent learners, capable of meeting the challenges of the academic content of the upper grades and beyond.

In Chapter 12, we described the structure of learning activity when it is fully formed. Primary-grade children have a long way to go before they develop learning activity. Depending on the content of the specific lessons and the methods of a particular teacher, children can only engage in elements of learning activity at this time. For example, because of its sequential structure and well-defined procedures, math can be used to provide practice in identifying specific learning tasks. Spelling allows children to practice elements of control and self-assessment as they compare their writing to correct models. In later grades, all aspects of learning activity are practiced within the same activity, but during the primary grades, certain subjects lend themselves to supporting different aspects of learning activity.

To ensure that children acquire and develop the elements of learning activity, classroom practices have to be designed so that they support learning in very specific ways. We will summarize some of the suggestions from the work of Davydov (1988), Elkonin (2001), and Zuckerman (2003) that focus on such elements as the defined learning task, learning standards, and self-reflection. Then, we will provide some guidelines on how to support the development of learning actions based on the work of Gal'perin (1969).

Supporting the Critical Elements of Learning Activity

Teachers can foster learning activity by modifying classroom practices to include some of the following specific elements of learning activity when they teach.

- Use models as a way to help children understand generalized actions.
- Help children see "through" the activity to the learning goal.
- Help children understand the concept of a standard and learn how to use standards to guide learning.
- Devise ways to promote reflection.

Use Models as a Way to Help Children Understand Generalized Actions

As children begin to learn concepts and generalized actions—the essential processes—specific external mediators can facilitate the process. This use of external mediators is especially effective if they, themselves, are a model of the primary principles being taught. For instance, manipulatives can be specifically designed to embody the concept being learned, such as the different length rods in Cuisenaire Rods that demonstrate the relationship between 1s and 10s. Graphic representations can also help children to internalize the principles being learned. To understand the beginning, middle, and end of a story, children can make storyboards with three sections, each standing for a part of the story. Both manipulatives and graphic representations help children learn the relationships that are at the heart of the concepts or the generalized actions being taught.

To use manipulatives and graphic representations to support the development of concepts, teachers must be careful to focus on the manner in which children use them rather than on what the child produces as a result of the process. A focus on the product can be misleading as one child's product might look like another child's product, although the mental processes used to create these products were different. Mrs. Shue's class is making the number 8 with different colored Unifix® cubes. She wants the children to see that when 8 is represented by two colors of cubes, it is possible to have different combinations adding to 8. She demonstrates by making the following groupings: 1 blue + 7 red, 2 blue + 6 red, 3 blue + 5 red, 4 blue + 4 red, etc. She shows the children the blocks and explains what she has done. Several children make the same pattern. When she asks Kenisha what she did, Kenisha says that "when you add one more blue, then the number of red goes down. When she asks Daren, he says, "It makes a cool stairs, so what I did, I just kept making the blue look like a stair step." Mrs. Shue soon discovers that only Kenisha comprehends the general principle she is trying to teach.

In fact, out of all the children in her room, only Kenisha understood the principle. The rest of the children produced the configuration of the cubes correctly, but for the wrong reasons. On the surface, looking at their products, it looked like all of the children understood.

Elkonin insisted children must be allowed sufficient time with manipulatives for them to really capture the concepts they model. If the manipulatives are removed too quickly or not used at all, children miss a critical phase in learning. This idea of providing children sufficient experience with the models of concepts provided by manipulatives was also championed by Gal'perin and is discussed at length in the following section. It is important to note that Vygotskians do not consider a calculator to be particularly useful at the early stages of learning how to add, subtract, multiply, and divide. It produces an answer but does not allow the child to engage in actions emulating the processes of addition, subtraction, multiplication, and division.

Help Children See "Through" the Activity to the Learning Goal

Children must understand the purpose of practice or of the activity they are asked to do. They tend to see the purpose as the product alone and think that if they make it look like the teacher's, that is enough. They do not readily see that it isn't just the product but the way they produce the product that is also important. Teachers must make clear that practice is assigned in such a way that the students repeat precisely the process they are learning. In one first-grade classroom, children were learning how to write the letter *a* in preparation for cursive writing. Several children wrote entire pages of *c* and then closed the figures to make *a*. When asked why they did that, the children said it was faster that way. They had completely missed the point that the purpose of the exercise was to produce an *a* in a specific way so that when they formed the cursive letter, it would be correct. Practicing the *c* and then later closing the figure did not teach children the correct hand movement. The teacher had not made it clear to the children why they were writing this letter in this particular manner.

Help Children Understand the Concept of a Standard and Learn How to Use Standards to Guide Learning

Related to the idea of understanding the learning goal for a particular activity is learning to compare one's performance to a standard. The standard describes the acceptable level of performance required to have mastered or performed that task successfully. It tells you that you know what is being taught. Understanding the standard, the student should keep working on his performance until it reaches this standard. As the standard is internalized, the student is able to work more and more independently, because he knows not only what he should learn but of what mastery consists.

In most schools, children find out many days after turning in their work whether their performance meets the teacher's standard for it. Vygotskians argue that the primary rationale for giving children feedback on their work is to promote their ability to self-correct. If children must wait for specific feedback, the intervening time period makes it difficult for them to reconstruct what their thinking was when they did the assignment. (Even adults have trouble reconstructing their thinking after lapses of time.) The more immediate the feedback, the greater the possibility that the child will be able to make self-corrections that will actually improve her performance.

Most teachers do not show children how to use the standard to analyze their performance, nor do they explain how to use it to analyze their errors. Following are several guidelines for teachers:

- Provide the standard ahead of time. Make sure children know what will be an acceptable performance.

- Provide children with answer books where they can check their work. Have a set of rules for how to use the books so children do not misuse them. For example, include the answers to the first five problems only, with directions on what to do if they miss them. Or provide the answers for odd- or even-numbered questions.

- When a child makes errors, walk that child through her thought processes to understand the errors that she made.

- Emphasize "what you know" and "what you don't know" when giving specific task-related feedback instead of general feedback like "nice try," sad faces, or a grade of "C." General feedback is of no help to students who are making errors. They often do not understand what they are doing wrong because if they did, they would not have made the error.

Devise Ways to Promote Reflection

The ability to reflect on thinking develops gradually during the primary grades. Like all the other intellectual capacities, for Vygotskians, reflection exists in a shared state first, before it is appropriated by an individual child. Reflection begins with the teacher helping children to think about their mental actions. Additional support can be provided by peers. Following are ideas to support reflection in primary grades:

- Have learning conferences to help children think about how they studied, practiced, and learned. Review papers and tests with children to identify error patterns or help children become aware of how they studied. Patterns of correct answers can be used to show children what they know just as errors show them what is not understood.

- Set learning goals that help children become aware of what they must do to learn more efficiently.

- Have children work as study buddies or partners. Have one child do the activity and the other child check to see if the task or solution is correct. This way children practice both doing and reflecting.

Step-by-Step Formation as a Way to Support the Development of Learning Actions

Gal'perin was interested in how external knowledge becomes internalized and represented by mental rather than actual physical actions (Gal'perin, 1969, 1992). He proposed that there are steps by which this happens. During the beginning stages of acquiring a new skill or concept, learning should involve concrete actions that are external and that exist in sequential steps. For example, when first learning how to count objects, the child touches each concrete object in turn and says the number. These actions are repeated in a sequence: first touch the first object and say its number, then move on to the next one, etc.

Once the learners know how to do something, Gal'perin argued, their actions are performed internally. They also become reduced, automated, and folded—meaning that many steps are unconscious. Instead of counting by touching, children can count in their head. In fact, the process may become reduced so that it is no longer necessary for them to count each object; by just looking at the five objects they know there are five. When actions are automatic, the steps that are necessary to count are no longer conscious and are done automatically. This also happens in reading. For skilled readers, so many of the processes are automatic that, at times, they are not even conscious of the words—just the ideas.

Gal'perin and his colleagues and students conducted many research studies to determine what steps are necessary for the novice to get to the level of internalization where he is able to act on a mental plane in a seamless way (Arievitch & Stetsenko, 2000). His ideas have been used to teach in many subject areas, and the children he worked with were able to perform at a much higher level than was typically expected of children of that age. Following is a summary of some of Gal'perin's major concepts that help teachers make instruction more effective:

- The importance of the *Orienting Basis of Action*
- The need for "materialized" action
- The importance of automatization
- The distinction between natural and avoidable errors

The Importance of the Orienting Basis of Action

In an analysis of traditional teaching methods where teachers taught parts of the whole and then built the skill from the parts, Gal'perin found that children were often left to their own devices to figure out how the parts fit together. Children formed their own naïve theories about the relationship between the parts and the whole. For example, the teacher demonstrates how to measure objects using a ruler. The children are then given rulers and begin to measure their own objects. However, they only have a vague notion about how to do this. Many of them do not understand that they have to make a mark at the end of the object they are measuring when it is longer than the ruler so they know where to put the ruler as they continue measuring the larger object. Consequently, every child in the classroom gets a different measurement for the same object.

Gal'perin's recommendation was to identify the basic principle that made the separate parts of the experience make sense. He reasoned that children have to learn not only this principle concept, but also the primary factors that influence its application. These things have to be woven together so that the child's actual behavior makes sense to her. Therefore, the teacher should provide a roadmap of what is to be learned, indicating the major principal and its major characteristics and applications. In teaching measurement, for example, the teacher needs to make it clear that length is continuous so the action of measurement should also be continuous.

The Need for "Materialized" Action

Gal'perin argued that mental actions start first as *material* or *materialized*. In a material action, a child is dealing with an actual object; in a materialized action, the child uses a representation of an object. For example, as children learn about 10s and 1s counting toward the hundredth day of school, they place individual sticks into bundles of 10 and tie them together (material action). They can also put a tally mark for each day they spend in school and then count these tally marks. In the latter case, children will be performing materialized action, since they will be counting the representations of objects and not actual objects.

Gal'perin argued that physical actions don't just precede mental actions; they actually shape them. The very way the child builds a number using Cuisenaire rods influences the thinking processes involved when counting. The rods convey the concept of units and how different-sized units are related to each other, thereby making a difficult idea concrete. The child uses the rods to create representations of numbers, thus engaging in materialized action. Until children understand place value, graph paper helps them to correctly use the 1s, 10s, and 100s places so they can add correctly. The graph paper makes the place value of the digits in a number concrete. When children write and solve addition problems using graph paper, they are engaged in materialized action. Another example of materialization involves the use of a "word window" where children place a cardboard frame around each word as they read. The window emphasizes the concept of "word" as a separate entity, one that is concrete and contained within the frame. The child's action of moving the frame from one word to another shapes her concept of words as distinct entities.

Gal'perin showed that there is a progression in how a mental action is formed: it goes from material or materialized (concrete and physical) to language-based to internalized. First, children physically perform a material or materialized action such as constructing a sum with Cuisenaire rods or moving a word window along the line of print. This materialized action is paired with private speech that both directs the child's action and begins the process of moving external action to an internal schema. Language turns the materialized action into a mental concept. Children may then discontinue the use of manipulatives and overt actions, but still need private speech to complete the mental action. Finally, the private speech becomes internalized and transformed into inner speech and eventually verbal thinking, which guides the mental action.

To return to the example of the Cuisinaire rods, the child makes the number 10 by putting together 10 one-unit cubes as he counts 1, 2, 3, 4, 5, 6, 7, 8, 9, 10. The private speech of saying the numbers as he uses the manipulatives facilitates the conversion of the physical action into a language-based concept. Eventually he internalizes the idea of a bigger unit (10) being composed of ten smaller units.

Skipping any part of this path leads to problems. In teaching older students, beginning at the language stage will sometimes lead to problems, because they may not have the previous building blocks in place. Gal'perin (1959) warned against skipping the material or materialized stage, arguing that students might develop an "empty" concept or skill devoid of its true content. Students who have developed an "empty" concept tend to tell you about the action they are supposed to perform instead of actually performing it. An example would be a student who can tell you that to add two-digit numbers, she needs to add 10s, then add 1s, and then add these two sums together. However, when asked to add 47 and 38, she will not be able either to add or to verbalize the concrete steps involved. For these students, teachers may have to return to the stage of material or materialized action.

For materialized action to be internalized into mental action, it has to be accompanied by private speech that carries it into the mind. Teachers have to not only plan for the use of the manipulatives and the procedures of their use, but also what children should say as they are using the manipulatives. Children who still point to words as they read will probably need the private speech of saying each word aloud as they point to it. Forcing them to read silently may slow down the development of mental actions.

Automatization of Mental Actions

Gal'perin believed that before any new concept, skill, or strategy is internalized, it exists for a period of time in an externally supported form. It can be observed from the child's verbalizations or by the way she manipulates objects. From these observations, the teacher can understand where the child is in learning the new skill and can offer help to facilitate the learning. Once the skill is internalized, it becomes *automatized* and *folded*, and some of the sequential steps are performed simultaneously. This means that the concept is not easily accessible to correction. When a skill becomes internalized, or automatic, it is very difficult for a teacher to correct a missing or defective part of it. The internalized form has become like a habit such as in the case of taking a specific sequence of turns. For example, if you usually turn right out of your parking lot to go home at the end of the day, it is probable that you will forget to turn left on the days you need to turn that way to go to the market. The behavior of turning right at the end of the day is so ingrained that it is automatic.

Automatization explains why it is difficult to correct things we have learned incorrectly, even though we know we are wrong. Some examples are incorrect spellings, mispronunciation of certain words, and incorrectly memorized math facts. In all these cases, we recognize the mistake after we have repeated it and wish we could have stopped ourselves beforehand.

The traditional way of correcting this kind of mistake is to point out the error after it has been committed. As most teachers can tell you, pointing out the error afterward has very little effect on error production the next time. First grader Katie reverses the number *6* when she writes it. She does not reverse any of the letters you would expect her to reverse, only the number *6*. Her teacher has tried many different strategies, including making her write 6 correctly on a separate sheet of paper or making her recopy math problems that contain 6. No matter what she tries, Katie seems to forget the new way of writing 6 and continues to revert to her backwards 6. Even the threat of a lower grade does not work.

To solve this problem using Gal'perin's approach, it is necessary to "deautomatize" the action by interrupting it and then having the child relearn it to the point of automatization. Katie needs to stop herself before she writes the 6 and then learn to do it correctly, step by step. To interrupt her actions, Katie's teacher has her write her math problems in pencil but when she comes to a 6 she is to stop and change to using a blue pen. When she uses the pen, Katie looks at the external mediator card where 6 is written correctly and says to herself, "Six goes this way," as she writes the 6 with a blue pen.

Then she returns to the rest of her math problems in pencil. After a few days, Katie easily stops herself from writing 6 incorrectly.

The Distinction between Natural and Avoidable Errors

Vygotskians recognize that there are different kinds of errors. Some of them require intervention, but others are natural or even beneficial. When errors occur for a short period of time and then are outgrown, they are a natural part of the learning process. Some examples are the use of baby talk by toddlers, drawing figures with no fingers or ears by preschoolers, and invented spelling in kindergarten.

Some errors are beneficial in the learning process by providing feedback to the child about her performance. By correcting these errors, the child can improve her performance. When a child reads the word *hat* as *hit* and the sentence no longer makes sense, the error makes the child look at the word and try to read it correctly. The child is able to think about the error and the reason for it. This type of error creates cognitive dissonance and may even trigger the child's curiosity.

On the other hand, some errors are not beneficial. These are errors that the child does not understand or cannot seem to correct even after feedback from the teacher or support from the social context. In some children, natural errors, such as reversing letters, do not disappear in a reasonable amount of time and consequently become a problem. After learning to read and write with left to right directionality, some children have trouble breaking this habit when they need to subtract two- and three- digit numbers. They subtract starting on the left instead of in the 1s column. Such errors are extremely frustrating and can have a negative effect on the child's motivation to learn. These *repeated errors* are very resistant to change and become a major problem in the classroom.

Gal'perin (1969) wrote of the benefits of *errorless learning* to help teachers prevent repeated errors and to help children correct them. First, he encouraged teachers to keep in mind the past mistakes of students when planning learning experiences. For example, if the teacher knows that children confuse the colors orange and red, when she presents those colors, she should point out right away that they are different. If she knows that the children's first reaction will be to confuse two concepts, she points this out as she starts. Thus, the teacher anticipates the elements that will be confusing.

Gal'perin points out that teachers should not leave the discovery of the essential elements of basic concepts to the children. He believed that trial-and-error learning was not beneficial in school. In school, learning by trial and error leads to repeated errors and is very frustrating because the child cannot guess what the teacher is getting at.

Once the teacher has explained all of the necessary elements of a concept or a skill, he has to monitor the process of its acquisition; provide various kinds of assistance, such as shared experiences and external mediators; and encourage the use of private speech. The teacher must make sure that the child's understanding reflects all the essential components and that she can apply the concept or skill to new problems without distorting it.

A typical error for second graders is to misuse capitalization. Using the idea of errorless learning, the teacher and the children generate a list of all the situations in which capitals are used. This list is placed on a card on each child's desk (external mediator). Children work on an assignment to practice capitalization using private speech and the external mediator. As they go down a list of words, they ask themselves at each word, "Should this be capitalized?" After several practice sentences, children discuss their results with a partner, and then the teacher comes by to monitor their progress. In a few weeks, most children will not need the card at their desks and will not use private speech. Some children may require external support for a while longer.

When repeated errors appear, according to Gal'perin, it is necessary to go back and see what caused the misunderstanding. Were all of the essential elements explicitly conveyed to the child, or did the child miss one of these? Did the child have enough practice, or was independent performance encouraged before the child was ready? Was enough support offered to the child to enable the child to master all of the pieces of the skill or concept?

Once the cause for the error is found, the teacher must compensate for the missing experience or help the child relearn the information. For example, the child may be missing a rule that will help him clear up the misunderstanding. In some cases, the child will need more practice, with the missing rule being emphasized or even visually highlighted, for example, with a different colored pen as in the earlier example in which Katie had to write all her 6s with a blue pen. In other cases, if a child has learned to spell a word incorrectly, she may need a visual representation of the appropriate rule and may need to say this rule to herself as she writes the word. An example of this would be having the child generate a page of visual reminders. Pictures and words that would stand for the most common uses of capital letters, such as a picture of a globe for the geographical names. The child would then be encouraged to say aloud whether each word in question falls into one of the categories listed on the page.

Scaffolded Writing—The Application of Step-by-Step Formation to Writing

Scaffolded Writing (Bodrova & Leong, 1998, 2001, 2003, 2005) is a uniquely American application of Gal'perin's ideas. Whereas in Russia, children are not usually expected to write sentences and entire stories until they already know how to read multiple paragraphs of print; in American schools, they are. Consequently, many American children engage in writing activities such as journaling or Writers' Workshop before they have fully developed an understanding of the concept of a word.

Many children who graduate from using scribbles and letter-like forms to using letters often do not leave spaces between the words, which makes it virtually impossible for them to read their own messages "or the words" (see Figure 13.1). As a result, these children miss out on opportunities to use the writing process to practice phonemic awareness, letter knowledge, and letter-sound correspondence.

Gal'perin's ideas of the steps involved in the formation of a new mental action became the basis of the Scaffolded Writing method, which we developed in 1995 (Bodrova & Leong, 1995). During Scaffolded Writing sessions, a teacher helps a child plan her own message by drawing a line to stand for each word she says. The child then repeats the message, pointing to each line as she says the word. Finally, she writes on the lines attempting to represent each word with some letters or symbols (see Figure 13.2). During the first several sessions, the child may require some assistance and prompting

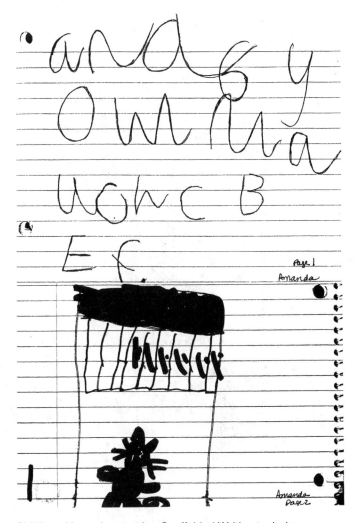

Figure 13.1   Child's writing prior to using Scaffolded Writing technique

from the teacher. As her understanding of the concept of a word grows, the child becomes able to carry the whole process independently, including drawing the lines and writing words on these lines (see Figure 13.3).

In designing a step-by-step protocol for emergent writing, we first identified the most critical aspects of the task, its *orienting basis* that could be supported by a specific tool. Although there are many tasks involved in the act of writing, and emergent writers may face difficulties executing any one of them, we focused on the *concept of a word* as the most critical aspect at this stage in the development of writing. A large number of studies of emergent writers indicate that children's developing concepts of a word affects significantly their learning of other important literacy prerequisites. Thus, the orienting basis for the action of writing has to explicitly focus a child's attention on the existence of individual words within a written message.

Figure 13.2   Child's writing one week after using Scaffolded Writing technique

The concept of a word is critical for learning to write, but in the earliest stages of writing young children experience great difficulty understanding what a word is. To scaffold the emerging concept of a word, an external mediator created to teach it has to be different from a written word and still retain some of the attributes of written words. We found that a line drawn to represent each word in an oral message serves as such a mediator. The lines separated by spaces represent the existence of individual words and their sequence in a sentence. At the same time, drawing a line does not present a young child with the same high demands on her orthographic knowledge and fine motor abilities as writing a word does. Thus, drawing a line presents the *materialized action* of the writing of the words in a message.

That *private speech* is encouraged during Scaffolded Writing helps emergent writers in at least three ways. First, when a child talks to himself when writing, it helps him remember more words from his initial message. Second, as a child repeats a word while drawing a line, he practices voice to print correspondence that reinforces the concept of a word. Finally, with lines reminding him of the other words of the message, the child

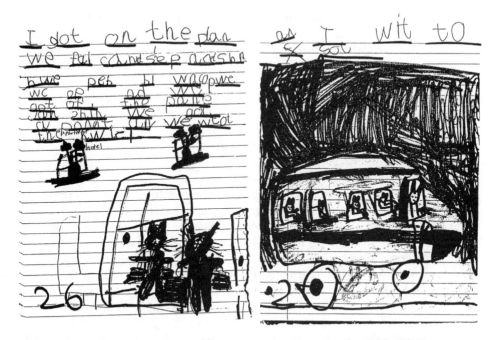

Figure 13.3   Child's independent writing two months after using Scaffolded Writing technique

can concentrate on repeating any word as many times as may be necessary to come up with some phonemic representations.

Scaffolded Writing begins as a shared activity, with the child contributing the message and the teacher writing the lines and then representing the sounds in the word with letters. Later, children are able to plan the sentence on their own and make the line for each word as they say it. After children write lines for each of the words, they go back and place letters on the lines representing the sounds in the corresponding words. Eventually, children grasp the idea of planning the sentence and writing words separated by spaces. When the concept of a word has been internalized, children drop the use of the line because they are able to perform the act without external cues. We have found a significant increase in the quantity as well as the quality of children's writing as a result of using Scaffolded Writing, demonstrating the applicability of Gal'perin's methods in American primary classrooms.

Supporting Primary-Grade Children Who Are Missing the Developmental Accomplishments of Preschool and Kindergarten Years

Many children enter the primary grades without the developmental accomplishments that make learning in the primary grades effective. Elementary teachers, however, cannot have children engage in play, which is the leading activity for preschool, in order to make up for gaps in their development. Emphasizing the role of games with rules as a transition between pretend play and learning activity, Vygotskians (Michailenko & Korotkova, 2002; Smirnova, 1998; Smirnova & Gudareva, 2004) advocate the use of various games to compensate for missing developmental accomplishments. These games have several characteristics that help the primary school child develop self-regulation, symbolic thought, and the capacity to follow the rules. The games have a pretend scenario, so children can engage in role-playing and planning, both of which are aspects of pretend play that support self-regulation skills. Learning games also help children internalize concepts, engage in other-regulation (checking to see if other children are playing correctly), and self-assessment.

Teaching games are a common feature of early childhood classrooms. They are often set out for children to play during their free time or as a part of center time. Most educational games are designed first as a game and secondarily as a way to help children learn a skill. They are often used more as an afterthought to the curriculum than as a planned way to help children practice skills in another context. Using educational games whose primary purpose is to bridge the gap between the leading activity of preschool/kindergarten and learning activity is a common feature of Vygotsky-based curricula for children of this age (Venger & Dyachenko, 1989). These researchers point out that games provide the support of shared activity, thus increasing motivation as well as assisting children who need extra help. The potential of games to provide real scaffolding for learning new concepts and skills is not fully exploited in today's early childhood classrooms in the United States.

To make games more effective and to turn them into something that helps children transition into learning activity, teachers can modify classroom games that they already have and devise new ones while keeping the following things in mind:

- The child who practices should win.
- The game should be self-correcting.
- The games for the beginning of the learning process should be different from those played when children are very familiar with the skill.

The Child Who Practices Should Win

Many teaching games are designed so that the child who is lucky enough to get certain cards wins, even if that child is not practicing the skill or concept being learned. Games should be designed so children who use the appropriate concept or skill win. Take, for example, a Lotto game where children are supposed to identify the picture on their card that begins with the same initial sound as the target card. If the game is organized so that only one child has the correct sound on his card, then only that one child can give the correct answer. The other children are supposed to check their card for that target sound; however, many children, particularly those who are unsure of their skills, sit passively and wait until the teacher or another child points out what they have on their card. In fact, a child may win even though he has not even looked at his cards.

It is better to redesign the same Lotto game so that every child has the target sound on their card, but each child has a different picture on the card. For example, each child has a picture with the *t* sound, but one child has a picture of a table, another child a picture of a tiger, and yet another a picture of a turkey. In this case, the children cannot just copy each other, but must search for the right pictures on their own cards. They all know that they will have the answer if they look. This provides more motivation and practice for the children who are not sure of their skills to find the correct matching pictures. The teacher will also be able to monitor what each child knows because they can all find answers on their cards. This is more effective because it increases the likelihood that they will all mentally engage in the game.

The Game Should Be Self-Correcting

The children should be able to check their performance against a standard so that the answer used in the game is correct or self-corrected. In an adding game where children take turns rolling dice and adding that number to a constant, a card is provided that enables children to check the answer. Only if the answer is checked and is correct can the child move forward on the game board. A means of checking is provided so that all children know what is correct.

The Game Should Change as the Children's Skills Change

Games played at later stages in the children's learning of a skill should provide less support and should rely on the children themselves to correct each other. It should also require faster, more fluent use of the skills. In an initial sound game, children try to identify pictures of objects that begin with the same sound as the target picture. At first, children play the game at their own pace. After they become familiar with the game, they time themselves to see if they can beat the group's personal best. This is similar to what happens in a chess game where the players time their moves. This technique can be used to encourage faster performance once children have mastered the fundamentals of the skill. The game can then support the development of skill automatization and fluency and not just practice of the skill.

For Further Reading

Davydov, V. V. (1988). Problems of developmental teaching: The experience of theoretical and experimental psychological research. *Soviet Education, 30,* 66–79.

Gal'perin, P. Y. (1992). Organization of mental activity and the effectiveness of learning. *Journal of Russian & East European Psychology, 30*(4), 65–82.

Zuckerman, G. (2003). The learning activity in the first years of schooling: The developmental path toward reflection. In A. Kozulin, B. Gindis, V. S. Ageev, & S. M. Miller (Eds.), *Vygotsky's educational theory in cultural context* (pp. 177–199). Cambridge: Cambridge University Press.

CHAPTER 14

Dynamic Assessment: Application of the Zone of Proximal Development

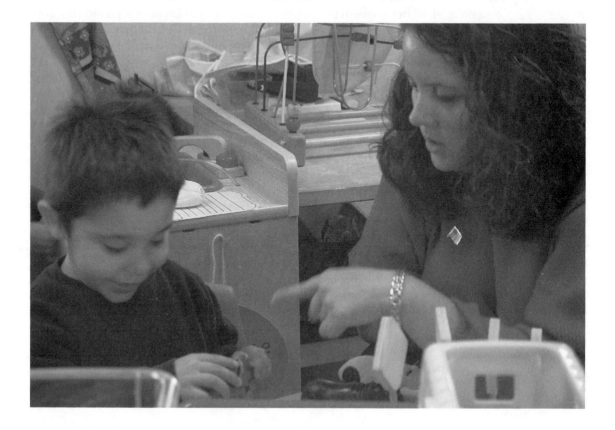

In *Mind in Society*, Vygotsky proposed a different way of looking at assessment and the measurement of abilities that moved away from static measures of child performance to ones that are dynamic and reveal something about how the child is learning (Vygotsky, 1978). The zone of proximal development (ZPD) is the organizing principle of this type of assessment. The focus is on measuring the dynamics of learning and development, which includes establishing both the child's current level of achievement and her potential to attain higher levels. For Vygotskians, development is defined not as a universal unfolding of abilities as children mature, but as the skills that emerge between the child's abilities and the supporting environment. Therefore, assessment should acknowledge that learning occurs within this social context and should include the influence of the support and assistance given to the child. From these principles, post-Vygotskians have developed the concept of the instructional experiment, which is currently known in the west as dynamic assessment. The goal of dynamic assessment is to help teachers to understand both what a particular child knows and the instructional steps needed to encourage his further learning.

Traditional vs. Dynamic Assessment

Vygotskians suggest that the following assumptions of the traditional testing paradigm reduce its effectiveness for assessing ongoing classroom learning (Guthke & Wigenfeld, 1992; Lidz & Gindis, 2003):

- Only fully developed competencies should be measured—those that the child can perform without support and assistance.
- The level of functioning revealed by the assessment accurately reflects children's inner capacities—what the child currently knows and can do.
- The purpose of assessment is to predict how the child will learn in the future and/or to classify the child according to a category, such as "ready for school" or "exhibits sensorimotor integration problems."

Vygotskians argue that examining fully developed competencies underestimates children's capacities because the information obtained pertains only to the lowest level of the ZPD. Knowing what the child can do independently does not measure anything that is in the process of being developed. Only when both levels of the ZPD are known—what the child can do alone AND what she can do with support—is the full range of the child's capabilities identified. The ZPD reveals the skills that are on the edge of emergence.

In Western psychology, it is customary to associate developmental accomplishments and learning outcomes with what a child can do independently. This mind-set affects people on all levels of education—from a classroom teacher who forbids children to help each other on a test to the authors of federal and state standards who describe grade level expectations in terms of a child's individual accomplishments. Consequently, all traditional assessment instruments are designed to minimize the effects of the interaction between the child and the administrator of the test, be it a teacher or another professional. Testers are specifically trained not to exhibit any sign of what they think about a child's answers and certainly not to assist the child in any way, even by rewording the test item or explaining what the child is supposed to do. As a result, practically all of the information collected by traditional assessment instruments reflects only what the child can do unassisted. This *independent performance* represents an important indicator of the child's current achievement—what the child can do alone—but for Vygotskians, it is not the only indicator.

Vygotsky argued that the independent level of performance was not sufficient to fully describe development. According to his Cultural-Historical Theory, child development involves the mastery of cultural tools through social interactions (Vygotsky, 1978). In this paradigm, how capable the child is in learning new tools is as important to his development as how well he can use the tools he has already mastered. And as social support is necessary for the acquisition of new tools, the child's use of support should also be assessed. Therefore, to capture all the nuances of a child's capacity, Vygotsky recommended evaluating the *level of assisted performance* when assessing a child's performance. The level of assisted performance represents what the child can do when given maximum help from the environment. This help includes, but is not limited to, the instructional support provided by the teacher. The level of assisted performance measures a child's potential ability to master new strategies, concepts, and skills by assessing the amount of help the child needs to complete a task successfully.

Responses to a traditional test may not reveal what the child is thinking as the task is performed and therefore may not accurately reveal his level of functioning. Many critiques of standardized testing indicate that a child's answers may not reflect her true understanding and are subject to misinterpretation of the question (McAfee & Leong, 2003). Children may also arrive at a correct answer using a wrong process as we have argued in Chapters 12 and 13. It is dangerous to extrapolate from the child's answers to only one or two specific questions the true potential of her inner capacities. Assessments that more fully probe the child's understanding produce responses that reveal more about what the child knows than the answers to only a few questions.

The purpose of traditional testing is to predict future functioning in general ways. Is the child ready for school? Does he read at grade level, equal to his peers? Only more specialized tests can give diagnostic information as to what particular problems a child has with learning. These specialized tests provide a narrow range of information that often is not useful for the day-to-day instructional decisions that teachers make. Traditional diagnostic tests tend to measure static abilities, producing snapshots of capacities at a given moment in time. Often they do not provide teachers with much guidance as to how to help a particular child.

Dynamic assessment is an alternative to a typical assessment in which only a child's fully developed competencies are measured and in which any intervention on the part of the test administrator immediately renders the test results invalid. On the other hand, in dynamic assessment, the interactions between the child and the tester are as valuable a source of information as the child's individual performance. Dynamic assessment reveals pieces of the "bigger picture" that are usually left out in a traditional assessment. This includes how well a child can perform a task with assistance and the extent to which the child is able to transfer this assisted performance to different tasks or tests. Further, dynamic assessments provide the teacher with information concerning which supportive interventions make a difference for a child. This helps her to make classroom decisions about how to teach a concept or skill.

What Is Dynamic Assessment?

In a typical dynamic assessment session, a child is first pretested individually to determine the level at which she can no longer complete the task independently. She is then retested but is no longer expected to act independently. She is given guidance and support in the form of cues, hints, prompts, or strategies provided by an adult. This support can also come in the form of a new context for learning in which specific materials or interactions with peers promote the child's performance at a higher level. Finally, the child is assessed in an analogous task where the same skills or concepts are used (Ivanova, 1976).

Unlike tests where children are given tasks that they should have already mastered, in dynamic assessment, the items are chosen to be within the child's ZPD, but not already mastered. The pretest is designed to expose what the child does not understand. Then, during the course of the assessment, the child is expected to learn the task being assessed. The task used in the dynamic assessment is chosen from among the classroom tasks that are part of the curriculum. Children at different levels can be given the same test. If a child shows mastery of the concept on the pretest, he is given a different, more difficult follow-up test to evaluate what further learning he is ready for.

Once the pretest has been administered, the teacher can begin the second phase of the assessment in which specific calibrated prompts, hints, and cues are given to the child. These supports are based on the teacher's knowledge of how the specific skill or concept develops—a developmental continuum of those skills or that concept; the use of teaching tactics—mediation, private speech, and shared activity; and knowledge about the types of errors commonly made by novice learners. The interventions are carefully planned and are designed to reveal what the child understands and does not understand, particularly if the concept is complex. The teacher should plan a number of supports that are contingent on the child's answers. It is expected that the supports will not be useful to all of the children, but will resonate with particular children, depending on their own specific comprehension level or pattern of errors. During the course of the assessment, the teacher notes not only what the child has said, but also the child's reaction to specific prompts and cues—which ones helped and which ones did not. Teachers obviously can skip certain levels of support if the child does not need them.

After the assessment is completed and the child has performed successfully, the teacher introduces an analogous task with the same elements as the one the child did with help. The child's performance is observed. Did the child incorporate the strategies that were just taught? Is the child able to perform independently? If the child cannot perform independently, does the reintroduction of some of the hints and cues seem to lead to successful learning?

Post-Vygotskian Applications of Dynamic Assessment

Like the concept of ZPD, the idea of dynamic assessment was first applied in the area of special education. This kind of assessment proved especially productive when it was used to determine whether a child's low level of mental functioning was caused by developmental delays or by educational deficits. In Russia, this approach was used initially to diagnose borderline cases of mental retardation (Ivanova, 1976; Rogoff & Lave, 1984; Rubinshtein, 1979). Later, when dynamic assessment had became more popular in the West, its use was extended to include a wider range of situations. These included ones in which the use of standardized diagnostic tools did not provide adequate distinction between neurological and environmental causes for low intellectual functioning or slow academic progress. R. Feuerstein and his colleagues are most often associated with this kind of assessment; they have applied the methodology of dynamic assessments to an increasing number of cognitive and linguistic competencies in children (Feuerstein, Feuerstein, & Gross, 1997; Tzuriel, 2001; Tzuriel & Feuerstein, 1992).

There have been fewer applications of dynamic assessment outside the area of special education. However, in a number of studies, dynamic assessment was found to be a better predictor of students' academic progress than more traditional static tests. Notably, many of these studies focused on the development of reading and writing. For example, Spector used dynamic assessment to assess children's phonemic awareness. In her study, children who could not segment a word into separate phonemes received a set of cues (Spector, 1992). These cues included pronouncing the target word slowly, asking the child to identify the first sound in the word; cueing the child with the number of sounds in the word; modeling segmentation using Elkonin boxes, and using Elkonin boxes jointly with a child while segmenting a word. The score the child received on this assessment reflected the number of prompts and the level of support each prompt provided. For example, saying a word slowly to a child requires less assistance from an adult than working with a child to move counters into Elkonin boxes. Spector found that the children's scores obtained as a result of the dynamic assessment procedure were a better predictor of their future reading progress than traditional static assessments, in which children were tested without an adult's assistance.

Abbot, Reed, Abbott, and Berninger (1997) investigated the use of dynamic assessments of reading and writing on later development and whether the approach yielded information that was useful in identifying children with language disorders. Gillam, Pena, and Miller (1999) used dynamic assessment to evaluate children's narrative and expository discourse abilities. Gindis and Karpov (2000) proposed the use of dynamic assessment for cross-domain problem solving. Kozulin and Garb (2002) developed a dynamic assessment of text comprehension.

Most of the studies that used the dynamic assessment methodology yielded results consistent with Vygotsky's claim that for an accurate and predictive assessment of child development, two measures are needed: one of a child's independent performance and one of his assisted performance. However, the further development of dynamic assessment measures and their application in various areas of development presents a significant challenge because of the very nature of this approach (Grigorenko & Sternberg, 1998).

One challenge is the compatibility of its results with the results of more traditional static assessments. Another is standardizing the testing procedures when the type of assistance provided varies significantly between the subjects as well as between the testers. Additionally, it is not clear whether dynamic assessment procedures measure various domain-specific processes such as how a child learns to carry in addition or spell with silent letters, or whether they measure a single characteristic that reflects a learner's ability to benefit from adult assistance that is domain-independent. Russian special educators use the term "obuchaemost" [*educability*] to describe this domain-independent characteristic; Feuerstein uses the term *cognitive modifiability*.

While these issues remain unresolved, there will continue to be a relatively slow increase in the development of new dynamic assessment instruments for educational testing purposes, even though the idea of process-oriented or assisted testing has gained recognition among educators. This new recognition can be attributed both to the growing dissatisfaction with traditional assessment methodology, especially when used with young children (see, e.g., Shepard, 2000) and to the realization that these static tests are not compatible with the increasingly popular instructional philosophies of active learning and construction of knowledge.

Up until this point, we have been discussing the use of dynamic assessment as a formal assessment. The common feature of formal assessments in that they use the same assessment protocol with every child and the prompts and cues used are prescribed ahead of time and are also the same for all children. Now we turn to dynamic assessment as it would be used in a classroom by a teacher as an informal assessment. Everyday decisions are made with informal information about a child. In informal dynamic assessment, the teacher tries out different levels of support to find out if the support moves the child forward in his learning. The conditions for the assessment may vary from child to child or from day to day. This lack of standardization is not important for day-to-day decisions that will be revisited often and for which actual performance relative to other children is not an issue.

In informal dynamic assessment, the emphasis is on finding the type of support that works for a child at this particular time. The teacher may try several approaches, trying to figure out what works the best. The following examples are of a child's attempts to write his name and the teacher's scaffolding support, based on the use of informal dynamic assessment.

Example of Dynamic Assessment in the Classroom

Asking a child to write his or her name is a common procedure often used by preschool and kindergarten teachers to quickly assess several literacy-related competencies in a young child. The first letters that young children are able to identify are in their names. Adding a dynamic component to this procedure allows teachers to assess these competencies more accurately and to be more effective in planning individualized instruction.

To conduct a dynamic assessment, it is necessary to have a developmental sequence that helps the teacher identify which critical elements to assess and that provides a framework for subsequent scaffolding. There have been a number of descriptions of the development of name writing in young children. Generally, these descriptions follow this sequence:

- The child can find his/her name given an array of names.
- The child scribbles or draws, and these marks are labeled as the child's name.

- The child makes a distinguishable set of marks that are labeled as *my name*.
- The child makes marks that resemble letters (letter-like forms).
- The name is distinct and some of letters are interspersed with letter-like forms.
- Several letters may represent the name. These may be formed correctly within the name but with some letters backwards or in a mirror image.
- All of the letters of the name are represented. Most are formed correctly. There may be letters that are backwards or in a mirror image.
- All of the letters of the name are represented and formed correctly.

The hints and cues used in scaffolding a higher level of name writing involve imitation and the use of Vygotskian tactics: mediation (the use of an example letter or colored pen to draw attention to specific elements of the letter), private speech (using words like *down-up-down-up* to describe the motor action of making a *W*) and shared activity (as when the teacher physically guides the child's hand or has him write only some of the letters of the name).

The following is an example of dynamic assessment in a preschool classroom:

Anthony: Assessment 1.   The teacher asks Anthony to write his name. He produces the following without support. This represents his independent level of performance. The teacher asks if this is his name and he says, "Yes."

The teacher shows Anthony a group of name tags with his classmates' names written on them. He is able to find his name when none of the other names begin with *A*. The teacher notices that he becomes confused between Anthony and Aaron.

The teacher places the child's name tag in front of him and encourages him to attempt a letter. She models how to write an *A*, saying "Down-Down-Across" to give him private speech to help him. He does not respond. The teacher places her hand over his and helps him to form the letter *A* and say "Down-Down-Across" as they jointly make the letter. She lets go of his hand and he makes the *A* on his paper as he says, "Down-Down-Across." The following is what he produced on his own after the teacher's support.

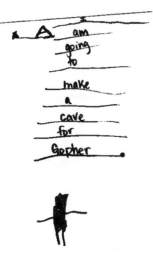

As you can see from these examples, assessing Anthony while providing him assistance reveals a higher level of writing than the assessment of his individual performance. Anthony's responsiveness to the teacher's help shows that while his ability to form letters is still "on the edge of emergence," his ability to control a writing instrument and his ability to follow directions is at the point where he can benefit from the teacher's modeling.

Anthony: Assessment 2.   Several weeks later Anthony attempts his name on his own. Only some of the letters are present, the name is backwards, and, although the letters are correct, they are in reverse order and written from right to left.

The teacher points out where he should start writing and places a dot under the spot. On the name tag, she places a dot with an arrow showing the direction of writing.

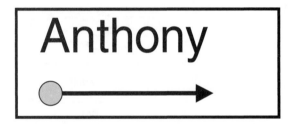

Verbally, she walks him through the process by saying, "Start your name here at the green dot." She does this once and then waits to see what he will write. He starts to write the letters he knows in the right order starting with the A on the left. He hesitates on the *n*, and she talks him through the act of writing it. The following is his writing after scaffolding.

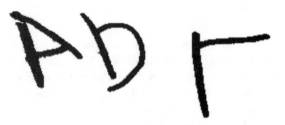

After comparing Anthony's writing with and without the model, the teacher realizes that Anthony needs help with the directionality of his writing and with the formation of certain letters. She starts bringing out his name card each time he writes his name. During the next few weeks, she makes sure that his papers are marked with a line with a dot underneath it where his name should go.

Anthony: Assessment 3.   Several weeks have passed since the last dynamic assessment. The teacher watches Anthony write his name. He now has learned to include most of the seven letters of his name. He writes five of them. Four of the letters are formed correctly. The *y* is not correct.

The teacher decides that it is more important for him to write his whole name all the way through than to form every letter correctly. She modifies the name tag she has given him earlier, removing the previous supports and underlining the letters he misses.

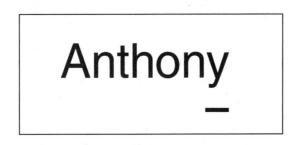

The teacher points out the missing letters and encourages Anthony to remember to write them. The following shows the effects of these scaffolds. He writes the other letters, but writes too many.

Next, the teacher places the name tag right above Anthony's name and shows him that there has to be a one-to-one match between his letters and the letters on his name tag. She also encourages him to look carefully at the *y*, pointing out that it has its arms in the air.

After these prompts, he produces the following:

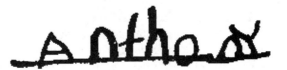

In subsequent weeks, as Anthony seems to need the name tag mediator card less and less, the teacher encourages him to write his name without the use of the card. Within two weeks of that assessment, Anthony can write his name without any support either from the teacher or from a mediator.

The teacher's supports were tailored to Anthony's individual needs. She would not provide the same supports to other children who started out in different places from Anthony, although the strategies used might overlap.

These examples of dynamic assessment are not done in one sitting. The teacher allows the children time to practice on their own and to absorb the support given to them.

Dynamic Assessment: A Tool for Instruction

Dynamic assessment provides the teacher with another tool to help make decisions on how to support children's learning. The teacher discovers which hints and cues make sense and seem to help a particular child. These supports are used whenever the child needs them. Once the child can perform the task without a specific support, another dynamic assessment occurs to determine what other support is needed. If the child can now perform well without support, the teacher removes supports completely.

It is important to keep in mind that the direct assistance provided by an adult is not the only kind of instructional assistance that can be used in dynamic assessment and subsequent instruction. Other kinds of assistance include such tools as external mediators, private speech, or writing, as well as various supportive social contexts like pretend play for preschool- and kindergarten-aged children. For example, the knowledge that a child only uses two-word sentences when talking to an adult but uses more mature grammatical structures when role-playing is helpful in determining effective ways of supporting a child's language development.

It is also important to remember that if dynamic assessment is designed and administered appropriately to facilitate instruction, the child should not be expected to perform the task perfectly until he has achieved complete mastery of it. In fact, perfection on a task in the dynamic assessment situation would mean that there is nothing in this assessment to inform instruction—the child has already mastered the task. Dynamic assessment is most informative in situations where there are tasks that a child can perform independently, harder tasks that require moderate assistance, and finally the most challenging tasks that the child can perform only when maximum assistance is provided. It is the performance on these challenging tasks that helps teachers determine the child's ZPD and individualize instruction to fit his zone.

Finally, the concept of dynamic assessment can provide teachers with an alternative format to frame their communication with parents. Instead of sending home letter grades or their verbal equivalents such as "mastered" or "needs improvement," a teacher can describe the child's progress in terms of "independent performance," "performing with moderate assistance," or "performing with maximum assistance" on a set of skills. These descriptions are appropriate for a wide variety of tasks, from following directions to solving word problems. Such language refocuses the dialogue with parents from an emphasis on a student's accomplishments and shortcomings to the establishment of continuity between the classroom and the home to provide the level of assistance the student needs to move forward.

For Further Reading

Gindis, B., & Karpov, Y. V. (2000). Dynamic assessment of the level of internalization of elementary school children's problem-solving activity. In C. S. Lidz & J. G. Elliot (Eds.), *Dynamic assessment: Prevailing models and applications.* Amsterdam, Netherlands: JAI, Elsevier Science.

Grigorenko, E. L., & Sternberg, R. J. (1998). Dynamic testing. *Psychological Bulletin, 124,* 75–111.

Lidz, C. S., & Gindis, B. (2003). Dynamic assessment of the evolving cognitive functions in children. In A. Kozulin, B. Gindis, V. S. Ageyev, & S. M. Miller (Eds.), *Vygotsky's educational theory in cultural context.* Cambridge, UK: Cambridge University Press.

Tzuriel, D. (2001). *Dynamic assessment of young children.* New York: Kluwer Academic/Plenum Publishers.

Epilogue

Eleven years have passed since the publication of the first edition of *Tools of the Mind,* and many changes have occurred in early childhood education. Vygotsky's ideas are now commonplace in developmental and educational psychology textbooks, and many programs now use his ideas as the basis for innovation. The Vygotskian approach continues to inspire teachers and to provide explanations for their practice. It provides teachers with a new way of looking at their role in leading their students' learning and development while encouraging the students to be active participants in the educational dialogue. The idea of scaffolding has become very popular among educators at all grade levels, signaling an increased emphasis on designing strategies to help students' perform at the highest levels of their Zone of Proximal Development. Some of the strategies now used in early childhood classrooms across the United States and abroad can be directly traced to their Vygotskian roots (e.g., Elkonin boxes). Others are based on more general ideas coming from the Vygotskian tradition.

One of the main strengths of the Vygotskian approach continues to be its emphasis on the underlying cognitive skills that parents and teachers are concerned about: self-regulation, deliberate memory, and focused attention. Many teachers have noted how changing these skills can have a radical effect on a child's entire outlook on school. As children gain in self-regulation—or in Vygotsky's words become "masters of their own behavior"—they begin to show great progress in academic tasks, improved social skills, and a more positive attitude toward school. Moreover, increased levels of deliberateness and intentionality resulting from children's use of the *tools of the mind* result in changes in brain functioning. This was discovered by Vygotsky and Luria in their pioneering research and is now being confirmed using modern methods of neurophysiology.

Another hallmark of the Vygotskian approach to early childhood education is its emphasis on play as the leading activity for preschool- and kindergarten-aged children. At a time when many are saying that play is no longer necessary and is in fact a waste of children's time, Vygotsky provides a rationale for retaining play's central role in the early childhood curriculum. More important, his approach and the work of his students and colleagues provide a clear way to help teachers strengthen play's contribution to childhood.

Vygotsky's work provides a way for teachers to guide and scaffold development while keeping a child-centered approach in the classroom. His work makes clear a role for the teacher that is central to the teaching process but still makes individualization possible. The difficult balancing act that teachers endeavor to maintain now has a set of principles that make that balance possible.

We have expanded the book's scope in reaction to the growing interest in the approach and the questions that we have encountered since the book's publication in 1996. We hope that this new edition will encourage even greater use of Vygotsky's ideas and will spur more research and innovative exploration of the aspects of child development that were the life's work of Vygotsky and his students.

Glossary

This glossary contains words that are referred to frequently in the text and that have different meanings in the Vygotskian framework than in general usage.

Amplification A technique for assisting behaviors on the edge of emergence using the tools and assisted performance within the child's ZPD; the opposite of acceleration, or pushing the child too fast.

Animation complex ("kompleks ozhivleviia") A complex reaction of babies to the appearance of a familiar adult that includes smiling, gesturing, and vocalizing.

Appropriation of knowledge The stage when the child has internalized or learned certain information or concepts and can use that knowledge independently.

Automatization A process by which a concept, skill, strategy, or action becomes internalized to the degree that its performance is seamless and its initial components are no longer discernable.

Complex A set of undifferentiated attributes used to categorize objects. For example, a child might use the complex "big-round-red" to understand "ball." Complexes exist before the development of concepts.

Control action A process students use to compare the outcome of their learning actions with a specific set of standards.

Cultural-Historical Theory The name given to the Vygotskian approach that emphasizes the cultural context of learning and development, and the history of the human mind.

Deliberate memory When children can remember on purpose, using memory strategies and mediators, they have deliberate memory. They no longer require many reminders from the environment but make the mental effort necessary to remember.

Developmental accomplishments The new cognitive and emotional formations that appear at different ages.

Director's play Play in which children play with pretend playmates or direct and act out a scene with toys without anyone else present.

Distributed Shared or existing between two or more people.

Double stimulation (microgenetic method) A research method in which the child is taught something new through the use of mental tools (e.g., symbols, categories). The researcher notes both what the child is able to learn and how the tools are being learned.

Dynamic assessment A classroom assessment technique that measures both the upper and lower levels of the ZPD.

Educational dialogue The exchange that occurs when the teacher sensitively guides the discussion and the child explains her understanding of the information; similar to the Socratic dialogue.

Emotional communication The emotional dialogue between the infant and the primary caregiver; the leading activity of infancy.

Enquiry motivation Intellectual curiosity that motivates children to learn on their own.

Errorless learning Learning that results from the use of Gal'perin's Step-by-Step Formation method. Errors avoided by the use of this method are the ones caused students' inability to focus on the essential properties of the problem or their internalization of ineffective strategies.

Everyday concepts Concepts based on intuitions and everyday experience. They do not have strict definitions nor are they integrated into a broader structure.

Focused attention The ability to attend deliberately and to ignore distractions.

Formal instruction School instruction in which information is taught in a prescribed way in a context often removed from the everyday tasks.

Games A type of play in which the rules are explicit and roles are implicit; most typical of children starting at age 6 and 7.

Higher mental functions Cognitive processes unique to humans and acquired through learning and teaching. They are deliberate, mediated, internalized behaviors built upon lower mental functions. Examples are mediated perception, focused attention, deliberate memory, self-regulation, and other metacognitive processes.

Informal instruction Instruction given in an informal setting or an apprenticeship.

Inner speech Speech that is totally internal, inaudible, self-directed, but retains some of the characteristics of external speech. People use inner speech to talk to themselves, hearing the words but not saying them aloud.

Instrumental activity Using objects as tools or instruments.

Internalization The process of appropriation or learning to the point at which the tools used are mental and their use is not visible to others.

Interpersonal (interindividual, inter-mental shared) Describing the stage of using mental tools with others or sharing the mental tools with others.

Intrapersonal (individual, intra-mental) Describing the stage when mental tools have been internalized and are used independently.

Leading activity A specific type of interaction between the child and the social environment that is most beneficial for the emergence of developmental accomplishments.

Learning actions The actions students use to solve learning tasks. Examples of learning actions include framing the problem, general and specific strategies of solving the problem, monitoring, evaluating the results, and self-correction.

Learning activity Adult-guided activity around specific, structured, formalized content that is culturally determined; the leading activity of the primary grades. Learning activity is found in schools where children begin to acquire basic literacies, such as concepts in math, science, and history; images in art and literature; and the rules of grammar.

Learning task A special kind of problem used in the context of formal instruction. When students engage in solving learning tasks, they acquire general strategies that they can apply to a broader range of problems.

Level of assisted performance Behaviors that the child can perform with the help of or through interacting with another person, either an adult or peer. Assistance can be direct or indirect, such as choosing a book or materials.

Level of independent performance Behaviors that the child can perform alone and without help; the lowest level of the ZPD.

Lower mental functions Cognitive processes common to both higher animals and human beings that depend primarily on maturation to develop. Examples are sensations, reactive attention, spontaneous memory, and sensorimotor intelligence.

Material[ized] action One of the beginning steps in Gal'perin's Step-by-Step Formation method. Students must engage in physical actions aimed at an actual (material) object or its materialized representation, such as schema or picture, to develop desired mental actions.

Maximally assisted performance Behaviors the child can perform with the most help or assistance from the social context; the highest level of the ZPD. These behaviors will become what the child can do independently at a later time.

Mediation The use of an object or symbol to represent a specific behavior or another object in the environment. For example, the word *red* mediates the perception of colors.

Mediator Something that stands as an intermediary between the child and the environment and that facilitates a particular behavior. A mediator becomes a mental tool when the child incorporates it into her own activity. Examples are a string around a finger, a list, a rhyme, and a clock face.

Mental tools Internalized tools that extend mental abilities, helping us to remember, attend, and solve problems. Mental tools are different in each culture and are taught to succeeding generations. They help the child master his own behavior. Examples are language and mediators.

Microgenetic Characteristic of the development (genesis) of a skill or a concept, over a relatively short period of time. Post-Vygotskians expanded the scope of the cultural-historical theory to add microgenetic studies to the phylogenetic and ontogenetic ones.

Nonpragmatic curiosity Interest that exists although there may be no tangible or practical payoff; similar to intrinsic motivation.

Object-oriented play Play that focuses on objects in which the roles and social interaction are secondary.

Ontogeny (or ontogenesis) The origin and development of an individual human being through the lifespan. Ontogenesis of higher mental functions is a part of Vygotsky's Cultural-Historical Theory.

Orienting Basis of Action (OBA) The first step in Gal'perin's Step-by-Step Formation method. OBA is the identification of the critical basis or central principle that enables a student to make sense of the learning experience.

Other-regulation The state in which the child regulates other people or is regulated by other people; the opposite of self-regulation.

Phylogeny (or phylogenesis) The evolutionary development and history of a species. Philogenesis of higher mental functions is a part of Vygotsky's Cultural-Historical Theory.

Play Interaction that involves explicit roles and implicit rules; the leading activity for preschoolers and kindergartners.

Private speech Self-directed speech that is not intended for communication to others. Private speech is turned inward to self and has a self-regulatory function.

Productive activities Activities that involve some tangible outcome such as storytelling, drawing, or block building. These are different from make-believe play that focuses on the process and not the product.

Public speech Language directed at others that has a social, communicative function. Public speech is spoken aloud and directs or communicates to others.

Repeated errors Errors that are not developmental or part of the learning process. These types of errors are often recognized by the learner as mistakes, but the learner cannot seem to stop repeating them. Repeated errors tend to persist in spite of efforts to correct them. They are often the result of having automatized an action incorrectly.

Scaffolding The process of providing, and gradually removing, external support for learning. During scaffolding, the task itself is not changed, but what the learner initially does is made easier with assistance. As the learner takes more responsibility for performance of the task, less assistance is provided.

Scientific concepts Concepts taught within a discipline that has its own logical structure and vocabulary.

Self-regulation The state in which the child is able to regulate or master his own behavior; the opposite of other-regulation. The child can plan, monitor, evaluate, and choose his own behavior.

Sensorimotor concepts A specific schema for interacting with an object based on senses and motor actions.

Sensory standard Representations corresponding to socially elaborated patterns of sensory characteristics of objects that allow for more accurate discrimination between these characteristics. "Sea green" or "pumpkin orange" are examples of sensory standards for color and "citrusy" or "woodsy" are sensory standards for smell.

Shared Existing between two or more people.

Social context Everything in the child's environment that has either been directly or indirectly influenced by the culture. This includes people (e.g., parents, teachers, peers) and materials (e.g., books, videos).

Socially mediated Influenced by present and past social interactions. Interaction with the environment is always mediated by others.

Socially oriented play Play that focuses on roles and rules.

Socially shared cognition Mental processes, such as memory and attention, that are shared or exist between two or more people.

Social situation of development The social context and the way the child interacts to this context.

Step-by-Step Formation Name given to Gal'perin's method aimed at assisting students in developing new mental actions. Teaching children how to internalize external knowledge using physical actions.

Symbolic function The use of objects, actions, words, and people to stand for something else. Examples are using a pencil as a spaceship or a book as a bed for a doll.

Symbolic substitution Using one object to stand for another in make-believe play.

Theoretical reasoning Reasoning that is not aimed at solving a specific practical problem but that focuses instead on revealing essential patterns, principles, and relationships. It requires discovery of the essential properties of a concept, which are mainly inferred and not observable.

Verbal thinking A type of thinking that is more distilled than inner speech and is what Vygotsky called "folded." When thinking is folded, you can think of several things simultaneously and may not be conscious of all that you are thinking.

Zone of Proximal Development (ZPD) Those behaviors that are on the edge of emergence. It is defined by two levels. The lowest level is what the child can do independently and the highest level is what the child can do with maximum assistance.

References

The names of the Russian authors in this reference list have been romanized in a number of different ways. We have used the most common spelling; alternative spellings are provided below.

Common	*Alternative*
Vygotsky	Vygotski, Vigotsky, Vygotskij
Luria	Lurija, Lur'ia
Elkonin	El'konin
Gal'perin	Galperin
Leont'ev	Leontjev

Abbot, S., Reed, E., Abbot, R., & Berninger, V. (1997). Year-long balanced reading/writing tutorial: A design experiment used for dynamic assessment. *Learning Disability Quarterly, 20*(3), 249–263.

Arievitch, I. M., & Stetsenko, A. (2000). The quality of cultural tools and cognitive development: Gal'perin's perspective and its implications. *Human Development, 43,* 69–92.

Atkinson, R. C., & Shiffrin, R. M. (1968). Human memory: A proposed system and its control processes. In K. W. Spence & J. T. Spence (Eds.), *Advances in the psychology of learning and motivation* (Vol. 2, pp. 90–195). New York: Academic Press.

Beilin, H. (1994). Jean Piaget's enduring contribution to developmental psychology. In R. D. Parke, P. A. Ornstein, J. J. Reiser, & C. Zahn-Waxler (Eds.), *A century of developmental psychology* (pp. 333–356). Washington, DC: American Psychological Association.

Berk, L. E. (1994). Vygotsky's theory: The importance of make-believe play. *Young Children, 50*(1), 30–39.

Berlyand, I., & Kurganov, S. (1993). *Matematika v shkole dialoga kul'tur* [Mathematics in the school "Cultural Dialog"]. Kemerovo, Russia: ALEF.

Blair, C. (2002). School readiness: Integrating cognition and emotion in a neurobiological conceptualization of children's functioning at school entry. *American Psychologist, 57*(2), 111–127.

Bodrova, E. (2003). Vygotsky and Montessori: One dream, two visions. *Montessori Life, 15*(1), 30–33.

Bodrova, E., & Leong, D. J. (1995). Scaffolding the writing process: The Vygotskian approach. *Colorado Reading Council Journal, 6,* 27–29.

Bodrova, E., & Leong, D. J. (1998). Scaffolding emergent writing in the zone of proximal development. *Literacy Teaching and Learning, 3*(2), 1–18.

Bodrova, E., & Leong, D. J. (2001). *The tools of the mind project: A case study of implementing the Vygotskian approach in American early childhood and primary classrooms.* Geneva, Switzerland: International Bureau of Education, UNESCO.

Bodrova, E., & Leong, D. J. (2003a). Chopsticks and counting chips: Do play and foundational skills need to compete for the teacher's attention in an early childhood classroom? *Young Children, 58*(3), 10–17.

Bodrova, E., & Leong, D. J. (2003b). Learning and development of preschool children from the Vygotskian perspective. In A. Kozulin, B. Gindis, V. Ageyev, & S. Miller (Eds.), *Vygotsky's educational theory in cultural context* (pp. 156–176). NY: Cambridge University Press.

Bodrova, E., & Leong, D. J. (2005). Vygotskian perspectives on teaching and learning early literacy. In D. Dickinson & S. Neuman (Eds.), *Handbook of early literacy research* (Vol. 2). New York: Guilford Publications.

Bodrova, E., Leong, D. J., Paynter, D. E., & Hensen, R. (2001). *Scaffolding literacy development in a preschool classroom.* Aurora, CO: McREL.

Bodrova, E., Leong, D. J., Paynter, D. E., & Hughes, C. (2001). *Scaffolding literacy development in a kindergarten classroom.* Aurora, CO: McREL. Communication and cognition: Vygotskian perspectives (pp. 21–34). Cambridge: Cambridge University Press.

Bogoyavlenskaya, D. B. (1983). *Intellektual'naya aktivnost kakkk problema tvorchestva* [Intellectual activity and creativity]. Rostov: Rostov University Publishers.

Bowlby, J. (1969). *Attachment and loss: Vol. I. Attachment.* New York: Basic Books.

Bretherton, I. (1992). The origins of attachment theory: John Bowlby and Mary Ainsworth. *Developmental Psychology, 28,* 759–775.

Brofman, V. (1993). Ob oposredovannom reshenii poznavatel'nykh zadach [Mediated problem solving]. *Voprosy Psychologii, 5,* 30–35.

Bronfenbrenner, U. (1997). Toward an experimental ecology of human development. *American Psychologist, 32,* 513–531.

Bruner, J. S. (1968). *Process of cognitive growth: Infancy.* Worcester, MA: Clark University Press.

Bruner, J. S. (1973). *The relevance of education.* New York: Norton.

Bruner, J. S. (1983). Vygotsky's zone of proximal development: The hidden agenda. *New Directions for Child Development, 23,* 93–97.

Bruner, J. S. (1985). Vygotsky: A historical and conceptual perspective. In J. Wertsch (Ed.), *Culture, communication and cognition: Vygotskian perspectives* (pp. 21–34). Cambridge: Cambridge University Press.

Campione, J. C., & Brown, A. L. (1990). Guided learning and transfer. In N. Fredriksen, R. Glaser, A. Lesgold, & M. Shafto (Eds.), *Diagnostic monitoring of skill and knowledge acquisition* (pp. 141–172). Hillsdale, NJ: Erlbaum.

Carlton, M. P., & Winsler, A. (1999). School readiness: The need for a paradigm shift. *School Psychology Review, 28*(3), 338.

Cazden, C. B. (1981). Performance before competence: Assistance to child discourse in the zone of proximal development. *Quarterly Newsletter of the Laboratory of Comparative Human Cognition, 3,* 5–8.

Cazden, C. B. (1993). Vygotsky, Hymes, and Bakhtin: From word to utterance to voice. In E. A. Formar, N. Minick, & C. A. Stone (Eds.), *Contexts for learning: Sociocultural dynamics in children's development* (pp. 197–212). New York: Oxford University Press.

Ceci, S. J. (1991). How much does schooling influence general intelligence and its cognitive components? A reassessment of the evidence. *Developmental Psychology, 27*(5), 703–722.

Chaiklin, S. (2003). The zone of proximal development in Vygotsky's analysis of learning and instruction. In A. Kozulin, B. Gindis, V. Ageyev, & S. Miller (Eds.), *Vygotsky's educational theory in cultural context.* New York: Cambridge University Press.

Clay, M. (1993). *Reading recovery: A guidebook for teachers in training.* Portsmouth, NH: Heinemann.

Cole, M. (Ed.). (1989). *Sotsialno-istoricheskii podkhod v obuchenii* [A social-historical approach to learning]. Moscow: Pedagogika.

Cole, M. (2005). Cross-cultural and historical perspectives on the developmental consequences of education. *Human Development, 48,* 195–216.

Cole, M., & Scribner, S. (1973). Cognitive consequences of formal and informal education. *Science, 182,* 553–559.

Cole, M., & Wertsch, J. (2002). *Beyond the individual–social antimony in discussions of Piaget and Vygotsky.* Retrieved January 8, 2006, from http://www.massey.ac.nz/~alock/virtual/colevyg.htm.

Copple, C., & Bredekamp, S. (2005). *Basics of developmentally appropriate practice: An introduction for teachers of children 3–6.* Washington, DC: National Association for the Education of Young Children.

D'Ailly, Hsiao, H. (1992). Asian mathematics superiority: A search for explanations. *Educational Psychologist, 27*(2), 243–261.

Davydov, V. V. (1988). Problems of developmental teaching: The experience of theoretical and experimental psychological research. *Soviet Education, 30,* 66–79. (Original work published in 1989)

Davydov, V. V. (Ed.). (1991). *Psychological abilities of primary school children in learning mathematics: Vol. 6. Soviet studies in mathematics education* (J. Teller, Trans.). Reston, VA: National Council of Teachers of Mathematics. (Original work published in 1969)

Davydov, V. V., & Markova, A. K. (1983). A concept of educational activity for school children. *Journal of Soviet Psychology, 21*(2), 50–76. (Original work published in 1981)

Davydov, V. V., Sloboduchikov, V. I., & Tsukerman, G. A. (2003). The elementary school student as an agent of learning activity. *Journal of Russian & East European Psychology, 41*(5), 63–76.

DeVries, R. (1997). Piaget's social theory. *Educational Researcher, 26*(2), 4–16.

DeVries, R. (2000). Vygotsky, Piaget, and education: A reciprocal assimilation of theories and educational practices. *New Ideas in Psychology, 18*(2–3), 187–213.

Dyachenko, O. M. (1996). *Razvitie voobrazheniya doshkol'nika.* Moscow: PIRAO.

Edwards, C., Gandini, L., & Forman, G. (1994). *Hundred languages of children: The Reggio Emilia approach to early childhood education.* Chicago: Teachers College Press.

Elkonin, D. (1969). Some results of the study of the psychological development of preschool-age children. In M. Cole & I. Maltzman (Eds.), *A handbook of contemporary Soviet psychology.* New York: Basic Books.

Elkonin, D. (1972). Toward the problem of stages in the mental development of the child. *Soviet Psychology, 10,* 225–251.

Elkonin, D. (1977). Toward the problem of stages in the mental development of the child. In M. Cole (Ed.), *Soviet developmental psychology.* White Plains, NY: M. E. Sharpe. (Original work published in 1971)

Elkonin, D. (1978). *Psikhologija igry* [The psychology of play.] Moscow: Pedagogika.

Elkonin, D. (1989). *Izbrannye psychologicheskie trudy* [Selected psychological works]. Moscow: Pedagogika.

Elkonin, D. B. (2001a). O structure uchebnoy deyatel'nosti [On the structure of learning activity]. In *Psichicheskoe razvitie v detskikh vozrastah* [Child development across ages] (pp. 285–295). Moscow: Modek.

Elkonin, D. B. (2001b). Psychologiya obucheniya mladshego shkol'nika [Psychology of education in primary grades]. In *Psichicheskoe razvitie v detskikh vozrastah* [Child development across ages] (pp. 239–284). Moscow: Modek.

Elkonin, D. B. (2005). Chapter 1: The subject of our research: The developed form of play. *Journal of Russian & East European Psychology, 43*(1), 22–48.

Elkonin, D. B. (2005). Chapter 3: Theories of play. *Journal of Russian & East European Psychology, 43*(2), 3–89.

Elkonin, D. B. (2005). The psychology of play: Preface. *Journal of Russian and East European Psychology, 43*(1), pp. 11–21. (Original work published in 1978)

Elkonin, D. B., & Venger, A. L. (Eds.). (1988). *Osobennosti psychicheskogo razvitiya detey 6–7-letnego vozrasta* [Development of 6- and 7-year-olds: Psychological characteristics]. Moscow: Pedagogika.

Erikson, E. E. (1963). *Childhood and society* (2nd ed.). New York: Norton.

Erikson, E. E. (1977). *Toys and reasons.* New York: Norton.

Ferreiro, E., & Teberosky, A. (1982). *Literacy before schooling.* Exeter, NH: Heinemann Educational Books.

Feuerstein, R., & Feuerstein, S. (1991). Mediated learning experience: A theoretical review. In R. Feuerstein, P. S. Klein, & A. J. Tannenbaum (Eds.), *Mediated learning experience (MLE): Theoretical, psychological and learning implications.* London: Freund.

Feuerstein, R., Feuerstein, R., & Gross, S. (1997). The learning potential assessment device. In D. P. Flanagan, J. L. Genshaft, & P. Harrison (Eds.), *Contemporary intellectual assessment theories, tests, and issues* (pp. 297–313). New York: Guilford Press.

Feuerstein, R., Rand, Y., & Hoffman, M. (1979). *The dynamic assessment of retarded performers: The learning potential assessment device (LPAD).* Baltimore, MD: University Park Press.

Flavell, J. (1979). Metacognition and cognitive monitoring: New area of cognitive-developmental inquiry. *American Psychologist, 34,* 906–911.

Fletcher, K. L., & Bray, N. W. (1997). Instructional and contextual effects on external memory strategy use in young children. *Journal of Experimental Child Psychology, 67*(2), 204–222.

Frankel, K., & Bates, J. (1990). Mother-toddler problem solving: Antecedents in attachment, home behavior, and temperament. *Child Development, 61,* 810–819.

Frawley, W. (1997). *Vygotsky and cognitive science: Language and the unification of the social and computational mind.* Cambridge: Harvard University Press.

Freud, A. (1966). Introduction to the technique of child analysis. In *The writings of Anna Freud* (Vol. 1, p. 3069). New York: International Universities Press. (Original work published as *Four lectures on child analysis,* 1927)

Gallimore, R., & Tharp, R. (1990). Teaching mind in society: Teaching, schooling, and literate discourse. In L. Moll (Ed.), *Vygotsky and education: Instructional implications and applications of sociohistorical psychology* (pp. 175–205). Cambridge: Cambridge University Press.

Gal'perin, P. Y. (1959). Razvitie issledovaniy po formirovaniyu umstvennykh dey'stviy [Progress in research on the formation of mental acts]. In *Psickhologicheskaya nauka v SSSR* [Psychological science in the USSR] (Vol. 1, pp. 441–469). Moscow: APN RSFSR.

Gal'perin, P. Y. (1969). Stages of development of mental acts. In M. Cole & I. Maltzman (Eds.), *A handbook of contemporary soviet psychology.* New York: Basic Books.

Gal'perin, P. Y. (1992a). Organization of mental activity and the effectiveness of learning. *Journal of Russian and East European Psychology, 30*(4), 65–82. (Original work published in 1974)

Gal'perin, P. Y. (1992b). The problem of attention. *Journal of Russian and East European Psychology, 30*(4), 65–91. (Original work published in 1976)

Garvey, C. (1986). Peer relations and the growth of communication. In E. C. Mueller & C. R. Cooper (Eds.), *Process and outcome in peer relationships* (pp. 329–344). San Diego, CA: Academic Press.

Gellatly, A. R. H. (1987). Acquisition of a concept of logical necessity. *Human Development, 30,* 32–47.

Gerber, M., & Johnson, A. (1998). *Your self-confident baby: How to encourage your child's natural abilities—from the very start.* New York: John Wiley & Sons.

Gillam, R. B., Pena, E. D., & Miller, L. (1999). Dynamic assessment of narrative and expository discourse. *Topics in Language Disorders, 20*(1), 33–37.

Gindis, B. (2003). Remediation through education: Socio/cultural theory and children with special needs. In A. Kozulin, B. Gindis, V. S. Ageyev, & S. M. Miller (Eds.), *Vygotsky's educational theory in cultural context* (pp. 200–222). New York: Cambridge University Press.

Gindis, B. (2005). Cognitive, language, and educational issues of children adopted from overseas orphanages. *Journal of Cognitive Education and Psychology, 4*(3), 290–315.

Gindis, B., & Karpov, Y. V. (2000). Dynamic assessment of the level of internalization of elementary school children's problem-solving activity. In C. S. Lidz & J. G. Elliot (Eds.),

Dynamic assessment: Prevailing models and applications. Amsterdam, Netherlands: JAI, Elsevier Science.

Ginsberg, H. P., & Opper, S. (1988). *Piaget's theory of intellectual development* (3rd ed.) Englewood Cliffs, NJ: Prentice Hall.

Grigorenko, E. L., & Sternberg, R. J. (1998). Dynamic testing. *Psychological Bulletin, 124,* 75–111.

Grossman K. E., & Grossman, K. (1990). The wider concept of attachment in cross-cultural research. *Human Development, 13,* 31–47.

Guthke, J., & Wigenfeld, S. (1992). The learning test concept: Origins, state of the art, and trends. In H. C. Haywood & D. Tzuriel (Eds.), *Interactive assessment.* New York: Springer-Verlag.

Horowitz, F. D. (1994). John B. Watson's legacy: Learning and environment. In R. D. Parker, P. A. Ornstein, J. J. Rieser, & C. Zahn-Waxler (Eds.), *A century of developmental psychology.* (pp. 233–252). Washington, DC: American Psychological Association.

Howes, C. (1980). Peer play scale as an index of complexity of peer interaction. *Developmental Psychology, 16,* 371–379.

Howes, C., & Matheson, C. C. (1992). Sequences in the development of competent play with peer: Social and social pretend play. *Developmental Psychology, 16,* 371–379.

Istomina, Z. M. (1977). The development of voluntary memory in preschool-age children. In L. Moll (Ed.), *Soviet developmental psychology.* New York: M. E. Sharpe.

Ivanova, A. Y. (1976). *Obuchaemost kak printsip otsenki ymstvennogo pazvitia u detei* [Educability as a diagnostic method of assessing cognitive development of children]. Moscow: MGU Press.

Ivic, I. (1994). Theories of mental development and assessing educational outcomes. In *Making education count: Developing and using international indicators* (pp. 197–218). Paris: OECD.

Jahoda, G. (1980). Theoretical and systematic approaches in mass-cultural psychology. In H. C. Triandis & W. W. Lambert (Eds.), *Handbook of cross-cultural psychology* (Vol. 1). Boston: Allyn & Bacon.

John-Steiner, V., Panofsky, C., & Blackwell, P. (1990). The development of scientific concepts and discourse. In L. C. Moll (Ed.), *Vygotsky and education: Instructional applications of sociohistorical psychology.* Cambridge, MA: Cambridge University Press.

John-Steiner, V., Panofsky, C. P., & Smith, L. W. (Eds.). (1994). *Sociocultural approaches to language and literacy: An interactionist perspective.* Cambridge: Cambridge University Press.

Johnson, D., & Johnson, R. (1994). *Learning together and alone: Cooperation, competition, and individualization* (4th ed.). Boston: Allyn & Bacon.

Karasavvidis, I. (2002). Distributed cognition and educational practice. *Journal of Interactive Learning Research Special Edition: Distributed Cognition for Learning, Vol 13*(1–2), 11–29.

Karpov, Y. V. (2005). *The neo-Vygotskian approach to child development.* New York: Cambridge University Press.

Karpov, Y. V., & Bransford, J. D. (1995). L. S. Vygotsky and the doctrine of empirical and theoretical reasoning. *Educational Psychologist, 30*(2), 61–66.

Katz, L. G., & Chard, S. C. (1989). *Engaging children's minds: The project approach.* Norwood, NJ: Ablex.

Kozulin, A. (1990). *Vygotsky's psychology: A bibliography of ideas.* Cambridge, MA: Harvard University Press.

Kozulin, A. (1999). Cognitive learning in younger and older immigrant students. *School Psychology International, 20*(2), 177–190.

Kozulin, A., & Garb, E. (2002). Dynamic assessment of EFL text comprehension. *School Psychology International, 23*(1), 112–127.

Kozulin, A., & Presseisen, B. Z. (1995). Mediated learning experience and psychological tools: Vygotsky's and Feuerstein's perspectives in a study of student learning. *Educational Psychologist, 30*(2), 67–76.

Kravtsova, E. E. (1996). Psychologicheskiye novoobrazovaniya doshkol'nogo vozrasta [Psychological new formations during preschool age]. *Voprosy-Psikhologii, 6,* 64–76.

Kukushkina, O. I. (2002). Korrektsionnaya (special'naya) pedagogika [Corrective (special) pedagogy]. *Almanac 5.* http://www.ise.iip/almanah/5/index.html.

Laboratory of Comparative Human Cognition. (1983). Culture and cognitive development. In P. Mussen (Ed.), *Handbook of child psychology: Vol. I. History, theory, and methods.* New York: John Wiley & Sons.

Leont'ev, A. (1978). *Activity, consciousness, and personality.* Englewood Cliffs, NJ: Prentice Hall. (Original work published in 1977).

Leont'ev, A. (1994). The development of voluntary attention in the child. In R. Van der Veer & J. Valsiner (Eds.), *The Vygotsky Reader* (pp. 279–299). Oxford: Blackwell.

Leont'ev, A. N. (1931). *Razvitie pamyati: Experimental'noe issledovanie vysshikh psikhologicheskikh funktsii* [The development of memory: Experimental study of higher mental functions]. Moscow: GUPI.

Leont'ev, A. N. (1981). *Problems in the development of mind.* Moscow: Progress Publishers.

Lidz, C. S., & Gindis, B. (2003). Dynamic assessment of the evolving cognitive functions in children. In A. Kozulin, B. Gindis, V. S. Ageyev, & S. M. Miller (Eds.), *Vygotsky's educational theory in cultural context.* Cambridge, UK: Cambridge University Press.

Lisina, M. I. (1974). Vliyanie obscheniya so vzroslym na razvitie rebenka pervogo polugodiya zhizni [The influence of communication with adults on the development of children during the first six months of life]. In A. V. Zaporozhets & M. I. Lisina (Eds.), *Razvitie obscheniya u doshkolnikov* [The development of communication in preschoolers]. Moscow: Pedagogika.

Lisina, M. I., (1986). *Problemy ontogeneza obscheniya* [Problems of the ontogenesis of communication]. Moscow: Pedagogika.

Lisina, M. I. & Galiguzova, L. N. (1980). Razvitie u rebenka potrebnosti v obschenii so vzroslym i sverstnikami [The development of a child's need for communication with an adult and with peers]. In *Problemy vozrastnoj i pedagogicheskoj psikhologii.* Moscow: NIIOP APM SSSR.

Luria, A.R. (1969). Speech development and the formation of mental processes. In M. Cole & I. Maltzman (Eds), *A handbook of contemporary Soviet psychology* (pp. 121–162). New York: Basic Books.

Luria, A. R. (1973). *Working brain: An introduction to neuropsychology.* New York: Basic Books.

Luria, A. R. (1976). *Cognitive development: Its cultural and social foundations* (M. Lopez-Morillas & L. Solotaroff, Trans.). Cambridge, MA: Harvard University Press.

Luria, A. R. (1979). *The making of mind: A personal account of Soviet psychology.* (M. Cole & S. Cole, Trans.). Cambridge, MA: Harvard University Press.

Luria, A. R. (1983). The development of writing in the child. In M. Martlew (Ed.), *The psychology of written language* (pp. 237–277). New York: John Wiley & Sons.

Matusov, E., & Hayes, R. (2000). Sociocultural critique of Piaget and Vygotsky. *New Ideas in Psychology, 18,* 215–239.

McAfee, O., & Leong, D. J. (2003). *Assessing and guiding young children's development and learning* (3rd ed.). Boston: Allyn & Bacon.

McAfee, O., & Leong, D. J. (2006). *Assessing and guiding young children's development and learning* (4th ed.). Boston: Allyn & Bacon.

Meshcheryakov, A. (1979). *Awakening to life.* Moscow: Progress.

Michailenko, N. Y., & Korotkova, N. A. (2002). *Igra s pravilami v doshkol'nom vosraste* [Playing games with rules in preschool age]. Moscow: Akademicheskii Proekt.

Moll, L. C. (2001). Through the mediation of others: Vygotskian research on teaching. In V. Richardson (Ed.), *Handbook of research on teaching* (4th ed., pp. 111–129). Washington, DC: American Educational Research Association.

Montessori, M. (1912). *The Montessori method.* New York: Frederick A. Stokes Company.

Montessori, M. (1962). *Dr. Montessori's own handbook: A short guide to her ideas and materials.* New York: Schocken Books.

National Council of Teachers of Mathematics (2000). *Principles and standards for school mathematics.* Reston, VA: National Council of Teachers of Mathematics.

Newman D., Griffin P., & Cole, M. (1989). *The construction zone: Working for cognitive change in school.* Cambridge: Cambridge University Press.

Newman F., & Holzman, L. (1993). *Lev Vygotsky: Revolutionary scientist.* New York: Routledge.

Nicholls, J. G. (1978). The development of concepts of effort and ability, perception of academic attainment, and the understanding that difficult tasks require more ability. *Child Development, 49*(3) 800–814.

Novoselova, S. L. (1978). *Razvitie myshleniya v rannem vosraste* [The development of thinking in toddlers]. Moscow: Pedagogika.

Obukhova, L. (1996). *Detskaya psikhologiya* [Child psychology]. Moscow: Rospedagenstvo.

Obukhova, L. (1996). Neokonchennye spory: Gal'perin i Piaget [Unfinished discussions: Gal'perin and Piaget]. *Psikhologicheskaya nauka i obrazovanie, 1.*

Ostrosky-Solis, F., Ramirez, M., & Ardila, A. (2004). Effects of culture and education on neuropsychological testing: A preliminary study with indigenous and nonindigenous population. *Applied Neuropsychology, 11*(4), 186–193.

Palincsar, A. S., Brown, A. L., & Campione, J. C. (1993). First-grade dialogues for knowledge acquisition and use. In E. A. Forman, N. Minick, & C. A. Stone (Eds.), *Contexts for learning: Sociocultural dynamics in children's development* (pp. 43–57). New York: Oxford University Press.

Palincsar, A. S., Brown, A. L., & Martin, S. M. (1987). Peer interaction in reading comprehension instruction. *Educational Psychologist, 22*(3–4), 231.

Paris, S. G., & Winograd P. (1990). How metacognition can promote academic learning and instruction. In B. F. Jones & L. Idol (Eds.), *Dimensions of thinking and cognitive instruction.* Hillsdale, NJ: Lawrence Erlbaum.

Parten, M. B. (1932). Social participation among preschool children. *Journal of Abnormal and Social Psychology, 27,* 243–269.

Perret-Clermont, A-N., Perret, J-F., & Bell, N. (1991). The social construction of meaning and cognitive activity in elementary school children. In L. B. Resnick, J. M. Levine, & S. D. Teasley (Eds.), *Perspectives on socially shared cognition.* (pp. 41–62). Washington, DC: American Psychological Association.

Piaget, J. (1926). *The language and thought of the child* (M. Gabain, Trans.). London: Routledge & Kegan Paul. (Original work published in 1923)

Piaget, J. (1951). *Play, dreams and imitation in childhood.* New York: Norton.

Piaget, J. (1952). *The origins of intelligence in children.* New York: International Universities Press. (Original work published in 1936)

Piaget, J. (1977). The stages of intellectual development in childhood and adolescence. In H. E. Gruber & J. J. Vone'che (Eds.), *The essential Piaget.* New York: Basic Books.

Piaget, J., & Inhelder, B. (1969). *The psychology of the child.* New York: Basic Books.

Pick, H. L. (1980). Perceptual and cognitive development of preschoolers in Soviet psychology. *Contemporary Educational Psychology, 5,* 140–149.

Poddyakov, N. N. (1977). *Myshlenie doshkol'nika* [Preschooler's thought]. Moscow: Pedagogika.

Pressley, M., & Harris, K. R. (In press). Cognitive strategies instruction: From basic research to classroom instruction. In P. A. Alexander & P. Winne (Eds.), *Handbook of educational psychology.* New York: MacMillan.

Rodari, G. (1996). *The grammar of fantasy: An introduction to the art of inventing stories.* New York: Teachers & Writers Collaborative.

Rogoff, B. (1986). Adult assistance of children's learning. In T. E. Raphael (Ed.), *The context of school-based literacy.* New York: Random House.

Rogoff, B. (1990). *Apprenticeship in thinking: Cognitive development in social context.* New York: Oxford University Press.

Rogoff, B. (1991). Social interaction as apprenticeship in thinking: Guided participation in spatial planning. In L. B. Resnick, J. M. Levine, & S. D. Teasley (Eds.), *Perspectives on socially shared cognition* (pp. 349–364). Washington, DC: American Psychological Association.

Rogoff, B., & Lave, J. (Eds.). (1984). *Everyday cognition: Its development in social context.* Cambridge, MA: Harvard University Press.

Rogoff, B., Malkin, C., & Gilbride, K. (1984). Interaction with babies as guidance in development. In B. Rogoff & J. V. Wertsch (Eds.), *Children's Learning in the "Zone of Proximal Development"* (pp. 31–44). San Francisco, CA: Jossey-Bass.

Rogoff, B., Topping, K., Baker-Sennett, J., & Lacasa, P. (2002). Mutual contributions of individuals, partners, and institutions: Planning to remember in Girl Scout cookie sales. *Social Development, 11*(2), 266–289.

Rogoff, B., & Wertsch, J. (Eds.). (1984). *Children's learning in the "zone of proximal development."* San Francisco: Jossey-Bass.

Rubin, K. H. (1980). Fantasy play: Its role in the development of social skills and social cognition. In K. H. Rubin (Ed.), *Children's play* (pp. 69–84). San Francisco: Jossey-Bass.

Rubinshtein, S. Y. (1979). *Psikhologia umstvenno otstalogo snkolnika* [Psychology of a mentally retarded student]. Moscow: Prosveshchenie Press.

Rubstov, V. V. (1981). The role of cooperation in the development of intelligence. *Soviet Psychology, 23,* 65–84.

Salomon, G. (Ed.). (1993). *Distributed cognitions: Psychological and educational considerations.* Cambridge: Cambridge University Press.

Sapir, E. (1921). *Language: An introduction to the study of speech.* New York: Harcourt Brace.

Saran, R., & Neisser, B. (Eds.). (2004). *Enquiring minds: Socratic dialogue in education.* Stoke-on-Trent, *England: Trentham.*

Saxe, G. B. (1991). *Culture and cognitive development: Studies in mathematical understanding.* Hillsdale, NJ: Erlbaum.

Schickendanz, J. A. (1982). The acquisition of written language in young children. In B. Spodek (Ed.), *Handbook of research in early childhood education,* (pp. 242–263). New York: Free Press.

Schickedanz, J., & Casbergue, R. M. (2003). *Writing in preschool.* Newark, DE: International Reading Association.

Scribner, S. (1977). Modes of thinking and ways of speaking: Culture and logic reconsidered. In P. N. Johnson-Laird & P. S. Wason (Eds.), *Thinking: Reading in cognitive science* (pp. 483–500). Cambridge: Cambridge University Press.

Shepard, L. A. (2000). The role of assessment in a learning culture. *Educational Researcher, 29*(7), 4–14.

Sirotkin, S. A. (1979). The transition from gesture to word. *Soviet Psychology, 17*(3), 46–59.

Slavin, R. (1994). *Practical guide to cooperative learning.* Boston: Allyn & Bacon.

Sloutsky, V. (1991). Sravnenie faktornoj struktury intellekta u semejnych detej i vospitannikov destskogo doma [Comparison of factor structure of intelligence among family-reared and orphanage-reared children]. *Vestnik Moskovskogo Universiteta, 1,* 34–41.

Smilansky, S., & Shefatya, L. (1990). *Facilitating play: A medium for promoting cognitive, socio-emotional, and academic development in young children.* Gaithersburg, MD: Psychosocial and Educational Publications.

Smirnova, E. O. (1998). *Razvitie voli i proizvol'nosti v rannem i doshkol'nom vozraste* [Development of will and intentionality in toddlers and preschool-aged children]. Moscow: Modek.

Smirnova, E. O., & Gudareva, O. V. (2004). Igra i proizvol'nost u sovremennykh doshkol'nikov [Play and intentionality in modern preschoolers]. *Vopprosy Psychologii, 1*, 91–103.

Spector, J. E. (1992). Predicting progress in beginning reading: Dynamic assessment of phonemic awareness. *Journal of Educational Psychology, 84*, 353–363.

Spitz, R. A. (1946). Anaclitic depression. *Psychoanalytic Study of the Child, 2*, 313–342.

Stetsenko, A. (1995). The psychological function of children's drawing: A Vygotskian perspective. In C. Lange-Kuettner & G. V. Thomas (Eds.), *Drawing and looking: Theoretical approaches to pictorial representation in children.* London, England: Harvester/Wheatsheaf.

Stipek, D. (2002). *Motivation to Learn: Integrating Theory and Practice* (4th ed.). Boston, MA: Allyn & Bacon.

Teale, W. H., & Sulzby, E. (Eds.). (1986) *Emergent literacy: Writing and reading.* Norwood, NJ: Ablex.

Tharp, R. G., & Gallimore, R. (1988). *Rousing minds to life: Teaching, learning and schooling in social context.* Cambridge: Cambridge University Press.

Thomas, R. M. (2000). *Comparing theories of child development* (5th ed.). Belmont, CA: Wadsworth/Thomson Learning.

Tronick, E. Z. (1989). Emotions and emotional communication in infants. *American Psychologist, 44*, 115–123.

Tryphon, A., & Voneche, J. J. (1996). Introduction. In A. Tryphon & J. J. Voneche (Eds.), *Piaget-Vygotsky: The social genesis of thought* (pp. 1–10). Hove, UK: Psychology Press.

Tzuriel, D. (2001). *Dynamic assessment of young children.* New York: Kluwer Academic/Plenum Publishers.

Tzuriel, D., & Feuerstein, R. (1992). Dynamic group assessment for prescriptive teaching. In H. C. Haywood & D. Tzuriel (Eds.), *Interactive assessment* (pp. 187–206). New York: Springer-Verlag.

Valsiner, J. (1988). *Developmental psychology in the Soviet Union.* Bloomington: Indiana University Press.

Valsiner, J. (1989). *Human development and culture: The social nature of personality and its study.* Lexington, MA: Lexington Books.

Van der Veer, R., & Valsiner, J. (1991). *Understanding Vygotsky: A quest for synthesis.* Oxford: Blackwell.

Venger, L. A. (1977). The emergence of perceptual actions. In M. Cole (Ed.), *Soviet developmental psychology: An anthology.* White Plains, NY: M. E. Sharpe. (Original work published in 1969)

Venger, L. A. (Ed.). (1986). *Rezvitije poznauatel'nych sposobnostey v protsesse doshkol'nogo vospitanija.* [Development of cognitive abilities through preschool education]. Moscow: Pedagogika.

Venger, L. A. (1988). The origin and development of cognitive abilities in preschool children. *International Journal of Behavioral Development, 11*(2), 147–153.

Venger, L. A. (Ed.). (1994). *Programma "Razvitije": Osnovnye polozhenija* [Curriculum "Development": Main principles]. Moscow: Novaja Shkola.

Venger, L. A. (Ed.). (1996). *Slovo i obraz v reshenii poznavatel'nykh zadach doshkol'nikami* [World and image in the preschoolers' cognitive problem solving]. Moscow: Intor.

Venger, L. A., & Dyachenko, O. M. (Eds.). (1989). *Igry i uprazhnenija po razvitiju umstvennych sposobnostej u detej doshkol'nogo vozrasta* [Games and exercises promoting the development of cognitive abilities in preschool children]. Moscow: Prosveschenije.

Vocate, D. R. (1987). *The theory of A. R. Luria: Functions of spoken language in the development of higher mental process.* Hillsdale, NJ: Erlbaum.

Vygodskaya, G. (1995). Remembering father. *Educational Psychologist, 30*(1), 57–59.

Vygodskaya, G. (1999). On Vygotsky's research and life. In S. Chaiklin, M. Hedegaard, & U. J. Jensen (Eds.), *Activity theory and social practice: Cultural historical approaches* (pp. 31–38). Oakville, CN: Aarhus University Press.

Vygotsky, L. S. (1962). *Thought and language* (E. Hanfmann & G. Vokar, Trans.) Cambridge MA: MIT Press. (Original work published in 1934)

Vygotsky, L. S. (1967). Play and its role in the mental development of the child. *Soviet Psychology,* 5, 6–18 (Original work published in 1933)

Vygotsky, L. S. (1977). Play and its role in the mental development of the child. In M. Cole (Ed.), *Soviet developmental psychology* (pp. 76–99). White Plains, NY: M. E. Sharpe. (Original work published in 1966)

Vygotsky, L. S. (1978). *Mind and Society: The development of higher mental process.* Cambridge, MA: Harvard University Press. (Original work published in 1930, 1933, 1935)

Vygotsky, L. S. (1981). The instrumental method is psychology. In J. V. Wertsch (Ed.), *The concept of activity in Soviet psychology* (pp. 134–143). Armonk, NY: M. E. Sharpe.

Vygotsky, L. S. (1987). *Thinking and speech* (Vol. 1). New York: Plenum Press.

Vygotsky, L. S. (1993). *The fundamentals of defectology (abnormal psychology and learning disabilities).* New York: Plenum Press.

Vygotsky, L. S. (1994a). The problem of the environment. In R. Van der Veer & J. Valsiner (Eds.), *The Vigotsky Reader* (pp. 338–354). Oxford: Blackwell. (Original work published in 1935)

Vygotsky, L. S. (1994b). The development of academic concepts in school-aged children. In R. Van der Veer & J. Valsiner (Eds.), *The Vygotsky Reader* (pp. 355–370). Oxford: Blackwell. (Original work published in 1935)

Vygotsky, L. S. (1997). *The history of the development of higher mental functions* (M. J. Hall, Trans., Vol. 4). New York: Plenum Press.

Vygotsky, L. S. (1998). *Child psychology* (Vol. 5). New York: Plenum Press.

Vygotsky, L. S. (1999). Tool and sign in the development of the child. In R. W. Rieber (Ed.), *The collected works of L. S. Vygotsky.* (Vol. 6, pp. 3–68). New York: Plenum Press.

Vygotsky L. S., & Luria, A. (1994). Tool and symbol in child development. In R. Van der Veer & J. Valsiner (Eds.), *The Vygotsky Reader* (pp. 99–174). Oxford: Blackwell. (Original work published in 1984)

Wadsworth, B.J. (2004). *Piaget's theory of cognitive and affective development* (5th ed.). Boston, MA: Pearson.

Wells, G. (Ed.). (1981) *Learning through interaction: The study of language development* (Vol. 1). Cambridge: Cambridge University Press.

Wells, G. (1999a). *Dialogic inquiry: Towards a sociocultural practice and theory of education.* New York: Cambridge University Press.

Wells, G. (1999b). The zone of proximal development and its implications for learning and teaching. In *Dialogic inquiry: Towards a sociocultural practice and theory of education.* New York: Cambridge University Press.

Wertsch J. (1979). From social interaction to higher psychological processes. *Human Development,* 22, 1–22.

Wertsch, J. V. (1979). The regulation of human action and the give-new organization of private speech. In G. Zivin (Ed.), *The development of self-regulation through private speech* (pp. 79–98). New York: John Wiley & Sons.

Wertsch, J. V. (1985). *Vygotsky and the social formation of mind.* Cambridge, MA: Harvard University Press.

Wertsch, J. V. (1991). *Voices of the mind: A sociocultural approach to mediated action.* Cambridge, MA: Harvard University Press.

Wertsch, J. V., & Tulviste, P. (1994). Lev Semynovich Vygotsky and contemporary developmental psychology. In R. D. Parke, P. A. Ornstein, J. J. Reiser, & C. Zahn-Waxler (Eds.), *A century of developmental psychology* (pp. 333–356). Washington, DC: American Psychological Association.

Whorf, B. L. (1956). Science and linguistics. In J. B. Carrol (Ed.), *Language, thought and reality: Selected writings of Benjamin Lee Whorf* (pp. 207–219). Cambridge, MA: MIT Press.

Wood, D., Bruner, J. S., & Ross, G. (1976). The role of tutoring in problem solving. *Journal of Child Psychology and Psychiatry, 17,* 89–100.

Zaporozhets, A. (1986). *Izbrannye psickologicheskie trudy* [Selected works]. Moscow: Pedagogika.

Zaporozhets, A. (2002). Thought and activity in children. *Journal of Russian & East European Psychology, 40*(4), 18–29.

Zaporozhets, A., & Lisina, M. (Eds.). (1979). *Razvitie obscheniya u doshkolnikov* [The development of communication in preschoolers]. Moscow: Pedagogika.

Zaporozhets, A., & Markova, T. A. (1983). Principles of preschool pedagogy: The psychological foundations of preschool education. *Soviet Education, 25*(3), 71–90.

Zaporozhets, A., & Neverovich, Y. Z. (Eds.). (1986). *Razvitije social'nykh emotsij u detej doshkol'nogo vozrasta: psychologicheskije issledovanija* [Development of social emotions in preschool children: Psychological studies]. Moscow: Pedagogika.

Zaporozhets, A. V. (1977). Some of the psychological problems of sensory training in early childhood and the preschool period. In M. Cole & I. Maltzman (Eds.), *A handbook of contemporary Soviet psychology.* New York: Basic Books. (Original published in 1959)

Zaporozhets, A. V. (1978). *Printzip razvitiya v psichologii* [Principle of development in psychology]. Moscow: Pedagogika.

Zimmerman, B. J., & Risenberg, R. (1997). Self-regulatory dimensions of academic learning and motivation. In GD Phye (Ed.), *Handbook of academic learning: Construction of knowledge* (pp. 105–125). Mahwah, NJ: Erlbaum.

Zivin, G. (Ed.) (1979). *The development of self-regulation through private speech.* New York: John Wiley & Sons.

Zuckerman, G. (2003). The learning activity in the first years of schooling: The developmental path toward reflection. In A. Kozulin, B. Gindis, V. S. Ageev, & S. M. Miller (Eds.), *Vygotsky's educational theory in cultural context* (pp. 177–199). Cambridge: Cambridge University Press.

Author Index

Subject Index